DANCEHALL: FROM SLAVE SHIP TO GHETTO

DANCEHALL: FROM SLAVE SHIP TO GHETTO

SONJAH STANLEY NIAAH

University of Ottawa Press
Ottawa

u Ottawa

The University of Ottawa Press acknowledges with gratitude the support extended to its publishing list by Heritage Canada through its Book Publishing Industry Development Program, by the Canada Council for the Arts, by the Canadian Federation for the Humanities and Social Sciences through its Aid to Scholarly Publications Program, by the Social Sciences and Humanities Research Council, and by the University of Ottawa.

LIBRARY AND ARCHIVES CANADA CATALOGUING IN PUBLICATION

Stanley Niaah, Sonjah, 1970–
    Dancehall : from slave ship to ghetto / Sonjah Stanley Niaah.

(African and diasporic studies)
Includes bibliographical references and index.
ISBN 978-0-7766-3041-0 (bound).–ISBN 978-0-7766-0736-8 (pbk.)

    1. Dancehall (Music)–Social aspects–Jamaica–Kingston. 2. Dancehall (Music)–Jamaica–Kingston. 3. Popular culture–Jamaica–Kingston. 4. Kingston (Jamaica)–Social conditions. 5. Inner cities–Jamaica–Kingston. I. Title. II. Series: African and diasporic studies

F1874.S72 2010   306.4'84246097292   C2010-903490-2

LIVICATION

In subverting the hegemony of English as used in the academies of the West, I wish to title my dedication a "livication," in the spirit of the Rastafari luminaries who have continually shown us the need to question our history and to write our own. In transforming the "ded" (dead) in dedication to its opposite, (a)live, I invoke Rastafari cosmology and linguistic protocol in my few words of praise:

> Every tree wants to bear fruit
> Every flowering plant wants to bloom
> Every human be beautiful and be seen to be beautiful
> Every created thing wants to know its beauty.

This book is livicated to all those who have ever known beauty, to those who want to know beauty and to the revolutionaries who will not stop until every hu(e)man being knows his or her beauty. It is also:

> For my father hero, Levi George Stanley,
> who taught me to strive for heights beyond the sky,
> and
> Pearline Codner (*née* James), Naomi Blackhall, John Blackhall
> (father and son),
> and
> Rebecca Blackhall (dancer, Revival bands member),
> who was present when I entered the world.
> This book lives because of You.
> Ashe!

CONTENTS

LIST OF ILLUSTRATIONS

LIST OF TABLES

"Kingston's Dancehall: A Story of Space and Celebration." *Space and Culture: International Journal of Social Spaces* 7:1 (2004), 102–18;

"A Common Genealogy: Dancehall, Limbo, and the Sacred Performance Space." *Discourses in Dance* 2:2 (2004), 9–26;

"Kingston's Dancehall Spaces." *Jamaica Journal* 29:3 (March 2006), 14–21;

"Making Space: Dancehall Performance and Its Philosophy of Boundarylessness." *African Identities* 2:2 (2004), 117–32;

"Readings of 'Ritual' and Community in Dancehall Performance." *Wadabagei: A Journal of the Caribbean and Its Diasporas* 9:2 (April 2006), 43–73;

"Mapping Black Atlantic Performance Geographies: Continuities from Slave Ship to Ghetto," in *Black Geographies and the Politics of Place*, ed. Katherine McKittrick and Clyde Woods. Toronto: Between the Lines Press, and Boston: South End Press (2007), 193–217.

PREFACE

Growing up in the 1970s, I was surrounded by what I later understood to be the intense unfolding of Jamaica's popular music and dance performance, in particular, the evolution of dancehall music. Songs such as Tappa Zukie's "Rocksteady," whose lines my mother had to correct when we sang "every time dem panty go" instead of "every time dem pass me go," established the ferment that inspired this book. At a more concrete level, I became acutely aware of this space through my own participation in the Jamaica Festival competition, school parties, Friday evening sessions at Pier One with Pieces Music, and my own sixteenth "birthday bash," at which a sound system delivered the latest tunes. By 1988, when Shabba Ranks emerged as the dominant DJ, my choice of entertainment was securely chosen. By 1989, after moving to Kingston from rural Jamaica, it became clear that Kingston was the centre stage for dancehall, indeed its largest "amphitheatre."

Up to that point I was far removed from anything but the sound of dancehall music. As my understanding of Kingston's population, layout and topography grew, I became committed to the need to write "a narrative of the city of Kingston," a concept which one of my former teachers, Mr. Clement Branche, had expressed. On the road between campus fêtes, listening to the likes of Buju Banton, Spragga Benz, Bounti Killa and Capleton during my own personal exile in the United States, and engaging in active research in 1999, I became convinced that I could contribute something to the documentation of Jamaican popular culture.

This book forms part of my writing of that narrative of the city of Kingston, a narrative of an unmapped heritage that can only profit the redevelopment plans for downtown Kingston in tangible ways and Jamaica's creative industries more broadly. I see this as part of my purpose for writing this book. Though I am an inside/outsider, in the sense that I am not, strictly speaking, from Kingston and not a dancehall creator, I am a stakeholder in documenting Jamaica's popular performance culture. Ultimately, my hope is to expose the multidimensionality of dancehall as an Afro-Jamaican creation, and as a space of celebration for ordinary people in Jamaica and beyond.

As I began to look critically at the dancehall space, there were initial questions that guided the research I conducted from 1999 to 2007. In taking the understanding of dancehall beyond its accessible and commodified musical form, I relied on insights from my grounding in geography, sociology and cultural studies. On the path to exploring key aspects of the performative spaces, the arena of the dance, movement and the types of events organized, the following questions helped to shape a broad-based inquiry into dancehall: What map of dancehall currently exists? What is missing? What does exploration of dancehall through its events, dance acts, dancers and general spatiality add to its definition? What is the value of dancehall to inner-city Kingston? To what extent is present-day dancehall a mirror of yesteryear's dance halls? Is there a generational bias in the definition of dancehall? What relationships exist between performance cultures across the Black Atlantic?

One important conclusion from my early research is that music-centred approaches have served to telescope research lenses along narrow and unsystematic lines, to emphasize and conjure excesses and obsessions rather than sociocultural, spatial and historically contextualized readings. Even as the dancehall musical genre has penetrated the world through the DJs' lyrics and performance styles, and the dissemination of research, details of dancehall topography, performance space, life/style and meanings, indeed its ecology, are lacking. The topography of the cultural production of dancehall life and style is foregrounded, therefore, to increase understanding of the dancehall context. Emerging from the marginalized youth of (mostly) Kingston's ghettos, dancehall is inextricably linked to the ghetto and the performance culture has given these spaces particular identities. Perceptions of "ghetto people" and their creations as outside the status quo have accounted for some censorship of dancehall, coupled with the real and imagined perceptions of the inaccessibility of these spaces, based on their location within poverty traps, or the inner city as underworld. This is consistent with the perception of ghettos generally, defined as uncontrolled groupings that are at the bottom of a hierarchy of power and wealth, and are spatially coherent. They can be considered "excluded spaces" because of their relationship to the hegemony of dominant social groups. Ghetto residents have "no use" in the eyes of the business class and political interests, who see "more to lose than to gain" in developing policies to benefit such residents (see Marcuse 2003, 277–78).

Grounded in a cultural studies approach that holds trans/multi-disciplinarity and inter/multitextuality as givens, I used the perspective on methodology that cultural studies brings to the study of complex social phenomena embodied in the term "bricolage." This is the tactical application of methods, especially as they allow for uses not necessarily intended. Cultural studies encourages the use of all methods and theories deemed applicable in highlighting the dynamics of power and negotiations within the cultural topography of a society. What is presented here are the findings facilitated by engagement with the dancehall space via a range of approaches in the use of primary and secondary sources, while drawing on techniques and theoretical explanations out of geography, anthropology and cultural studies, in mapping a cultural terrain that is local, regional and transnational.

Developing an understanding of dancehall ecology, dancehall as geocultural construct, with space implicated in the very origin of the name, necessitated entering dancehall research through the arena of "the dance." Importantly, when someone in Jamaica asks "Yuh waan go a dance?"—that is, "Do you want to go to *the dance*?"—they are referring to a specific activity that implies a particular space/venue, a particular event of a known purpose and character, with particular acts and actors. This book reclaims these three "missing texts"— space, event and actors/acts—that widen the definition of dancehall. This is the rationale for separating the representations of the well-known musical genre "dancehall" from the explicitly spatial "dance hall," with its unique sociocultural manifestations. The "dance" is visualized in a holistic way, placing it in the context of its uniquely urban Jamaican nuance. In deconstructing the term "dancehall," this phenomenon is disaggregated into the three interrelated parts, dance as event, space, actors/acts. These are in turn linked to basic elements of dancehall performance. The act of dancing is done by dancers/patrons generally and has a link to creators of movement at its highest level. The dancers and patrons generally enter the space at observable times. The event has a purpose onto which the power of the gathering/group is centred: it attracts patrons (increases in appeal and affect) and therefore marshals power onto itself. Everyone knows why they are there. The event takes place at a particular venue, which has its own geography, land use, spatiality and geopolitics, and its own relationship to class structure/ boundaries and community.

In looking at dancehall's terrain and the relationship among its component parts, this book advances an ecological agenda that is consistent with the cultural studies agenda. To understand dancehall's component parts, varying bodies of knowledge and systems have to be engaged with. To take an ecological approach is also to attempt a social systems approach, that is, to look (among other things) at actors beyond the DJ, such as embodied acts, spatiality, geopolitics, urban-centredness, land use patterns and social identity production. It allows inclusion of elements underexposed up to present, so that lyrics, stage, performer, performance space and patrons can interact, giving depth to what has been a (research) stage dominated by dancehall music to the exclusion of other important factors. In using space as a holistic paradigm, this book allows for a mapping of context(s) and the "very identity that brings the context into focus" (Slack 1996, 125), which is "the dance." Entering dancehall through the arena of "the dance" allows the articulation of a new perspective, adding rich material to this process of cultural-history-making.

With no adequate cultural history of dancehall (see Scott 1999), research has to take account of political, historical and spatial relations. One of the key components is that of African traditions, and their continuities within Jamaica and the Diasporic space more generally. Exploring these sheds light on the systems, symbols and philosophies at work. For example, the important associations between dancehall, plantation dances and traditions in Africa, where cross-cultural studies could present new readings, are not to be missed. As a start, both secular and sacred dance practices originate in an African system including a wide range of worship, ritual and other praise methods (see Ryman 1980 and Hazzard-Gordon 1996, 103). Second, religion is inextricably tied to Caribbean ontology/ies, psychology/ies, epistemology/ies and cosmology/ies (see Mintz and Price 1976), while, as a system of strongly held views, Western religion, with its concept of the sacred, often engenders intolerance of other religious views and practices. Third, "the sacred" is a conceptual category made manifest as nature on Earth. It is culture specific, arising out of a universal human need to "overstand" the foundation and function of the universe, and, in particular, the relationship of human beings to cosmic totality. Cultural differences emerge as each group concretizes its perception of the universe in myths based on the specific environment of the group (see Ajayi 1996). Africans generally have a holistic concept of the universe as a single unifying entity where a multiplicity of sacred forces are found, rather than limited solely to the creator deity as in Judaism, Christianity and Islam. Dance practices, then, are sacred: indeed, they are a medium for worship in its broadest sense. By extension, so too could be the dance practices of the dancehall, based on historical continuities with both sacred and secular performance systems.

Perhaps embodiment in dancehall performs the same function as some forms of erotic art among a variety of peoples in, for example, South America and India. In some Indian temples, erotic art tells the story of the return of woman and sex after the sexual repression. This return of sex, ultimately the uni/verse of creativity, is depicted in sculptures of people in all manner of sexual poses, as vulgar as vulgar can be, as obscene as obscene can be. Kanwar Lal (1967) has documented these erotic sculptures and contends that it is only when things are brought to the extreme that the pendulum can shift. The extreme or excess is manifested in different ways within and beyond the dance hall. Broader perspectives such as these and many others can in fact be applied to dancehall if it is located in a wider scholarly field and everyday practice.

Studying dancehall posed interesting challenges. I argue that dancehall has seen a number of high points, including the periods 1989–1994 and 1999–2004. By the end of 2000 I realized that I was witnessing the emergence of another high point. In such performatively euphoric moments the temptation is to try to capture everything, search for systems of analysis not previously applied and seek to present the definitive dancehall story. Such thoughts were shelved. One of the challenges presented was the way in which "slackness" loomed large, not only as a defining feature, but as something that each researcher entering the field has to contend with. In this way it has functioned as a "gatekeeping concept." Discussing the Caribbean in anthropological theory, Michael-Rolph Trouillot (1992) concludes that the region has no gatekeeping concepts, in contrast to, for example, India, but I borrow the concept here to indicate that slackness has functioned similarly, forming signposts or stamps on particular regions to block full investigation of complexity (Trouillot 1992 pp. 21–22). In this way this book serves to open up closed or partially fixed designations of dancehall, collapsing boundaries and gates, and, in some respects, barricades. Collapsing these boundaries became crucial to reducing "slackness" from a master narrative, preventing deeper research beyond the lyrics and female stage performances, to its everyday place, where it no longer overshadows the practice but forms part of the wider milieu of cultural codes in a common field of representation. Even as the researcher stayed aware of ways in which the gatekeeping concept functioned, it became clear that there was definitional obscurity, as well as contradictions. For example, slackness becomes conflated with "nastiness," the term used by older folk to refer to illicit sex and sexual impropriety at several levels. Slackness has also been reified by academics, while dancehall adherents have to some extent moved away from this concept.

Finally, this is not a definitive study of dancehall. This book proposes no generalizations and holds no truths, it only places signposts for the next traveller on the research route.

OUT OF MANY ... ONE DANCEHALL

DANCEHALL is synonymous with Jamaica. Its very identity is reflective of Jamaica's motto, "Out of many, one people," unifying yet divisive and exclusionary. Who are these "many" and, by logical deduction, what is this "one"? The famous maxim is that 99 percent of the Jamaican population is of African descent (although in fact, according to the World Bank, as of September 4, 2008, the population of African descent totalled 97.4 percent). Those who are not reflected in this statistic feel excluded by such a motto. Dancehall is created by the people, the "many" disenfranchised youth of African descent who continually seek tomorrow's dinner from a "noisy" space that has been snubbed by the upper classes.

What is this dancehall? What map of dancehall currently exists? What is missing? Most persons familiar with dancehall might feel a rhythm, hear the "sound system drum" (Brathwaite 1994a, 9) or recall a tune such as the Tenor Saw original "Ring the Alarm" or Baby Cham's "Ghetto Story," with infectious drums and bass line, and a tempo pounding through the veins to make them want to "drop legs." The image of the cassette/CD man, who makes his living from reproducing the latest dancehall mix, might come to mind. Still others will imagine the space, the inner city, the dancers, the fashion, the gender politics, and want to hear the story that must accompany such a music and its space of production, its habitus.

This chapter seeks to outline many of the perspectives on dancehall served up by critics and scholars, locally and internationally. It highlights some of the tensions that surround dancehall, while locating it within a wider scholarly field and everyday practice. There is consensus that the definition of dancehall goes beyond the musical genre to encompass a wide creative economy, global network and culture. I see dancehall as developing from, and coterminous with, its reggae predecessor. Together, their contribution to Jamaica's economy, national identity and development is to some degree unquantifiable.

This is some of what we know. Dancehall emanated from the poor and continues to receive its creative sustenance from them. Many have found their livelihoods in the creative work around producing and consuming dancehall music and culture, from as early as the 1950s. With more than 6,000 people directly employed, supporting up to 43,000 others, and some 200 recording studios, approximately 170 sound systems, estimated revenues of 800 to 900 million Jamaican dollars a year from more than 10,000 concerts, dances, shows, and other music events (as of 2008), and an estimated 15.5 million US dollars in sales of music goods, the total value of the Jamaican market for music goods and services is estimated at between 31 million and 35 million US dollars, or about 10 percent of the nation's GDP. Estimates of the value accruing from the international market in respect of Jamaican music stood at 450 million dollars in 1998 and 60 to 100 million US dollars in 2000 (see Stanbury 2006). It was estimated in 1999 that Jamaican music generated more than 1.2 billion US dollars, and in 2000 estimates of overall worldwide earnings from exports of reggae music went as high as 2.5 billion US dollars, yet Jamaican earnings from recorded music were estimated at only 300 million US dollars. Bruce Lehman, the founder and president of the International Intellectual Property Institute, a non-governmental organization, has suggested that the Jamaican economy could expand by 10 percent if the country were able to capture all the earnings from Jamaican music on the world market (see Jamaica Intellectual Property Office).

With music as such an available text, it is often the entry point for persons who come into contact with the dancehall phenomenon, but there are important distinctions to be made. A progeny of reggae, contemporary dancehall music is now Jamaica's most popular indigenous music, and the sociocultural manifestations around its consumption constitute Jamaica's premier popular street theatre. This phenomenon first flourished around the 1950s, along with local music, but with unique manifestations of sonic dominance and innovation, dance, fashion, lyrical content, and delivery style since the 1980s.

The antecedents of dancehall are in popular sacred and secular forms such as the slave-ship Limbo, Jonkonnu, Dinki Mini, Gereh, Revival and Brukins Party, among others. There is something very old, therefore, and simultaneously new and renewing about Jamaica's dancehall. As it draws on the old, so it invents and reinvents itself. Its navel string (umbilical cord) is firmly rooted in African performance, evolving in the New World from slave-ship and plantation dances, and from the social dances organized at, for example, Marcus Garvey's Edelweiss Park, inaugurated in Kingston in 1931, and, later, Liberty Hall. Beverly Hamilton (1994, 100) notes that "both Edelweiss Park and Liberty Hall ... were venues for public dances, places where the general public could go for an evening of social dancing." Advertisements signalled the events, which generally took place between 7:30 p.m. and midnight. Dancing was also encouraged at other events organized by Garvey's Universal Negro Improvement Association, occasioning demonstrations of the latest moves from "dance-mad youths." More importantly, Hamilton cites Ivy Baxter (1970, 296), who noted that "Marcus Garvey had been one of the first people in the 1920s to consider the public recreation and entertainment of the poorer people in the Kingston and St Andrew area."

The venue for "subcultural dance" (see White 1984) or "sound system dance" (see Stolzoff 2000) is that place in which consenting individuals meet in a cultural system. Here, the sacred and the secular, politics and economics merge in the celebration ritual of the patrons, DJs, sound system, promoters, selectors, dancers, vendors and musicians. In most cases, earth was the floor, sometimes bounded by a metal fence along the perimeter. Arguably, dancehall was created out of nothing but the need to celebrate in the face of adversities that negated the very existence of those brought to the New World. There is a deep and primal connection to survival, performing subjectivity and agency.

Dancehall is space, culture, attitude, fashion, dance, life/style, economic tool, institution, stage, social mirror, language, ritual, social movement, profile, profession, brand name, community and tool of articulation for, especially, inner-city dwellers, who continually respond to the vibe expressed through the words "without the dancehall a wha' wi woulda do, reggae music call you must answer to ... " (from Buju Banton, "Pull It Up," 1999).

OUT OF MANY ... PERSPECTIVES

Dancehall occupies a tenuous place, a "war zone," in Jamaican society: there are relations of tension between this mostly lower-class performance practice and the middle- and upper-class status quo, and positives as well as negatives have been said of dancehall. Among the many criticisms levied at dancehall, the most prominent are music-centred challenges regarding the persistence of lyrics about women's body parts and violence. Many interpretations and histories of dancehall have come from academics, journalists, wellwishers, soothsayers and purveyors of doom, using a variety of disciplinary perspectives. From literary and cultural studies, psychology, anthropology, sociology, ethnomusicology, politics and history, these interpretations have given dancehall "cartographic representation," and their contributions to the construction of a cultural history and ecology of dancehall are invaluable.

Nevertheless, David Scott (1999) argues that "there is as yet no adequate cultural history of dancehall." Much of the work on dancehall to date, particularly that published before 1980, appears as part of the reggae continuum. Often, chapters or subsections within histories of reggae have been dedicated to dancehall recordings, music, musicians and artistes, and, to a much lesser extent, its wider practice, sartorial and other fashioning, economic benefits, choreography, and wider performance. I wish to examine briefly some of the arguments in these texts that directly relate to dancehall.

3

Dancehall is largely understood as an incarnation of reggae from the 1980s to the present, or as part of the continuum of Jamaican popular music since the rhythm and blues of the late 1950s, music that has largely been consumed in dance halls. However, the difference in the dancehall era is the degree to which live dancehall styles influence what appears on vinyl, developing performing styles, a new generation of singers, bands with fresh playing styles, reliance on digital rhythms, explicit lyrics, new dance moves and sound clashes.

The DJ used to perform live in the dance as a word artist, a Griot in the broader African sense, one who chants or sings or talks on a rhythm to keep the dance event lively by toasting the fans (see Brewster and Broughton 1999, Cooper 1993, and Stolzoff 2000). Then technological advances, commodification and increased demand meant that vinyl was used for playing recorded music within the dance space. The DJ's presence in the dance decreased as that of the selectors of recordings increased, a phenomenon precipitated by migration to studios and the radio stations (airwaves) as new arenas. It has also been claimed that during the 1980s increase in the drug trade and guns, facilitated by the neoliberal shift in political policies (see Katz 2003 and Gilroy 1987, 188), a new sense for quick wealth and the evolution of an exaggerated (ostentatious, fabulous) selfhood, in which "ghetto fabulous," a term first used by citizens of the inner city, began to blossom in a real way. Lyrics began to reflect this new sense of self, and DJs such as Yellow Man and Shabba Ranks are seen to mirror a roundabout turn away "from the social concerns of the seventies," fuelling the "'new' dancehall era with songs replete with sexual braggadocio, misogyny and violence, pandering to concerns earlier reggae artists might call 'Babylonian'" (Foster 1999, 157).

This view is reflected by Salewicz and Boot (2001, 172), who explain dancehall as a distinct musical genre characterized by "the marriage of digital beats and slackness: that moment and music in which lyrics about guns, women's body parts and men's sexual prowess come together" in songs such as "Wicked inna Bed" by Shabba Ranks (see also Barrow and Dalton 2001). This definition highlights technology and slackness as two distinctive features, but it is slackness in particular that has almost become the brand name by which dancehall is signified. This "Babylonian" brand of liturgy, this slackness narrative, is by far the largest source of debate about dancehall among scholars, social commentators, journalists and cultural critics. It is manifested through arguments in various ways, using moral, social, historical and pathological overtones.

A multidisciplinary approach presents a more comprehensive account. Some write from the perspectives of cultural studies, sociology, anthropology, (ethno)musicology, literary criticism or feminism, or combinations of these. For example, Norman Stolzoff (2000) uses the lens of the development of the sound system to anchor his ethnographic engagement with dancehall. Stolzoff establishes a history of dancehall from slavery to the Second World War, consistent with my own understanding of the space as having its inception in the earliest history of the New World. The dance is acknowledged for its role in the regulation of social relations and the maintenance of the cultural identity of slaves, a role that it plays for ghetto youth today. Stolzoff traces the rise of the sound system in the 1950s and 1960s, while contextualizing its role in the political tribalism of the 1960s and 1970s, as well as the decline of big bands, the roles of migration and technology in the evolution of the practice, strategies of record acquisition, the class influence and driving force of competition in the early era, among other issues. Attention is also given to the production arena of dancehall through discussions of the career path of a dancehall entertainer, and of the recording studio as a distinct and central space. In discussing the power of dancehall culture, its centrality to "cultural creation and intersocial negotiation," Stolzoff questions whether dancehall is socially beneficial, unleashing creative potential, or a constellation of negatives, tending to implosion or destruction by way of received notions of "'indiscipline,' 'lawlessness,' 'vulgarity,' 'slackness' and 'violence'" (Stolzoff 2000, 228).

Carolyn Cooper's literary approach to the study of Jamaican culture through the prism of dancehall is drawn mainly from DJs' lyrics, especially those of Lady Saw, Capleton and Shabba Ranks. Making use of the slackness/culture dichotomy, Cooper (1993) presents dancehall as an arena of erotic play using word art in the form of metaphors, verbal and other clashing, and role play as key devices in what is considered an African-centred system. Cooper identifies the place of the DJ's art as a site of tensions in Jamaican society. Further, consistent with a feminist approach and a focus on female performers in dancehall, particularly Lady Saw, Cooper (2000, 50) visualizes dancehall culture "as an erogenous zone in which the celebration of female sexuality and fertility is ritualized." With fantasy as a vehicle of the imaginary, and with the "pleasures of disguise" made manifest in their dress and performance, women destabilize the order established for the censorship of the black female body. Perspectives on the historical link and break between Bob Marley's musical and political themes, on the one hand, and those of contemporary artists such as Capleton or Shabba Ranks, on the other, have also occupied Cooper's analysis.

Tracey Skelton (1995, 1996 and 1998) works within cultural studies and social and cultural geography to examine the ways in which ragga music becomes a "space for women to voice their opinions and desires" (1995, 86). By using and critiquing notions of respectability and reputation from the work of Peter Wilson, Skelton discusses dominant forms of representation, particularly dominant black masculinity, that have been challenged by female performances of music and dance. She argues that by inverting submissive dance forms, and traditional notions of respectability and reputation, and demonstrating indifference to male consumption of their sexuality, women performers of ragga use stage space to empower themselves.

Donna Hope (2004 and 2006) challenges the view of dancehall as characteristically violent by deconstructing violence as both lyrical and real within the performance space and the wider society. Hope sees dancehall music and culture as a historically specific composite of DJs, sound systems, stage shows, clubs and dance moves following Yellow Man's rise to prominence in 1981 and the technological advances that produced the sleng teng rhythm in 1985. She uses this moment both to locate dancehall music historically and to dissociate it from all preceding genres of Jamaican popular music. She also focuses on the politics of gender to include a masculinist perspective using the male crews, DJs and their performances as important sites of analysis, and draws conclusions about alternative constructions of viable identities at the local, national, and global levels.

Louis Chude-Sokei's article "Postnationalist Geographies" (1997) presents a reading of ragga sound as a marker of African Diasporic identity that articulates a spatial understanding. He depicts various levels in the urban geography of the Third World: ragga as inner city, ragga as national, and ragga as postnational/transnational/Diasporic space and representation. Within this tripartite view he gives examples of how ragga operates and claims that these spaces are shown in the way music is manufactured, represents native knowledge, new "national belonging" beyond politics and geography, and new identities.

Consistent with the reading of ragga as a transnational space and sound, Marvin Dale Sterling (2000) traces the oral music tradition, fashion and dance, gender, and Rastafari consciousness in Japanese dancehall. He explores through ethnography the way in which Japanese selfhood negotiates space "in the shadow of the universal Jamaican other."

Subcultural studies have examined ways in which social groups collectively assert their identities, disturb norms, and reconcile or dissolve issues of class, race, ethnicity, age and sexuality. As definitions of subcultures suggest, the prefix "sub" refers to the secondary, subterranean and subaltern elements of either self-definitions or definitions of the other. Their internal positioning and representation as secondary other, a "beneath, but within" (Gelder and Thornton 2005, 4) outside the mainstream and somewhat liminal, make them identifiable. Some of the biases against subcultures include classifications as "'outsiders,' 'perverts' and/or 'radicals.'" Dancehall as a practice emanating from the lower class and embodying tensions over race, class, law, gender and the body therefore invites analysis within a subcultural frame of reference.

Kingsley Stewart (2002, 17–28) defines dancehall as a subculture. In this space actors live their cultural imperatives and complexities through their music and dance performances. Stewart concludes that violent conduct seems to be linked to influences rooted in the wider Jamaican sociocultural setting and that the dancehall worldview represents a Jamaican cultural prototype that helps us interpret violence in Jamaica. The essential argument is that cognitive and behavioural forms in dancehall can help in comprehending the social push and pull factors of violent behaviour.

Sociocultural analyses have also been combined with the subcultural perspective, especially in the unprecedented exposition by Garth White (1984) of the distinctive development of what he calls the "subcultural dance event." White's discussion centres on local musicians between 1950 and 1980, along with the urban spatiality of their practice within shanty towns, the bands that worked the upper- and lower-class scenes, their decline, and the rise of early sound systems such as Tom Wong's The Great Sebastian, Lord Coo's The Universe, V-Rocket and others. White details the technology, innovations, economy and industry that propelled the development of these sound systems, the competition for records, and the reliance on sailors and farmworkers for their importation. His summary of the overall significance of the sound systems, and of popular dance events and moves, documents direct contributions such as the development of a local electronic enterprise, increased demand for technology and local music, the diminished role played by radio stations, the creation of underclass "culture heroes," self-awareness and intra-group communication, the rise of "edutainment," the dissemination of underclass views, and the validation of Africanness and indigenous ways of being. White defines the subcultural events as "occasions for pleasure," not ritual. (I extend the idea of ritual space as a perspective within which to view dancehall in Chapter 5.)

Reggae and dancehall as musical genres and cultures, like Rastafari, have been spoken of as subcultures in Jamaica. This is established by Dick Hebdige in his book *Subcultures: The Meaning of Style* (1979), as well as in his article "Reggae, Rastas, and Rudies" (1997), where he clearly classifies reggae and Rastafari as subcultures. This subculture analysis and, by extension, subculture theory, which George Lipsitz (1994) identifies as having defined the scholarship on the culture of reggae and Rastafari, pose some difficulties. Dancehall and its reggae ancestor, as both literal and metaphorical Caribbean reality, challenge the definition of a subculture, in that they define a national identity while embodying national and postcolonial tensions. They are therefore not strictly peripheral, for, as the dancer Rex Nettleford, Artistic Director and Choreographer of the National Dance Theatre Company, has affirmed (2000, xi), "'mainstreams' get sluggish without replenishment from life-giving tributaries"—that is, there is a symbiotic relationship inherent in flows of creative energy. Developments in subcultural theory have culminated in collections of papers such as Ken Gelder and Sarah Thornton's *Subcultures Reader* (2005), and are summarized by Andy Bennett (2000, 11–27), who acknowledges the work of the Centre for Contemporary Cultural Studies (founded in 1964 and closed in 2002) at the University of Birmingham in England, especially Stuart Hall and Tony Jefferson's *Resistance through Rituals: Youth Subcultures in Post-War Britain* (1976).

Beth-Sarah Wright (2004) adds analysis of visual culture to further extend the definition of dancehall. She introduces perspectives on the creation, distribution and consumption of dancehall images, particularly the dancing black female body, in dancehall docuvideos. The role of the video camera in objectifying women's bodies, through a focus on isolated body parts such as the pudenda, is counterposed with a reading of female "communication rituals" that, she argues, ultimately create transformation beyond narcissistic pleasure, or more broadly pleasures in self-indulgence and excessive visibility.

Bibi Bakare-Yusuf (2006) takes the discussion of dancehall's visual culture and aesthetic into the relationship between the lived reality, embodied practice and adornment. She attempts a systematic analysis of the relationship between fashion and play, arguing that, through extravagant designs, colour and pageantry, dancehall women of all body types creatively register "anxiety, vulnerability, violence, joy," and "historical, cultural, economic and technological changes." For example, violence and history are reflected in the pervasiveness of guns, knives and other weapons that characterize ghetto life and are visually woven into the sheered tops, or the motif of bulletholes in jeans that can be read as part of the fabric of dancehall designs. While dancehall fashion cannot be seen as a homogenous construct, Yusuf argues that women's use of fashion allows for visual and other pleasures through creativity, and poses a challenge to puritanical male-dominated and class-based distinctions.

These perspectives have served to colour the landscape of dancehall scholarship, giving it greater depth and breadth of focus, engagement and analysis. Beyond these engagements, however, much is left to be unearthed. Through the prism of space, this book continues the data gathering process and analysis of dancehall.

MANY "RELATIONS OF ABNORMALITY"

The many perspectives on dancehall outlined above are matched by tensions that riddle the performance culture and indeed the performance geography. Violence, the decline of moral values and battles with the state feature prominently is this milieu.

Let me use a concrete example to demonstrate some of these tensions. It was the occasion of English's Birthday Bash on January 27, 2003, with the sound system Stone Love on hand for a night of celebration at the frequently used La Roose Restaurant and Nightclub, a venue that has hosted countless dance events. As the dance event approached its height at 2:00 a.m., members of the Jamaica Constabulary Force reportedly opened fire on patrons at the St Catherine nightclub. Whatever the reason for their opening fire, five persons, including "Pinkie" (Doreen Prendergast), sister of Jamaica's media-proclaimed "dancehall queen" Carlene Smith, were victims of gunshot injuries. This incident was matched by the debacle at the British link-up dance held at the same venue on March 22, 2007, when approximately eight persons were shot and injured after police interrupted the dance proceedings to shut down the sound system.

Both these incidents highlight some important issues about Jamaica's popular cultural/dance space. Typically, news of such incidents is reported on the front pages of the main newspapers under headlines such as (in the case of the earlier incident at La Roose) "Four Injured in La Roose Shooting" (*Daily Gleaner*, January 28, 2003) or "Dance Mayhem: Five Injured as Cops Fire into Crowd" (*Jamaica Observer*, January 28, 2003). These incidents occurred during what was arguably a major high point of dancehall activity (1999–2004), which has generally been snubbed by the upper classes.

Characterized by a proliferation of artistes, hit songs, dance moves, dance events, hyperreality and consumption, dancehall high points have a distinct character. At specific time periods they are characterized by hit songs of a style and spirit that make an indelible mark on the space and its collective memory. In the early 1990s it was Shabba Ranks and Buju Banton whose styles and energy entered the dancehall music-making and agenda-setting canons. By 1999 the recording artiste Elephant Man, then a member of the Scare Dem Crew, started a new wave, characterized by songs about dance moves such as "Log On" (2001) that have infectiously captured the patrons of dancehall. Inevitably, the high points see an increase in dancehall consumption. This is followed by decline because of such factors as stasis in the reproduction of the DJ style, negative publicity, conflict between artistes, violence and state intervention.

By observing these high points, one can identify the life cycle that is inherent in the (social) production of dancehall space, styles, music, meanings, artistes and dancers, as well as its decline. Among other things, the shooting incident at La Roose in 2003 could be read as a sign of the impending decline of the high point of 1999–2004. What is significant, however, is that, even with these rises and falls, and despite state intervention over the period of its development, the form proliferates.

Incidents such as these shootings draw attention to general apprehension about the "end of days," the supposed oversecularization of society, and signs of the decline of moral values and respect in Jamaica, with dancehall culture as an embodiment of such signs. Some might argue that incidents of violent attacks on various publics, for example, are commonplace, as reflected in the general increase in crime and the high murder rates of 1999–2007, a trend that made an indelible mark in the period 1999–2002 (see Headley 2002, vii). Yet, as Harriott (2000) and Headley (2002) both point out, police misconduct, the drug trade and domestic violence combined account for the high murder rates. There is no evidence that dancehall as a practice contributes to the nation's violence. On the contrary, with police misconduct and paramilitary operations introduced as crime control mechanisms, dancehall activity has suffered negative effects. Popular dance activity has increasingly come under pressure from police officers and constitutes another site of tension. Anxiety over the staging of dancehall events—their sonic proportions and their associations with criminal elements—has precipitated legislation either being created or being revised for enforcement. Though the 1960s saw its own share of police presence in dance halls, the Noise Abatement Act 1997 offered an exploitable framework through which money could be extorted in exchange for permitting dance events. This speaks to the policing of entertainment activity, as well as issues of corruption and the willingness on the part of the authorities to exploit regulations for personal gain.

There are also unreconciled issues of law and governance, and battles for space, power and personhood in the postcolonial context. In defining brands of postcolonial power and political institutions, Achille Mbembe (2001, 102) highlights the particular brands that mirror old colonial structures and are manifested as "regime[s] of violence" that inscribe their power in postcolonial Africa and, undoubtedly, the Caribbean. Unfortunately, a result of this brand of power is the challenge it poses to African and African Diasporic embodiment, performance practice and memorializing.

Since the 1950s, however, there have been increased associations made between dancehall and violence. Though there is no empirical research that supports the claims that have been made, several commentators within the media suggest that dancehall is a contributor to the violence that pervades society, and at the same time there are those who have offered alternative views (see, for example, Stewart 2002, and Boyne 2002a and 2002b).

Representations of dancehall have increased in the media generally, and reports of "cass cass," or quarrels between artists, are common, alongside sexual or violence-based readings increasingly allowed in various media because they attract large audiences. Media studies have identified rituals of media in handling special events that revolve around three categories, "contests," "coronations" and "conquests" (see Liebes and Curran 1998, 3–22). The portrayal of dancehall being discussed undoubtedly falls within the categories of contests and conquests, with obvious connotations of conflict, into which some sporting and other popular performances also fall. The reality is that sex and violence, and the tensions over them, constitute the power conceived by various media houses to capture audiences. Generally, conflicts between artists, between artists and law enforcement officers or the courts, between police officers and patrons, and among dancers are all highlighted. One noteworthy set of incidents is the engagement, marriage and separation of Moses "Beenie Man" Davis and Michelle "D'Angel" Downer, dubbed the biggest dancehall celebrity saga. A whirlwind courtship led to the wedding, which took place on August 22, 2006, at one of Kingston's posh resorts, but the marriage ended within one year. The saga was covered by all the major daily newspapers, as well as television and radio stations. The irony is that Jamaican popular music and culture, its purveyors and their lifestyles, did not feature in the media before programmes such as *Teen Age Dance Party*, produced by Sonny Bradshaw, were initiated at the former Jamaica Broadcasting Corporation in 1959 and became popular in the early 1960s. That single programme featuring Jamaican music and dance culture was broadcast on radio from Mondays to Fridays, and on television on Fridays, then moved out of the studios on Saturdays. The first venue was the Broadcasting Corporation itself, but then it moved to the Rainbow Club (formerly Skateland in Halfway Tree), the Glass Bucket Club, and Johnson's Drive Inn.

1.1 Photographs showing scenes from Teenage Dance Party (c.1963)
Source: The Jamaica Gleaner Company

The way in which dancehall is packaged and promoted by the media in the public sphere, and the role of the media in perverting boundaries that were put in place often by participants themselves, have to be accounted for in a holistic reading of dancehall. Dancehall's movement from private to public spaces, including those beyond the immediate boundaries of Jamaica, is therefore significant in the account of tensions. Many questions could be posed. In what ways has dancehall demarcated, transformed, maintained or disrupted post-colonial tensions over the popular space? What has the media's role been? In order to widen the focus on these tensions, I want to turn my attention to other dimensions of the space and place of popular culture in Jamaica, that which occupies the margin as much as the centre of national fervour. David Scott (1999, 191) argues that one index of the contemporary postcolonial project's crisis is the deep and loud disquiet over "the popular," the anxiety over the moral values embodied in contemporary popular practices, among them music and dance creations and celebrations (see also Cooper 1993, 171). The consistent and prevailing influence of the popular on the youth is comparable to, if it does not exceed, the influence of the churches. For the critics, this reflects an erosion of fundamental values and structures of society, and for others a profound synthesis in Caribbean identity through the creative imaginary.

Here I want to use the example of the Trinidadian David Rudder's carnival song "High Mas" (1998), which is profoundly expressive of the Caribbean popular ethos, and speaks directly to this perception of crisis and the countervailing creative potential. The lyrics are as follows:

> Our father who has given us this art
> so that we can all feel like a part
> of this earthly (lesser) heaven
> ... amen
> Forgive us this day our daily weaknesses
> as we seek to cast our mortal burdens on this city
> ... amen
> Oh merciful father, in this bacchanal season
> Where some men will lose their reason
> But most of us just want to wine and grine and have
> a good time because we feeling fine, Lord ... (as we seek our lost
> humanity)
> ... amen

In cajoling the bacchanalian revellers to "give Jah his praises"

Rudder uses the structure and sentiment of the Lord's Prayer, as well as the style and rhythm of spirituals and church choruses such as "If you're happy and you know it, say amen!" to blur the boundaries of the sacred and the secular. Similar examples from Jamaican DJs include Beenie Man's single "Gospel Time," (1999) which encourages one to "shake that boody that Jesus gave you, shake that boody in the name of the Lord," and is set to the tune of a traditional church chorus. To the arbiters of moral values, this would seem blasphemous and a further sign of the decay of values. Rudder's plea for the healing that carnival brings would not factor into their analysis, for no colonial history, performance rituals, literary imagination or metaphors could explain to them the kind of ontology that would produce such a song.

The space that Caribbean popular culture occupies is one of tension with the establishment, particularly the church and state apparatus that denies a Caribbean sense of being rotating holistically around the symbiotically juxtaposed sacred and secular, with spaces of creation in between. The sacred and the secular are not antithetical in character, but coexist in the synthesis they create, which renders the contradictions that some might see as mere omens in the mind. Jamaica's popular cultural space is a cutting-edge site of autonomous creation and negotiation of identity for mostly disenfranchised families and, especially, the inner-city youth. For them the popular space is where the "area politics" that results from partisan political affiliations metamorphoses into vibrations of family or community and deeper "bonds of solidarity" (Patterson 1974, 38; this topic is discussed further in Chapter 2).

These bonds among the urban poor of Kingston are not necessarily based on a "sense of community," but rather on the basis of class or common interest. I would challenge Orlando Patterson's reading of "community" as being too narrow. The work done by social anthropologists and cultural geographers since Patterson's report appeared in 1974 has broadened the way in which "community" is perceived by relating it to wider cultural and social processes, including the worldview as a necessary factor in recognizing one's space as a discrete entity in relation to other spaces, through which notions of "me and you" and "us and them" take shape. It is this perspective that I draw on here to look at performing artistes who strongly mirror the sentiments of their communities of origin, but also those of the wider community of dancehall participants, formed by the lived practice of "community" beyond place of residence and feelings of attachment. Community thus also operates in the popular dance spaces that have served to integrate peoples even beyond their areas of origin. With the opening up of spatialities, diasporas also constitute even broader forms of community due to interconnection and distinctiveness (see Keith and Pile 1993, 18). In the words of Frantz Fanon, these are "zone[s] of occult instability where the people dwell that we must come to; and it is there that our souls are crystallized ... [and] perceptions and lives are transformed with light" (Fanon 1963, 183). Often deemed an occult zone (even if not in those words), the performance space is a collective construct that has spawned communities, diasporas, and transnational geographies.

This double-edged sword of the popular, this contradictory, seemingly deconstructive yet constructive ethos, has been a central part of how Jamaican identity has been (mis)understood. Dancehall can be read as metaphor for the Jamaican popular entertainment culture, which, as if violating some performative boundary, is regulated by the state in ways reminiscent of the past four centuries of plantation entertainment (see Beckles 2000). I would like to draw from Barbara Browning's understanding of "relationships of abnormality," at the global level between 'black' Diaspora performance practice and white perception, and at the local level Kingston's popular dancehall as situated in the wider Jamaican society. In Browning's words (1998, 1 and 5–6),

> the rumble of bass drums so bass they sound for all the world like thunder.... This is a war zone, this is a party.... The beat could be rhumba, hip hop, juju, reggae, samba. Or it could be a combination of all these, layered, one over the other, gaining intensity and significance with every rhythmic line.

Hip hop is one moment in the history of the dispersion and popularization of black musical idioms, a process of cultural exchange that was concomitant with the first processes of global economic exploitation, that is, colonization. Reggae represents another such moment. All were infectious rhythms, all spread quickly, transnationally, accompanied by equally "contagious dances, often characterized as dangerous, usually overly sexually explicit, by white critics" (Browning 1998, 5–6).

Browning explains (1998, 6) that the purpose of her book is to "consider a model with a lengthy and complex history: the Western account of African Diasporic culture that relies on the figure of disease and contagion." She uses the frequent association between the AIDS pandemic and African Diasporic cultural practices as her starting point to illustrate the ways in which "disease and contagion" play a major role in the perception of such practices (1998, p. 6) and cites statistics from the World Health Organization and the U. S. Centers for

Disease Control (1998, 17–49) to show that in 1995 "all twenty of the countries worldwide with provisional HIV infection rates topping 3 percent of the population were in Africa and the Caribbean," while in the United States up to March 1997, more than 50 percent of AIDS cases were among blacks and Hispanics. According to Browning, when "African Diasporic cultural practices" are called upon by Europeans the associated metaphors of contagion may seem harmless. However, their use can result in "violent reactions to cultural expressions," thus reinforcing the "Western depiction of Africans as virulent and dangerous." Further, "it is the conflation of economic, spiritual, and sexual exchange that has allowed for the characterization of Diasporic culture as a chaotic or uncontrolled force, which can only be countered by military or police violence" (1998, 7).

While Browning's project details the African Diasporic cultures as contagion in the European imaginary and the relationship of that configuration to current discourse on the AIDS pandemic, her point of reference is useful for a contextualization of the popular and for a portrayal of the space that dancehall occupies. Its space, though regenerative in its capacity for entertainment, is seen as volatile, as that which can erase the work done by centuries of missionaries trying to Christianize and civilize. Plantation entertainment culture with its contemporary manifestations such as dancehall has been maintained outside the state apparatus, as legislation, state sanctions and marginalization are overshadowed by persistent (re)creativity.

Dancehall life and style exist at the margin of tension between the dispassionate middle and upper classes and the impassioned lower class, as they creatively assert their sense of a disenfranchised self in postcolonial Jamaica (a point I can make with far more clarity thanks to a discussion with Abiona Pape). For some, dancehall is the positive equivalent of the violence that pervades the concentrated but spatially and aesthetically differentiated population of the Kingston Metropolitan Area (a topic further developed in Chapter 4). Dancehall occupies marginal spaces and is simultaneously central to national identity. Dancehall culture is mainstream not only because its spatial centre is the capital city of Jamaica but because of the pervasiveness of its tempo and rhythm, whether displayed in an ordinary television advertisement or its music. Dancehall culture occupies a tenuous place in the popular consciousness of Jamaica. Sentiments vary as to the life-giving nature of the space, as much as over the need for censorship. Among the national stories told by this performance practice is the fact that Jamaica's reputation as a cultural Mecca is unsurpassed due to the inextricable link with the indigenous creations of reggae, Rastafari and dancehall, representations of which frequently appear in tourism campaigns used to attract the next willing visitor. Cursory mention of Jamaica in any country brings the light of recognition on faces that tell of their familiarity with Bob Marley, who is not a national hero at home. Ultimately, therefore, Jamaica self-identifies with these cultural forms in visualizations of the nation beyond its shores. However, ironically, all these indigenous cultural manifestations have received their ample share of criticism, snobbery and censorship at home, and there still has been no government that has addressed issues such as the persecution of Rastafari in the Coral Gardens massacre of April 1963, the establishment of sustainable venues for dancehall culture, or the allocation of resources for infrastructural development that could produce, market and distribute Jamaican music, or for investment and incentive schemes for Jamaican musicians and producers.

ONE DANCEHALL FROM SLAVE SHIP TO GHETTO

I have adapted the Jamaican motto in the title of this chapter to read "Out of many ... one dancehall." This is not some essentializing project that sees all dancehalls as having their antecedents in the plantation dances of the West Indies, or some fundamentalist basking in the Jamaicanness of the product, with exclusive genealogical rights accruing to the "one" Jamaican citizenry. Rather, I want to use the transformed motto to highlight many overlooked dimensions of a unified and unifying cultural practice, in particular, those dimensions related to its spaces of operation, its habitus, historical antecedents, migratory networks, ritual manifestations, as well as the transnational terrain. This book recognizes that there is a broader field and practice in which Jamaican dancehall can be located, compared and analyzed, and that there are many sites through which Jamaican dancehall has even greater significance.

First, spaces of performance can be classified based on the musics consumed in them, their association with secular or sacred practices, the classes, races and ethnicities they originate from, their urban versus rural manifestations, their levels of commercialization, and the events associated with them. Even before the current phenomena of dancehall culture and music began, dance halls have been primary spaces of celebration, especially throughout the Black Atlantic world—from the West Indian plantation dance shrubs, ring shouts or shuffle shouts (Baraka 1968, 42); through "the purely social function of the early Negro Christian churches," which "is of extreme importance if one is trying to analyze any area of American Negro culture" (Baraka 1968, 47), or indeed New World Negro culture more broadly; to

Congo Square and the slave barracks where Afro-Rican Bomba ruled supreme; to juke joints famous for gutbucket cabarets, Chicago's taxi-dance halls in the 1930s, the Savoy or the Palladium ballroom and theatres that were the Jazz and Mambo headquarters of Manhattan; to British basements that housed blues dances, shebeens in Johannesburg, dance yards in Kingston, decorated *casitas* or shacks built by Newyoricans that serve as dance clubs, and the ubiquitous streets. There is a common genealogy, as it were, among New World performance practices, which is an important dimension of the expansive field and practice within which dancehall has to be contextualized. What is this common genealogy?

Dance halls date back to plantation culture. In tracing the story of the dance from the earliest records of dance activity on the slave ships through plantations and colonial cities, it is apparent that the kinds of marginal spaces negotiated for performance have mostly been consistent. Whether on ship decks, in school rooms or shrubs, or on the streets, the enslaved and, later, the freed Africans or peasantry settling across the island of Jamaica, and especially in Kingston, occupied marginal lanes, river banks and gully (ravine) banks, not only for housing and subsistence, but for performance as well. Articulation of the self in these spaces was, and continues to be, potent, as their marginalization is at once their power. Marginalization implies that little or no life can exist in these spaces, only scarcity, idleness, worthlessness, all of which have long been attributed to marginalized peoples. The recoding of mainstream perception of the margin, in deploying its potential to create and communicate a sense of identity, is indicative of power. Creations such as Jamaican dancehall that achieve global recognition emerge in only a few centres on Earth, with power enough to interpolate, even disturb, state consciousness.

There are historical moments, performance ethos and geographical instances, such as in the Blues and the slave ship dance before the settlement of the New World plantations, that I wish to implicate in this discourse of a common genealogy. Among the antecedents of contemporary dancehall are, for instance, both the slave ship dance (or limbo) and the plantation dances reported in the early 19th century by the Reverend Hope Masterton Waddell (1970, 147 and 161–62), with their unique revelry, space and tensions with the ruling class. In many ways dancehall functions as ritual memorializing, maintaining a memory bank of the old, new and dynamic bodily movements, spaces, performers and performance aesthetic of the New World, and of Jamaica in particular. There are continuities of performance, masking, philosophies of space, political processes and fashioning of selfhood, and parallels can be drawn.

One of the first performances recorded in the history of the New World was of limbo, the "slave ship dance." Slave ship logs as early as 1664 document this dance in the experience of enslaved Africans who travelled across the Middle Passage (Fabre 1999, 33–46). Known for its effectiveness as a "ritual of rebirth" based on the healthy exercise received from the dance (Fabre 1999, 42), limbo forms part of the entertainment repertoire in the contemporary tourism industry, and in 1993 to 1994, and 2007 it was a popular dance in dancehall, along with the tatti, the world dance and the erkle. The use of these dances in this way highlights the attempt to locate the history of dancehall in the ancient practice of free Africans and, later, the enslaved peoples. Kamau Brathwaite's poem "Limbo" (1973, 194–95) brings this dance to life in the literary imagination. Brathwaite uses "limbo" as a metaphor to read the Middle Passage experience, with the spiritual and physical pain of dislocation from the African's past. The dance, which involves the body moving under a stick, is thought to have emerged out of the lack of space available on the slave ships, necessitating the slaves bending themselves like spiders. The dance reflects this in the constant lowering of the stick, ostensibly till it touches the ground, and clearing the stick with a lowered back and bent knees presents an ordeal increasing proportionately with the lowering of the stick. This ordeal produces triumph for the dancer who can endure to survive the challenge. The African home and life lost are represented by the bending ordeal, and the promised land to be reached by the triumph of clearing the lowered stick.

There are concrete ways in which limbo can be read as a metaphor for what is missing in the theorization of Caribbean performance, a metaphor of the sacred, a "gateway" (see Harris 1999), as well as a trope through which we can therefore appreciate the common genealogy within performance practices of the Caribbean. First, limbo calls our attention to the dance movement and the space (its limits and potential) in which the movement was (and still is) performed. Second, limbo is a "ritual of rebirth" (Fabre 1999, 33–46): beyond the slave ship during the Middle Passage, it has been linked to puberty and war rituals within Africa, to Kongolese cosmology in particular, as well as to funereal rites (Ahye 2002, 250–54, and see Warner-Lewis 2003, 242–43). Similarly, the plantation dances and urban dancehall events hold memories of aspects of daily life celebrated without any space made available to accommodate or encourage them.

This conversation between limbo and dancehall at the metaphorical and literal levels forms an important platform for understanding performance geography (explored in Chapter 2). By juxtaposing dancehall and limbo, our understanding of performance in the New

World generally, and in contemporary Jamaica specifically, becomes complicated. New World performances such as limbo, especially as it continues to be recreated, hold untapped knowledge that can be excavated for application to contemporary performances. Indeed, when Brathwaite asserts that limbo, as performed in dance events today, is a ritual "being performed in memory of the Middle Passage and it is a transformatory image" beyond the actor's consciousness, he calls attention to the "long-memoried" common genealogy it shares with performances such as contemporary dancehall. So, when limbo appeared in 1994 and again in 2007 as a popular dance move, there was a reliving of this ritual, this connection to the slave ship past. This connection, this common genealogy, is placed squarely into focus by Brathwaite (1994b, 22), for whom limbo is a ritual of arrival, of performance and of history. Limbo is a ritual of rebirth, a recreative response to the condition of the New World, but a ritual with a particular character.

Such a reading allows us to engage with other spaces used for celebration within dancehall and, before dancehall, the plantation and the city, as well as the slave ship, as encounters of sacred and secular practices, and as spaces between centre and periphery, unreflected in any national development agenda. As changing ideologies and terrains have spawned new spaces and acts embodied within memories of the old, these new spaces, acts and actors require new interpretations of their lived rituals.

Dancehall, by virtue of its incorporation of the traditional (in terms of ritual celebration), stands between the Old World and the New World, and the movement/concept of limbo, as well as its invoked extension, liminality, is useful for understanding this. Limbo and dancehall symbolize an everyday life that occupies shrubs, streets, yards, the cracks and margins, but yields tremendous power in philosophy, transcendence and transformation of space. Therefore dancehall can be understood as liminal performance space, a sort of crossroads by virtue of its location at the margin while it simultaneously makes space within the mainstream. As Barry Chevannes (2001) has noted, the crossroads is the meeting place of cardinal points, of loss and gain, the sacred and profane, joy and sorrow, which are important aspects of Caribbean reality, while liminality, which implies ambiguity, is a part of everyday life in many cultures, some of which have deities who preside over it, especially at the crossroads. It is important to note that such deities, as bequeathed to Caribbean experience from West African societies, have survived within folk religions in Haiti, Cuba, Trinidad & Tobago, and Grenada, as well as in Jamaica.

From the time of their arrival, the enslaved participated in a sort of revelry referred to as "seasoning." In an account first published in

1796, John Gabriel Stedman describes the seasoning of the enslaved: on arrival after the debilitating journey across the Middle Passage, enslaved Africans would pass the day away "dancing, hallooing, and clapping hands on board the vessel" (Stedman 1992, 95). This practice of new arrivants is akin to that of aeroplane passengers who clap to give thanks for a safe landing: there is a philosophy of celebration and thanksgiving here. Parallels can be drawn with the present day dancehall patron who is thankful for the release and the opportunity that dancehall provides to escape quotidian social and economic challenges.

Hilary Beckles concludes that the cultural work on the plantations was more than just the search for pleasure; it was "spiritual ideological liberation" (2002, 224), ultimately linked to "political conscientization and organization" (2002, 243). The dance event, Beckles says, was a persistent affair that had within its rubric political endeavours that attracted the attention of legislators. As dancing became a sign of spiritual strategy and liberation for the enslaved, so too did it find seething hearts within the planter class. Dress regulations were enforced in some colonies, and there were prosecutions for "rebellious conspiracy" (Beckles 2002, 231 and 240). A distinct celebratory culture emerged as the enslaved "fashioned a life of their own beyond their owners' corporate boundaries, so that organized activities moved beyond the bounds of plantations to encompass broader geographical boundaries."

This is paralleled by other performance traditions, such as those of Congo Square in New Orleans, to which the enslaved were brought from the surrounding areas by their masters who policed their playing, singing and dancing in regular gatherings (Baraka 1968, 71–72). Social containment was maintained by the New Orleans Black Codes, which allowed the enslaved Sundays off. Many used the day to dance, sing and play instruments in Congo Square (c. 1804–1820). Later, policed spaces of performance were legitimized by the segregation laws (c. 1894). Formerly privileged creoles lost their jobs as performers because of these laws, while blacks gained employment playing music in the saloons and dance halls, at which older brass bands were the staple.

A close examination of the history reveals that "shrubs" were made for the slave dances in the early and mid-19th century, as reported by a contemporary witness, the Reverend Hope Masterton Waddell (1970, 17–18, 147 and 161–62). They were sometimes constructed with bamboo and as often as they were erected they were demolished after the event. Waddell reports that slaves in Jamaica had three holidays at Christmas, which lasted one week among the town slaves, "who made a Saturnalia of a Christian festival, spending the time in the grossest rioting." His report of the character of slave entertainment, and the physical and philosophical spaces it occupied, is revealing. There was "unbounded revelry" in the "shrub made for the occasion", with crowds dancing "Johnny Canoe," singing and drumming, and set girls. There were "rude and demoralizing 'balls and suppers,'" as well as "the soirée," of which the first one, in the school house, an official space, was introduced "to promote the great cause of temperance and of social improvement." Waddell recounts "revelling and rioting" in the negro yards by "ill-disposed, disorderly people … pervert[ing] their freedom" with singing, drumming and dancing in "the booth" constructed in a certain yard, which the powers of the plantation society were not able to prevent. One resident of the yard was later arrested and jailed for staging the ball and threatening the life of a constable, and Waddell and other "quiet good people rejoiced" that this person would no longer be able to "disturb all their neighbours" with revelry into the morning. The conception that the soirée, not the so-called meetings, balls and suppers, would "help the process of transformation which was going on from slavery to freedom" prevails in contemporary Jamaica, and is manifested in the tensions over popular cultural expressions.

The use of booths for the events reported by Waddell is consistent with reports of the dance scene in Jamaica by Erna Brodber (2003, 90–96), who highlights the setting of rural dance activity based on interviews conducted with octogenarians. One of them, Mass Levi, with his reference to the "boother" who collected the entrance fee, reveals much about the operation of such booths in rural Trelawny.

1.2 French Set Girls & Jonkonnu Dancers (Jamaica) by Isaac Mendes Belisario
Source: The Atlantic Slave Trade and Slave Life in the Americas Collection, University of Virginia

22

These witnesses' memories are confirmed by the reports of the an-thropologist Jozef Obrebski and his wife Tamara, who observed the presence and popularity of booths in St Elizabeth as part of their im-portant record of dance activity in the New World in the late 1940s. Booth dances commenced at around 8 p.m. and often continued till midnight, escalating in intensity as they celebrated various aspects of life, including marriage and death. They were held in small spaces, sometimes in yards or shops or adjoining them, and, depending on the booth, only six dancing couples could be accommodated at any time, although larger booths could accommodate up to twenty couples. The Obrebskis reported (1948, 7) seeing

> seventy men outside the dancing hall.... There were about eleven women, including those standing at the window. There were about twenty couples on the dance floor. The place was congested, but somehow the dancing continued, largely because the dancing was of the rumba and jitterbugging type. There were also, at this time, about ten to fifteen people in the bar.

To solve the problem of space, groups of dancers rotated in and out of the booth between sets of approximately five songs. Jive, jitter-bugging, "jogging," arm-swinging, rolling, hip-wagging, shaking and waltzing were typical for the rumbas, waltzes and mento played by live bands using guitars and violins.

The Obrebskis also underscored the importance of women in the dance space, dance and music styles, use of space, spectatorship, and the method of paying. Women were central to these dances, as partner dancing was required. Women did not pay to gain access to the dance floor. Rather, they were escorted by men who chose them as partners.

Some of the music they danced to in the booths came from the United States. In the late 19th century thousands of black migrants had experienced and taken advantage of their "out-of-placeness" to travel from place to place throughout the Southern United States in search of work or a new sense of self. Blacks in the Mississippi Delta created their music in the context of their everyday troubles and prob-lems, and their experience is bound up in the blues. Poverty, political disenfranchisement and legal segregation, the violence of lynchings, beatings and shootings: a conglomeration of oppression and disen-franchisement is articulated in the music and the writings of blues per-formers. The space and ethos of "blues people" were similar to those of plantation dwellers in the West Indies. Blues as a form of musical expression highlighted themes of frustration, lack of love, loneliness, anger, life in the slums and rejection, many of these being universal themes. Beyond musical themes, Michelle Scott (2002) has defined blues culture as the

> various forms of communication and the creation of community that occurred in such recreational environments as saloons, vaudeville houses, tent shows, juke joints, and street corners. In these spaces, blues music became more than just entertainment, but music of self-definition and personal liberation.

Such spaces, some of them with different local names, can be found throughout the Black Atlantic world.

Alan Lomax (1943), Amiri Baraka (1968) and David Grazian (2003) all explicitly acknowledge that space and place are critical to an understanding of the blues, as is its origin in slavery. The Delta, the swamps of New Orleans and the South Side of Chicago were key points for the blues, each with its own unique symbols and icons. The blues originated from the field hollers, the chain gang chants, and the choruses of roadbuilders, clearers of swamps, lifters and toters, with all the anger of work songs rooted in African singing tradition. Places of locational importance included highways and streets, yards and verandas, juke joints, and back alleys. It is thought that blues music came from the back alleys, the equivalent of the lanes of early Kingston, and portrayed the ways of the alley and its lifestyle (Murray 2000, 50). There are memories and myths of the blues bound up in certain locations, such as the "blues crossroads," at the intersection of Highways 61 and 49, which run through the Delta, where, it is said, Robert Johnson, a foundation bluesman, sold his soul to the Devil in exchange for his musical genius (King 2004, 466). Not unlike dancehall in Jamaica, blues performances also spilled onto streets, or the streets were their actual site.

What is distinctive about the blues is that its emergence was in displacement, "out-of-placeness," transport and travel, touring and migration, flows and networks. The concept of "Traveling Riverside Blues" (the title of one of Robert Johnson's songs) encapsulates the nomadism firmly embedded in blues music and performance. Like the movement of Jamaican mento bands in the 1940s and 1950s, itinerant bluesmen traversed the Mississippi Delta up to the 1930s, using trains, trucks and carts. The popular singer Ma Rainey, for example, "toured the South for years with a company called the Rabbit Foot Minstrels and became widely known in Negro communities everywhere in America" (Baraka 1968, 89).

As a popular site, juke joints or honky tonks were commonly associated with jukeboxes. By the early 1920s, and before the popularization of radio, coin-in-slot phonographs in public spaces had become the primary mass medium for the consumption of popular music, which at that time meant orchestral and classical instrumental music. By the 1930s, however, jukeboxes had emerged, and could be found in roadhouses and taverns or juke joints. Every American innovation finds its way to Jamaica, and the jukebox is no different. (In the 1960s my grandfather purchased a jukebox, which provided the music for weekend dances organized by my aunts and uncles.)

According to Amiri Baraka (1968), you had to go to the "gutbucket cabarets" to hear real blues played live. Gutbucket cabarets were lower-class venues where tripe or chitterlings (pig guts) was served. While the blues developed and was consumed in more commercialized settings, it also maintained a strong presence in the more marginal/informal lounges and shacks, including many impromptu jam sessions, on street corners, at family or public barbeques, in roadhouses, and at private and semi-private parties. Many of these venues for entertainment were an imperative produced by the condition of oppression.

Of course, some early perceptions of the blues in the United States mirror the perception of dancehall in Jamaica by purists who embrace the Judeo-Christian ethic as the high water mark of spirituality. It was thought to be the Devil's music, not the music of the church or God. The underlying racial discourse here is not to be overlooked, as the church and state apparatuses colluded to shroud blacks and their performance practices within a cloud of inferiority and evil. However, church space and religious aesthetic share a strong relationship with the blues, as explicitly seen in the experiences of those blues stars who had to go to church and were not even permitted to go to the weekend blues. Ma Rainey, W. C. Handy and Jelly Roll Morton, among numerous others, blended the practice of Protestant church musicians with their own.

An examination of blues performance through the lens of space shifts the focus from linear, musical, lyrical or celebrity analyses to incorporate other perspectives, theoretical orientations, histories and national contexts. Without referencing fixed points of origin, I want to highlight the presence within the blues of a common spatial imagination that is relevant to an understanding of dancehall. While this book is not centred on historicizing the blues, I have implicated historical antecedents such as the blues in connection with dancehall in order to underscore the similarities in their production and consumption of culture within policed, marginalized, ritual spaces, in a context of displacement, state intervention and sanctions. This relationship between place, performance and identity extends beyond national contexts, therefore, to a wider Diasporic space of musical trajectories.

Research on the blues also confirms that there are continuities in terms of the spaces of operation, the creators and the mechanisms for identity construction. The obvious influence that the blues has had on Jamaican culture can be seen, for example, in the Blues Busters, a vocal group often in the top ten musical chart in Jamaica, with regular bookings at musical showcases at the Majestic and Carib Theatres; blues dance, a popular entertainment for the youth based on the sound system culture; blue beat, which is what ska came to be called; and Clue J and the Blues Blasters. The early importance of the blues is also evident in the advertisements in the *Daily Gleaner* that announced the latest blues records for sale, as on July 26, 1924, when they publicized such tunes as "Mobile Blues" and "Limehouse Blues." There were also many Jamaican imitations of the American big bands, the blues and jazz bands that emerged in the 1930s. Some twenty to thirty bands were playing mento and jazz in Kingston by the 1940s, all of them modelled on American big bands and using "fake books" that contained the musical repertoire. Rhythm and blues (R&B) found favour with Jamaicans in the 1950s in the sound system dances, and by the 1960s ska had developed as a combination of rhythm and blues with Jamaican forms such as mento. The lingering influence of the blues through R&B continues today in the staple of American artists played in rotation on the Jamaican airwaves.

Perhaps a metropolitan U. S. equivalent of Jamaican dance halls is to be found in Paul Goalby Cressey's study of the "taxi-dance halls" of Chicago, which was first published in 1932 (see Cressey 2008). These halls boasted beautiful ladies of "unique" reputation who were available to dance with desiring men for a fee. The system was not far removed from the mechanism of booths discussed above, but what is different is the extent to which documentation of the dance scene—the mapping of its spaces and its prohibiting as well as encouraging factors—has been undertaken.

Contextualizing Jamaican dance halls takes us forward to the mid-1950s in Kingston, when sound system operators such as Tom "The Great Sebastian" Wong or Clement "Sir Coxsone" Dodd reigned supreme around the area of downtown Kingston that came to be known as Beat Street, in the North Street area. From Foresters Hall, Bull Head Lawn and Chocomo Lawn to clubs such as Cactus and Asylum, Kingston's rich history of dance halls is the focus of this book, alongside the engagement with dancehall through a discourse of space. It is important to note that spaces that have been used for dance events in Jamaica have intrinsic character and tell stories about the politics and culture of these spaces. Among these—the theatre stage, the school house, the market or the street, be it for the class-specific mass "dhaance" or the upper-class "dawnce theatre"—dance activity prevails in the Afro-Jamaican way of life with specific features. As mentioned earlier, these include a tense relationship between the state and what emerges from the lower class, as well as notable differences between the sanctions placed on the street versus those that affect the stage. In their location can be seen class and geopolitical characteristics. For example, one is uptown, the other downtown, one is on the gully bank or street occupying marginal space, the other is on the managed and "cultured" proscenium stage.

This chapter has set the groundwork for privileging the idea of space as a holistic category that allows for engagement with dancehall through indigenous lenses that take account of the spatial. The discussion in ensuing chapters builds on the (performance) sociology of the subcultural dance contributed by Garth White (1984), for example, but also on the long tradition of recorded dance activity in the New World that highlights space as a significant feature of the performance practices. In Chapter 2 these ideas are solidified within the concept of performance geography.

INTRODUCING PERFORMANCE GEOGRAPHY

THE WORLD is a stage that forms the core of how we navigate or perform our being in the many worlds we occupy. Humans, then, can be seen as performing beings who live simply because they can act or perform, rather than merely observe.

The term "performance" had early denotations (c. 1500s) of completion, executing action, restored behaviour, but from the 1960s it came to be used in academic circles to represent the visual effect of actual performance on stage, as distinct from the dramatic scripts that give birth to the artistic productions (Taylor 2003, 2–7). Since then the field of performance studies has sought to engage with various aspects of performance as an object of study and a method of analysis. The analysis of performance events and acts has revealed much about how humans perform themselves in the context of their everyday lives (see Pelias 2008), and the field has established connections with such disciplines as anthropology and sociology. One unique area of performance studies is performance ethnography, which takes account of theatre practitioners and academics who have adapted ethnographic field notes in order to stage them (see McCall 2000). With such cross-disciplinary terrain being created between sociology, anthropology and the performing arts, this book seeks to further interdisciplinary engagement by introducing performance geography.

Performance is defined in different ways in different cultures. Broadly speaking, African performance stands somewhat apart from performance in the West because it is seen less as an object than as part of the fabric of life. For example, as Africans view it, music is not a thing of beauty to be enjoyed in isolation. Rather, it exists only as woven into the larger milieu, which also combines games, dance, words, drama and visual art. As Ruth M. Stone observes (1995, 258):

> The words that mean "performance" or "event," whether the *pele* of the Kpelle [in West Africa] or *lipapali* of the Basotho [in Southern Africa], are applied not only to music-making, dancing and speaking, but also to children's games and sports.

Similarly, according to John Comaroff (1985, 111), among the Tswana "the verb *go bina* connoted 'to sing,' 'to dance,' *and* 'to venerate,' implying the act of honouring by means of the aesthetic of harmonious collective performance" (emphasis added). The arena of performance can therefore be much wider than the staged performances that are the objects of inquiry into "the performing arts."

A cursory examination of academic disciplines suggests that performance studies is different from geography. Performance is focused on the act and the stage, while geography concerns the locational features of the physical, cultural and material world. With debates in cultural geography, and in cultural studies more widely, revolving around relationships of time and space, and the politics of space and identity, an increase in the use of spatial metaphors, such as mapping, location, centre/margin, global/local, liminal space, the city, is apparent (see Keith and Pile 1993, 1 and 67). The reassertion of space, be it real, imaginary, symbolic or a combination of these, makes it clear that space can no longer be constituted as a passive void, but that a new spatial imagination allows for a reading of its structures or surfaces of articulation, which include the body, the cosmos and the city. For example, Edward Soja (1993 and 1996) has argued for an integrative approach to the study of social existence. He documents the historical perspective as a master narrative through which temporality is set up against spatiality, constructing and configuring existence and its interpretation. Soja calls for a critical awareness of space as an interpretive context, and argues that comparable attention should be centred on the geographical imagination as on the historical. Here, Soja is engaging with Michel Foucault's perspective on space. Such works bring into focus an understanding of spatial epistemology, the spatial imagination as a critical piece of human existence and therefore a significant part of the critical insight into, and interpretation of, this existence.

Reference to Foucault (1986) highlights another dimension, that of the lived social space as a complex of sites and their relations to each other, in a social ecological perspective. Sites, then, are delimited by the set of relations among them. Sites speak to particular relations, and those such as the cemetery, the church or the brothel and the colony, determine how society views itself and is viewed. Power also lies in the juxtaposing of several spaces and their attendant relations. According to Soja (1993, 143), Foucault created another understanding of space in the world of spatial imaginings, conceptualizing an "actually lived and socially created spatiality, concrete and abstract at the same time, the habitus of social practices. It is a space rarely seen, for it has been obscured by a bifocal vision that traditionally views space as either a mental construct or a physical form."

Engagement with space in cultural studies of the Caribbean is critical. What can the relations of time, space and social being tell us about the dancehall lifeworld, for example? I argue that the social being in dancehall is constantly performing and being performed. History is the record of this performance, with its attendant relations of domination and exclusion, and geography is its site, a spatiality that is contested yet is creatively used at the margins of existence. Both history and geography are engulfed in power relations. Space and, consequently, its web of spatialities are therefore critical to an understanding of cultural groupings, as they throw into relief issues of power: how space organizes, reproduces, produces or destabilizes power. Ultimately, such an understanding helps us in reconsidering what the Caribbean is, not only historically, but also spatially, through the site(s) it (under)represents and those it is juxtaposed to. This sheds light not only on the macropolitics but also on the schemes of the habitat, the home and the street.

My intention is not to outline a lineage of spatial language or its criticism, or even to add to the theorizing that has culminated in postmodern conceptions of space. I wish to apply what Soja offers as examples of spatial epistemologies, not only at the level of discourse but to postcolonial materiality, where identity is understood as lived spatial narratives of, for example, the street, nomadism or siege, at personal and communal levels. Postcolonial realities are manifested in, for example, the African Diaspora in the Caribbean, residing at the centre of modernity and postmodernity. By their very existence these realities complicate the prisms that emanate from linear and binary perceptions of cultures within contact zones such as the Caribbean.

The nexus of historical and social production of space is present at varying levels of the approach to dancehall in this study, including, among others, space as space of work, as home, as celebration, pleasure, barrier and identity. Space has to be understood as both unifying and differentiating, as produced and as product, as an apparatus of domination, as having knowledge, struggles, narratives, and as sites of negotiation. Dancehall displays an emphasis on space and locality in the movement and lyrics highlighting the city, the area, the ghetto, the street or other sociospatial data. These data help us in mapping the cultural production of significant performance sites and identities. Identities are life stories that have a geography, a locale, a habitat by which thought and action are motivated. Coupled with the historical, which influences action and the story line, the spatial imagination sets the stage of the theatre, as it were.

With renewed interest in space and its implied discourse of spatiality, and building upon the work of Foucault, Soja and others, performance geography expands the work of Nigel Thrift (1997) and Catherine Nash (2000) on the role of performance, and specifically embodied practices, in cultural geography. Cutting-edge directions in geography point to the nexus between cultural geography, cultural studies and performance in the study of music and dance. For example, John Connell and Chris Gibson (2003) provide a geography of popular music, its meaning, its relationship to identity, and its links to and between sites, in a range of musical genres. Acknowledging that perceptions of space are mediated by popular cultural forms such as music and television, space is implicated in the sites where music is created, consumed and disseminated across time, through various local and global flows, and at all geographical scales. Identities are shaped by music. Social movements from Rastafari to the Civil Rights movement in the United States have used music as a medium, in rituals, praise and proselytizing. Music may be seen as an institution around which process, economy, identity and heritage are organized; as a product that gains mobility through networks, tours and technology; and as a medium for the transmission of sacred, profane, oppositional, transnational and political elements, operating in a cartographic web of cultural production. In short, there is a link between sound and setting.

Catherine Nash (2000, p. 657) calls for a move away from representation towards analysis of performance practices. She notes that performativity, seen through embodied practices such as dance, opens spaces for new theoretical, imaginative and material understanding, and points to the way in which "work on cultural histories and geographies of specific dance forms offers alternative directions for thinking about practices and performance." Examples of what she calls "choreocriticism" embrace such questions as who could dance "where, with whom, for what audiences and how, tell of contests over culture, masculinity, class and nationhood, the legitimate, the civilized, the respectable, the primitive, the authentic and the exotic" in various local, national and global sites. I consider such engagement with music and embodied performance, and their relationship to the spatial, as important building blocks on which to develop an understanding of performance geographies.

What, then, is performance geography? Using dancehall as the site for introducing this perspective, performance geography is as an integral and unexplored dimension of cultural studies and cultural geography that expands the definitions of cultural geography and performance studies to include the ways in which people living in particular locations give those locations identity through certain acts. By "performance" I do not refer to a narrow context and analysis of what is staged. Rather, I want to take account of the physical, mental, emotional and spiritual acts in the process of enacting one's being, in such historical and political experiential contexts as the Black Atlantic, between violation, ruptured roots and self-(re)construction. Performance is a requirement for life. It consists of labour, the work of being or having status in the world one occupies. I focus here on acts or performance practices that implicate space in tangible ways that can be, and need to be, theorized by virtue of the weight given to these (socio)performative acts. For example, when the Jamaican Olympic and world 100-metres record holder Usain Bolt performed the "no linga" dance during his victory lap at the Beijing Olympics in 2008, what was the significance of this event for dancehall performance as well as for Jamaican identity, and Jamaica's geopolitical and cultural distinctiveness?

Performance geography provides innovative ways to conceptualize space, place and their interconnectedness. It is about the link between the self, identity, place and certain acts. Developing a perspective on the link between location and performance requires engagement with individual and collective power that transforms a space into a place through acts of display. In looking at the ways in which people living in specific contexts give those locations identity through performance, I analyze the interplay between spatial use, character, citizenry, identity construction and community building strategies. I use performance geography to refer to a mapping of the material and spatial conditions of performance: entertainment and ritual in specific sites/venues, types and systems of use, the politics of their location in relation to other sites and other practices, the character of events/rituals in particular locations, and the manner in which different performances and performers relate to each other within and across different cultures.

There is also the level of the spatial philosophies that govern systems of use, boundaries and boundarylessness, gendered spaces, and the urban, and that form part of the rubric of performance geography. How do performances imprint themselves on space? What spatial identities do performances bear? How is the performative self to be defined in any given space? Are there distinctions to be made between the local and the global self in performance? An understanding of the performance of self and the collective in space is an important dimension of performance geography. Performance geography is built on an understanding that acts of performance are linked across space through ritual, dance movement, production and consumption practices, as well as the movement of aural and visual images. There are spatial texts that can be read at various levels in and around performance. Here lies the constitution of the explorations in this book.

Consistent with the ecological approach mentioned earlier, entry into dancehall via its space allows for illumination of the relations among elements such as venues, events and embodied elocution, especially in the form of dance moves. Here, emphasis is not placed on music performance, even though it is used to elucidate central points about dancehall spatiality. Rather, the performances of DJs and selectors, and the recordings of their practice, are used as sites to talk about movement, tours, flows and routes, while simultaneously expanding perspectives on performance geography.

While dancehall's macro- and microgeography is the main site used to explore performance geography, this book is also concerned with applying the concept to other Black performance practices, looking specifically at the history that grounds it as far back as the Middle Passage slave ship dance (limbo), and its delineation in plantation, city and ghetto contexts, where performance practices such as the blues in the United States, kwaito in South Africa or reggaetón in Puerto Rico emerged and have their creative homes. Out of such marginal spaces as the ghetto, performance cultures are consistently emerging, challenging the very contexts that militate against their emergence. Like the enslaved who arrived at Kingston Harbour after the ordeal of the Middle Passage, inner-city youth survive the challenges of the urban experience through their strategies of performance, voluntarily or not.

Spatiality is a central concern for geography, and performance is a vital part of human existence, so a mapping of the nexus created by these elements is crucial to our understanding of humanity and the sociocultural systems that humanity has fashioned. I therefore introduce a geography that is performer-centred, "geography as citizenry" constantly performing their identities as economic, psychic or cultural imperatives dictate.

Space is a significant element in New World performance. My analysis of performance geography in the context of Blackness, the New World and its Middle Passage history invokes Paul Gilroy's conception of the Black Atlantic as a "counterculture of modernity" (see Gilroy 1993), although there are ways in which I depart from Gilroy's reading even as my work continues the tradition. Acknowledging the criticisms of Gilroy's discourse—from Peter Sutherland (1999), who highlights the virtual absence from it of examples from Latin America, Africa or the wider Caribbean, Norman Corr, Jr., and Rachel Corr (1999), who emphasize the absence of the Middle Passage history of suffering, and Don Robotham (2005), who points to Gilroy's lack of attention to material forces—I concur with Gilroy when he states (1993, 111),

In the space and time that separate Robert Johnson's "Hellbound on my Trail," the Wailers' exhortation to "Keep on Moving," and the more recent Soul II Soul piece with the same name, the expressive cultures of the black Atlantic world have been dominated by a special mood of restlessness. These songs, like so many others in the same intertextual sequence, evoke and affirm a condition in which the negative meanings given to the enforced movement of blacks are somehow transposed. What was initially felt to be a curse—the curse of homelessness or the curse of enforced exile—gets repossessed. It becomes affirmed and is reconstructed as the basis of a privileged standpoint from which certain useful and critical perceptions about the modern world become more likely. It should be obvious that this unusual perspective has been forged out of the experiences of racial subordination. I want to suggest that it also represents a response to successive displacements, migrations, and journeys (forced and otherwise) which have come to constitute these black cultures' special conditions of existence.

Gilroy's geographically themed study speaks to a spatial imperative in the black experience in terms of restlessness, homelessness, displacement, migration and other journeys. On a point of convergence with Gilroy, I would like to continue the unearthing of New World performance geographies, indeed, of popular culture and space.

In the tradition of Kamau Brathwaite, Wilson Harris and Geneviève Fabre, who have etched clear images of the slave ship dance limbo in Black Atlantic scholarship, let me return to the limbo dance as one of the first moves to be recorded in the New World. It presents an opportunity to illustrate some key points for laying the groundwork of what I am calling performance geography. Limbo offers an intellectual context, a framework, literal and artistic, to unearth meaning and narratives in the culture of entertainment in the New World, particularly dancehall in Jamaica and beyond. Limbo holds memory and marks continuity among performance practices of the New World. This memory is evidenced in the way in which movement patterns such as the limbo have been preserved throughout the past 300 years, emerging among the Jamaican Maroons, in Jamaican tourist entertainment in the 20th century and as a wake dance in Trinidad & Tobago (Ahye 2002, 247–61). The dance presents a historical, spatial and performance instance. Space is an important element in New World performance and the limbo dance brings this sharply to mind, emphasizing the importance of not only the historical imagination but also the spatial imagination.

The plantation dances and urban dancehall events evoke memories of celebratory events held within spatially restricted, heavily policed and marginal settings. As mentioned in Chapter 1, the limbo is thought to have emerged out of the lack of space available on the slave ships. This lack of space is also obvious to anyone who visits slave-trading posts such as Elmina Castle in Ghana, with its low thresholds that the enslaved navigated to move from dungeon to holding room to the "door of no return"—now renamed the "door of return"—before boarding the slavers (as I saw for myself on November 9, 2003). Consistent with certain African beliefs, the whole cycle of life is reflected in the dance, culminating with the dancer's head clearing the pole as if emerging in a triumph of life over death (see Ahye 2002).

The slave ships, like the plantation and the city, reveal particular spaces that have produced magical forms of entertainment and ritual. An average of 78 inches by 16 inches per person was available to the enslaved below deck, from which they had to emerge invigorated. This closely parallels the narrow lanes and walkways, and the cramped yards and rooms, in the inner-city spaces of Kingston. In these cramped spaces inner-city dwellers use their "shuffle shoes" to ease the tensions of their immediate everyday lives—the hunger, the guns, the brutality, the margins. Having been performed on the slave ships, where hardly enough space existed limbo focuses the issue and crisis of space at the empirical level and within critical discourse. Transporting the enslaved for such long journeys in restricted spaces necessitated exercise to keep them alive. Performance was a requirement for life. It pushed the boundaries of limitation to avail spaces of liberation from oppression and dislocation, even as these spaces were limited, liminal and often ephemeral with nomadic events.

The slave ship, just like the urban spaces of downtown Kingston, Jamaica, or Laventille, Trinidad, from which dancehall and steel band cultures respectively have come, produced particular "brands" of performance, with unique citizenry and community-building strategies. Viewing contemporary dancehall more precisely from the perspective of limbo, and its spatial and performance dimensions, enables analysis of its core creative energies among the population residing in for example, Kingston's inner city, a space compounded by what I call "triple exile," as a way of illustrating just how far from origins postcolonial actors are. Inner-city dwellers are removed from their ancestral origin, but they are also exiled by physical, political and economic marginalization, and this in turn is compounded by a third form of exile, through the way in which the former militates against progress toward personal and collective aspirations, visions of self, and advancement generally. The research published by Horace Levy (1996) and Herbert Gayle (1997) on the ways in which inner-city communities are stereotyped, so that their location functions as a kind of negative passport when they try to obtain jobs, speaks to some of these issues.

Viewing contemporary dancehall from the perspective of limbo also allows a view of spatialities and philosophies of space not yet engaged. For example, the street figures into many venues, whether events are on the street or spill onto the street, possibly as a way of transcending the boundaries inherent in the layout of the city. What does this street narrative tell us about dancehall as style and practice? When and how does the street make its transformation into ritual space? Are there any inherent philosophies about space, possibly linked to notions of success and failure, and the spirit of the collective? The inclusion of a problematization of its space and spatiality, its practice, practitioners and spaces of practice that have been excluded, widens the definition of dancehall beyond the scholarship currently available.

I focus here on performance, especially that of marginalized people. I am particularly interested in the spatiality of performances, and the performers' ability to produce and reproduce space through their practice, particularly participants' negotiation of contested and unreconciled issues of space while they create spaces of celebration and valorized identities as key survival strategies. The work of living beyond the odds for persons outside capitalist mainstreams is bound up with performativity as a means for public as well as private advancement. As Dwight Conquergood states (1991, 189),

> Particularly for the poor and marginalized people denied access to middle-class "public" forums, cultural performance becomes the venue for "public discussion" of vital issues central to their communities, as well as an arena for gaining visibility and staging their identity.

These marginalized citizens, whether on the slave ships or in inner-city communities, wield power in their performance modes. By "performance" I therefore refer to the movement, the drama, the cultural work of enacting one's identity; physical, mental, emotional and spiritual performance; performance as a requirement for life that pushes the boundaries of limitation to avail spaces of liberation from oppression and dislocation, even as these spaces continue to be limited, policed and nomadic.

A PERFORMANCE GEOGRAPHY OF THE CITY

While the history of popular music and dance culture in Jamaica, particularly the emergence of mento, ska, rocksteady and reggae, has to acknowledge the role of rural-based traditional music and dance forms, a cartographic representation of reggae and its contemporary expression, dancehall, would locate its central nervous system within the city of Kingston. Most of the musicians, sound systems, recording studios, DJs, dance venues and patrons, were and still are located in the urban complex known as the Kingston Metropolitan Area (KMA), which includes the parishes of Kingston and St Andrew. The citizens who have inspired, performed and consumed dancehall lifestyle include dancers, such as the late Gerald "Bogle" Levy, a foremost dance master, or Denise "Stacey" Cumberland, Dancehall Queen 1999; the early DJs U Roy, Tappa Zukie, Brigadier Jerry, Tenor Saw and Yellow Man; and today's DJs such as Elephant Man, Bounti Killa and Capleton, whose practice reveals strong ties to what is loosely known as inner-city Kingston.

The inner-city communities are mostly located around Kingston Harbour and along the gullies entering it. The Harbour operates as an aquatic drum on which the sounds from the inner city are amplified and sent out to the world. While this is a figurative rendering of how reggae music and later dancehall spread globally, it is also a visual representation of the sacred drum, the echo chamber that Kingston Harbour has become for Kingston's sound systems. Kingston, with its backdrop of mountains overlooking the natural harbour, is both physically and metaphorically the amphitheatre in which daily life is performed for both the self and the world as its spectator. I argue that performance is the lifeworld of actors: they are not merely subjects in a postcolonial script but agents in the creation and recreation of their own urban life stories.

When Elephant Man proclaimed "Me an' my crew got di whole city lock," he was referring to the fact that, from high to low, from uptown to downtown, in clubs and streets, and on radio and television, dancehall has the attention of the entire city. Kingston is one of the spaces where New World Africans settled their minds on the task of performance, enacting their being in that space between violation, ruptured roots and self-(re)construction. I turn attention to the space that is synonymous with dancehall, centring on inner-city Kingston and its citizenry, their culture and everyday life, and, to a lesser extent, the wider KMA. I look at the kinds of spaces that are used by dancehall, where they are located, and how everyday spaces, even uninhabitable ones, are transformed into ritual spaces through events that are ultimately celebrations of life and death. This section explores multiple geographies evidenced in the performance world of the dancehall, in the spatial divides, systems and descriptors revealed by the research. Spaces of the self and community are overarching pillars on which the performance geography is built.

Kingston—King's Town, "Jah Jah City", amphitheatre and once auction block—is where the drum and later the drum machine beat one of the world's most popular musics, to which bodies the world over move, a signal of something new and ancient. It is the city that Jah made, that garden with the Hope River running through, where rhythm signals the pulse of life in the redefinition of violated selves that are renewed in the complex process of re-enacting memories from a ruptured past. The development of the parish and city of Kingston was a consequence of the destruction of Port Royal by earthquake in 1692, and the move on the part of colonialists to capitalize on the trade made possible and strategic by the world's seventh largest natural harbour, Kingston Harbour. The city, modelled on English-style residential squares, grew slowly, with the population being concentrated in the southern sections from its inception (see Bailey 1974).

From the days of Captain Morgan and other pirates in Port Royal, life and style in Jamaica attracted world attention even before the development of Kingston, mostly for the negatives of corruption, piracy and violence. The "high life" of Port Royal, Jamaica's first metropolis, attracted so many explorers and exploiters that it soon became the den of iniquity that history recalls it to have been. In some ways, the disasters that plagued Port Royal and southern Kingston were the only solutions to a history gone bad. The harbour between Port Royal and Kingston today stands as a kind of spirit glass or mirror in which memories lie, as it is simultaneously a drum's echo chamber. The harbour could also be seen as a goblet or cup, from which the somewhat bitter-sweet wine of celebration is drunk, especially by those closest to the rim. Indeed, dance venues at the edge of the harbour, such as Jamaica Gates (now defunct) or the New Little Copa Club, have functioned in this way for countless celebrants. Today life and style in the KMA are reminiscent of Port Royal: politicians exploit the poor, violence is the Achilles heel, and agents come as explorers wanting to find the latest pulse of the reggae beat. The DJ Capleton (a.k.a. Clifton Bailey) says this of "King's-to(w)n" in his song "Jah Jah City" (2000): "Jah Jah city, Jah Jah city, dem a tu'n it inna dead man town." The Rastafari rendering of Jamaica is "Jah mek ya" ("God made here"), which is consistent with notions of sacred space heralded by DJs such as Capleton.

In outlining the development of dancehall in urban Kingston, critical components include mapping of the historically and politically orchestrated lifestyle of the urban poor and the ordinary persons' orchestration of their own survival, or survivalism (see, for example, Harriot 2000, 100), of which the dancehall space forms a central part. Bob Marley's song "Dem Belly Full (But We Hungry)" (1976) captures the sense of frustration, inequality, injustice and attendant creative survivalism in the very making of the music and the sound/dance nexus that is at the core of the city identity:

> Dem belly full but we hungry
> A hungry man is an angry man ...
> A pot a cook but the food no 'nough

> You're gonna dance to Jah music, dance ...
> Forget your troubles and dance ...

Twenty-six years later the DJ Mr. G (formerly Goofy) claimed in a television interview (2002): "Over the years we've got our support, not from the government or the court," lamenting the lack of institutional support for the music industry in general, but also for the citizenry at the heart of this music culture. The systems that sustain indigenous forms are at best underresourced. It is in these conditions that reggae music was birthed and its progeny dancehall has thrived. No study of dancehall can ignore this citizenry. The next section, in conjunction with ensuing chapters, provides answers to the following questions: Who are these citizens and what is the condition of their everyday life? Where do they live and have their being? What are the spaces and habitus of their creativity? What are the symbols, fantasies and products of their imaginings? All these questions become critical to an understanding of dancehall and to the elaboration of a performance geography of Kingston.

SELECT CITIZENRY, SELECT SPATIALITY

The KMA occupies only about eight square miles, a tiny fraction of Jamaica's total area of 4,444 square miles, but it is home to nearly 652,000 people, or 23 percent of Jamaica's total population of about 2,825,000. The city has contradictions as well as its own internal logic and consistency. West, Central and East Kingston, forming an almost horizontal corridor that borders the Harbour for approximately three miles, is the creative home of Jamaica's popular music and dance culture. This is Kingston's inner city and the people here—increasingly marginalized, with some degree of cartographic non-existence since the outmigration of the merchant class—occupy one of the world's poverty traps. Arguably, this is Jamaica's sustained laboratory of cultural production, a highlight of which is Trench Town with its reputation as the home of reggae.

All elements of culture, politics and economics in Jamaica converge on and around Kingston. It is the capital city, the seat of government, the centre of commerce and industry. Recent arrivals from the rural areas carry their traditional or localized representations of culture as they come in search of work, escape, opportunity, pleasure, freedom, while staying with relatives or friends, often near the marketplace. Flows of consciousness, bodies, resources and rhythm make Kingston in general Jamaica's crossroads, but Cross Roads is also the actual name of one of its major junctions, in the southern central part of the KMA, used interchangeably with Torrington Bridge as a geographic and class divide.

Social distinction is spatial as well as economic and temporal. By day, members of the upper class descend and mix with the lower class as they meet in the commercial districts downtown, but by evening, as "upper" suggests, they retreat to their mansions, sometimes with their adjoining ghetto, that often allow "high rise" views of the city. Conduct by day is therefore separated from conduct by night, but downtown and uptown are inextricably linked, constituting each other even as they exist in a tense relationship. It is not to be missed, however, that the popular cultural space has remained an open frontier and those who are so tempted sneak out of their resorts to mingle by night in the community dance events.

Orlando Patterson, in his novel *The Children of Sisyphus* (1964), set what was, when he wrote it, the pathbreaking stage for a view of inner-city Kingston. The physical setting is described in what have since become stereotypical terms, highlighting waste and detritus, stench, shacks, deteriorating structures, and inadequate building material. Patterson uses the ancient Greek myth of Sisyphus as a trope embodying the themes of frustration, futility and non-achievement. The superficial transition from "negro yards" to government and tenement yards, from plantation to city, meant that the face of Kingston did not change. In the 18th century the negro yards were located at the rear of the merchant's houses and the enslaved accessed them through back entrances on lanes. Today the merchants' houses and shops are mostly closed, and corroded metal fences have replaced wooden ones. Yet the squalor and poverty observed in the 1890s (see Moore and Johnson 2001) and in the 1930s (see Fullberg-Stolberg 1990) was also observed by Lisa Douglass (1992), and can still be found in areas such as Denham Town, Drewsland or Seaview Gardens. Narrow lanes—Tulip Lane, Luke Lane, Matthews Lane and others—are common features, where living conditions bear striking resemblance to the limited space in which the enslaved travelled the Middle Passage. Visiting one of the collaborators in this project, I entered a zinc gate and walked through a narrow passage bounded on either side by a newly built concrete wall, which concealed small rooms on the premises. When I arrived at her room, which was home to three people at the time, it was so full that we had to squeeze through the door to enter. Within the space, which was seven feet by seven feet by seven feet, there was a television, a dressing table, a single bed, a fan, a cabinet and a footstool, so there was hardly any space to manoeuvre without encountering furniture. Cooking, washing and bathing facilities were shared, with water and electricity illegally connected to each room. It was suggested by one resident that the water and electricity were effectively paid for by uptown residents, who get billed for inner-city consumption.

Space acquires meaning through use, that is, through practice and movement. Michel de Certeau (1984, 117) distinguishes "practised place" as the space whose meaning is derived through use and action. Planned areas, therefore, are often transformed through use and occupation beyond the projections of planners and the control of the state. Many officially uninhabitable areas, such as gully banks and derelict buildings, are transformed by the poor into habitable sites, using the characteristic zinc and cardboard fixtures that pervade the Kingston lanes (Patterson 1964, 7). Transformation also occurs when a street is used for dance events, or communities block roadways and erect barriers to impede movement. The gated community is often represented as a middle-class phenomenon, but especially since the 1970s many of the inner-city community borders have had semi-permanent policed checkpoints, mimicking the middle-class gated communities above Cross Roads, because of gang feuds and partisan political upheavals. In some cases communities themselves erect these manned barriers to hinder the movement of rival gangs. Similarly, the area called "lock the city" or "no man's land" between the Rema and Jungle communities was not officially planned as a war zone, just as Cross Roads and Torrington Bridge were not officially designated as class divides (Douglass 1992, 76–77). Markets extend each weekend to every sidewalk and street West of King Street and South of Heywood Street, outside the planning and control of either Metropolitan Parks and Markets or the Kingston & St Andrew Corporation, evidencing the control and influence of informal commercial culture. Similarly, legal drafters and parliamentarians did not provide for the "road code," the greeting of the dominant Shower Posse, the consistent use of "Shower!" as a sign of respect, and as a passport that determines location, identity and loyalty.

Horace Levy (1996) describes communities with high levels of unemployment, general social apathy, gang violence and vandalism as a result of days and nights of political shoot-outs, the abandonment of whole streets, and decades of gun violence. The interlocking of space and sense of self is a dominant map that each inner-city dweller carries. Residents of communities plagued by violence and other socioeconomic incivilities are stigmatized, and every young man from such a community is considered a criminal. There are few jobs generated within the inner city and few prospects for employment outside. Residents speak with bitterness about the injustice of area stigma because it attacks the very core of their being.

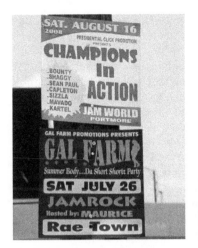
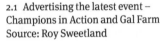

2.1 Advertising the latest event – Champions in Action and Gal Farm
Source: Roy Sweetland

2.2 Advertising the latest dance event
Source: Sonjah Stanley Niaah

The don or area leader is a major figure in this inner-city milieu. He has "soldiers" who report to him within what is best described as a paramilitary framework. The don is expected to be hard and cold, and his domain is intertwined with a degree of criminal activity, such as random, arbitrary killings, along with respect from some and, of course, significant patronage. The don is also a source of financial support for various community dwellers. Horace Levy (1996) notes that some inner-city residents condemn the illegal activities of dons, but the gun remains a big part of these communities and identities are constructed around it. It brings respect, fame, quick money and girls. Gangs also form part of the character of many communities. There are adult as well as youth gangs that are attractive to many youth. For example, if the youth have uneducated parents, with no parental example or guidance in many instances, they join gangs because that is the common practice (Levy 1996, 11).

Dons are visible in dancehall events as participants, spectators and promoters. For example, the alleged leader of the Presidential Click gang, Christopher "Dudus" Coke, is the promoter and host of events such as "I'm the World's Greatest" (2003) and the annual Champions in Action stage show. Dons are also visible at community events such as Passa Passa, held on Spanish Town Road in Tivoli Gardens, West Kingston. Similarly, Donald "Zeeks" Phipps, the now-imprisoned former don affiliated with the People's National Party (PNP) in the

Matthews Lane area, promoted dance events such as Mother's Day Fiesta, Peace Day and Millennium Niceness.

According to the Jamaican Census of 2001, only 96,052 people out of the 235,960 born in the parish of Kingston were usually resident there, highlighting the size of the migrant and commuting population. Of the 100 communities in the city, as identified by the Statistical Institute of Jamaica, more than twenty-five, covering approximately one sixth of the area of the KMA, were reported in 1996 to have inner-city conditions, including, from East to West, Rockfort, Backbush, Rae Town, Dunkirk, Nannyville, Tel Aviv, Southside, Matthews Lane, Tivoli, Hannah Town, Denham Town, Craig Town, Rema, Concrete Jungle, Rose Town, Trench Town, Glock Corner, Payne Land, Olympic Gardens, Waterhouse and Riverton City (*Daily Gleaner*, September 15, 1996). Corin Bailey (1999) established that approximately one fifth of the KMA had three or more persons per household, 33 percent or more of the population living in one room and 33 percent or more aged fourteen years and younger.

These patterns continue today. Poverty maps released on July 24, 2008 by the Planning Institute of Jamaica were based, like those preceding in 1996 and 2002, on assessments of unsatisfied basic needs and levels of consumption, using per-capita consumption levels from the Jamaica Survey of Living Conditions conducted in 2002. Members of households that had consumption levels below the poverty line for the area in which their households were located were deemed to be in poverty. The proportion of persons in poverty in each community was then used to rank 829 communities across the country. In the parish of Kingston, 19.5 percent of communities were ranked in the first and second quintiles, or the highest levels of poverty. In the KMA as a whole, 14.5 percent of communities were in the highest levels of poverty.

The inner city is considered by "polite society" as the underworld, even though most of Jamaica's middle- and upper-class citizens are unaware of the day-to-day experiences of this select citizenry. Generally speaking, the perception of uptowners is that everyone living below Cross Roads belongs among the "ghetto people." The leadership of these communities is seen as being organized by the dons around drug-dealing and guns. The space that dancehall occupies has consistently been subjected to police raids to apprehend either criminals thought to frequent dance halls or smokers of marijuana, or to enforce the Noise Abatement Act 1997. For some, it is not easy or even desirable to enter this world, especially the "garrisons" or political strongholds (see Figueroa and Sives 2002). Some implore you to make sure on approaching some streets that men are visible, because if they are not it could mean they are inside and armed for attack. Circuitous routes

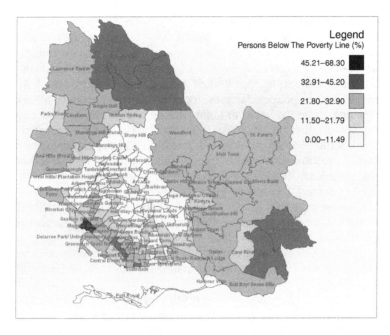

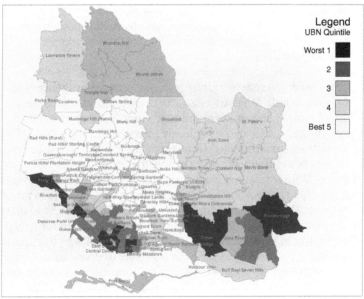

2.3 Poverty Maps of Kingston Metropolitan Area (2008)
Source: Planning Institute of Jamaica

(Levy 1996, 16) are safety strategies employed by inner-city dwellers while exiting and entering their areas to avoid "enemy territory." Some of the streets are blocked with barbed wire to signal no-entry zones, and police and army contingents are posted at volatile "garrison" borders. Residents fear the bark of guns during conflicts, especially those between political factions. A child with bullet wounds, others sleeping under the house or hiding during conflicts and a clinically depressed father are not unusual. The zinc and cardboard façades that mask rotting homes, hungry and barefoot children, and daughters turned prostitutes are some of the signals of the lack of resources that these residents struggle to overcome. Among other things, a pervasive "gang geography" or "geography of violence"—and "institutionalized warfare with the police, political banditry, and the quieter brutality of being bulldozed or torched out" of homes (Gunst 1995, 65)—is part of inner-city Kingston's urban life.

Jamaica Kincaid (1988, 34) points to violence perpetrated by colonizers as one of the things the peoples of the New World learned well:

> Have you ever wondered to yourself why it is that all people like me seem to have learned from you is how to imprison and murder each other, how to govern badly and how to take the wealth of our country and place it in Swiss bank accounts? Have you ever wondered why it is that all we seem to have learned is how to corrupt our societies and how to be tyrants? You will have to accept that this is mostly your fault.

This seemingly systemic violence, also discussed by Frantz Fanon (1963) and Achille Mbembe (2001), is manifested at several levels. Within the inner city, or life at the edge, there is a way in which violence, life and death are more closely intertwined. The value of life and death was reinterpreted throughout the era of slavery, as seen in such acts as infanticide and suicide, and it is so even in today's ghettoes. Murder rates are high, gang violence is prevalent, survival is at the edge and residents seek more risk-centred avenues to make ends meet. These avenues can involve violence to others or to oneself. For example, Spandex, a participant I interviewed in the course of my research, was considered a "drug mule," one who transports drugs across national boundaries by ingesting or inserting pellets in the vagina for income. Not being able to meet her daily needs through dancing alone, she existed at the economic fringe, taking the type of risks that are mandatory for survival given the inner-city experience. Some of these experiences parallel the act of jumping overboard from the slave ship. In the midst of the violence that marginal existences offer, death, even suicide, becomes a choice.

BONDS OF SOLIDARITY, ECHOES OF COMMUNITY

However, Kingston's inner city embodies constructive elements as well as destructive ones. While everyday conditions militate against longevity, there are other realities to be considered.

Based on his sociological research in Drewsland, Seaward, Salt-lane, the McIntyre Lands and the Shantytown area of Wareika Hill, Orlando Patterson argued (1974, 153) that

> the city offers a more exciting ... altogether more stimulating way of life than the country. A considerable number of migrants, especially male, ... migrate for this reason. The truth is that there is a thriving lower-class culture in Jamaica, one that is infinitely more creative than anything yet generated by the imitative "mimic men" of the middle classes. This new, creative lower-class culture is, however, almost entirely concentrated in the KMA and other major urban areas. Lower-class culture centres on the reggae music and dance halls, on the cinema, and on intense and varied group activity.

Patterson recognized "bonds of solidarity" (1974, 36) around child-rearing, feeding and other activities in the tenement and government yards of inner-city Kingston, in which households share water, toilet and bathing facilities, and provide services such as childminding to each other (see also Brodber 1975 and Alleyne 1988, 158–59). Patterson described the urban poor surviving their daily conditions through a sort of "patterned interaction" (1974, 36) that was not necessarily based on a "sense of community," but rather, in the absence of community and social bonds, on class or common interest. Some of these interests cut across areas and others integrated groups of people smaller than the total population of an area. Bonds based on common interest or economic arrangements could include intermittent projects, such as staging dances, and dancehall can provide a *raison d'être* for some social groups, including youth gangs: "many gangs of the fifties ... were centred on [the] owner and/or disc jockey of sound-system dances" (Patterson 1974, 38). Today, too, some youth gangs operate as "crews" or groups formed around fashion, dance moves and music. Well known dancehall crews include the Pow, Ouch, and Scare Dem Crews. Above A Dem Squad, Black Blingers, and Ravers Clavers are examples of dancing crews.

Patterson concluded that "every community should have its dance hall and sound system" as "a regular feature of urban community life" (1974, 175). While the state has not formally acted on this recommendation, today virtually every inner-city community has its own dance hall(s) and sound system(s). Even with the decline of dance activity in the face of violence in the 1990s, restrictions by the state and harassment from police officers, sound men continually set up their systems on the streets for community celebrations. Each community has its corner shop, bar, and dance yard or lawn, mainly the rear of a typical yard that accommodates dance events and often the nucleus around which social life, especially on the weekend, comes alive with, dominoes, the "three card man" mobile casinos, dances and music. The Sound System Association of Jamaica currently has some 150 registered sound systems and there are countless others operating informally. Most of these communities are smaller units within the larger communities identified by the Statistical Institute of Jamaica as "special areas."

Despite the state's neglect of dancehall and reggae culture generally, its economic and spiritual benefits are constant. Outside the obvious financial returns, community leaders, researchers, selectors and dance promoters believe that crime and discontent both decline when dancehall is allowed to reach its expressive height, as evidenced in the author's interviews with Marcia Hemmings, promoter of Super D (2002), and with Marcia Davis, co-promoter of the Frontline and Top Line events (2002), as well as in remarks by the sociologist Herbert Gayle (2002) and the selectors "Bop" Campbell (2003) and Señor Daley (2003). Buju Banton's popular song "No Respect" (1993) extends this idea, asserting that "A wi a guard unu life an' unu nuh know, when oonu a sleep wi a patrol outa door" ("We are guarding your life and you don't know, when you are sleeping we are patrolling outdoors"). The equation being developed here is that, when community celebrations around the sound systems proliferate, contentment increases, and violence and rivalry decrease. Dancehall constitutes a ritual of protection, whether through the staging of these activities and the gods they appease or through the very act of channelling the energies of the disenfranchised: as we sleep, gods protect and patrol as part of their duty. Therefore dancehall has within its rubric a "geography of refuge," whereby the performance is strongly correlated with social cohesion and protection.

THE SOCIAL "PSYCHOSCAPE"

I derive the idea of the social "psychoscape" from the work of Arjun Appadurai (1990) and of George Lipsitz (1994, 5). Lipsitz in particular delimits the importance of reorganizing space beyond local experiences or landscapes, especially those of urban areas, to address concurrent ethnoscapes, mediascapes, technoscapes, finance-scapes and ideoscapes. This entails the development of new ways to envision a worldwide cultural economy, based on the active movement of images, techniques, ideas and capital, which can occupy different places and spaces simultaneously, rather than being limited to one continent or one country. Thus, I use the term "psychoscape" with the recognition that all inner-city urban settings, regardless of location, are likely to breed certain conditions that make them more susceptible to experiencing instability and producing varied recreative responses.

The Caribbean historical space is inscribed with a number of unique concerns, including relative smallness; the absence of an indigenous ancestral culture; openness to, and developed relations with, metropolitan centres; and high levels of international and internal migration. Some of these factors have resulted in the breakdown of life-giving institutions, such as the family (see Minott and Branche 1994). The response has been aggression against the self, a high degree of colour and class awareness, and increased vulnerability (see Branche 1998). Constructions around identity and self-negation have been seen as a major overarching factor, alongside identity and self-creation. Dancehall lifestyle has evolved in the same context of identity formation, and has amplified and, in some cases, publicized these themes. As an illustration of this, the practice of skin-bleaching among some inner-city dwellers and dancehall patrons has been analyzed by some scholars as self-negation, but others (see Charles 2003) point to the way in which skin-bleaching is used as a means of increasing one's chances for upward mobility on the social ladder, indicating that, far from being a signal of self-negation, it is an opportunity grasped by those who feel disenfranchised by their dark skins.

The extent of the struggle to re-engineer self and society can be explained by the creole term "smadditizin'." A development from the word "somebody," "smadditizin'" is an active Jamaicanism explaining the process of becoming somebody. Added to this are the factors of class and hierarchy that dominate the process of becoming somebody, especially for those who are at the bottom of the class and race ladders, or not on the ladders at all. Charles Mills asserts (1997, 55) that smadditizin' should be understood as a "struggle for, the insistence on, personhood ... in a world where, primarily because of race, it is denied," and thus, essentially, smadditizin' is a political, cultural, moral, epistemological, and ontological (metaphysical) struggle that is not yet complete, as the structures against which it struggles are "in many ways intact." This is where the ontological and psychological reality of the inner-city dweller rests: the creative process of making and remaking self and identity in a world that privileges the colour and class of the colonial and metropolitan ideal, compounded by the competition inherent in the urbanscape.

Additionally, dancehall's habitus, in some respects, breeds a psychology of the fantastic among its citizenry, expressing itself in "drama" and the "will to adorn" in the latest fashion. This characteristic of African expression has been acknowledged and theorized from as early as 1933, by Zora Neale Hurston (1999, 293–97). The dramatic also encompasses the display of real and imagined (sexual) prowess, and overinflated, larger-than-life selves. The entrance of the video camera assisted in the transformation of ordinary selves into fantastic ones that could now be seen on screen, with the video light shining on their fineries, shining them into stardom.

I use "fantastic" here in the sense that it is used by Wole Soyinka (1976) in his discussion of Euro-centred perspectives on the African's inner world, into which he sometimes withdraws. He defines this inner world as "fantasy," invoking "a primal reality, the hinterland of transition," and asserts that "The community emerges from ritual experience charged with new strength for action," based on the procuring of knowledge from the realm of embodied wisdom during that ritual experience. It is not the individual's withdrawal from conscious reality, but rather, the tapping of consciousness by the "embrace [of] another ... reality" (Soyinka 1976, 33). This differs from the use that Carolyn Cooper (2002) makes of "fantastic" in the Ancient Greek sense of making visible or showing. In Soyinka's sense, dancehall cannot be understood simply as a "world of make-believe" (see Cooper 2002), but rather as an intense personal and communal ritual. (The role of the video light and ritual manifestations in dancehall are further discussed in Chapters 4 and 6.)

The city's performance identity is seen not only through its citizenry, locations and use of space, but also at the psychic level, where meanings take shape, and inform action and process within particular spaces. The use of space, then, is not to be interpreted as merely action, but as process, operating on several economic, psychic, religious/ spiritual, political and sociological planes. Among other things, I have developed a definition of performance geography and extended it to an understanding of what makes Kingston unique as a performance site. This forms the basis on which texts such as dancehall venues, located inside and outside specific areas of the KMA, as well as within and beyond Jamaica more broadly, are analyzed. It provides the foundation through which I also engage with the embodied elocution of dancers as underrepresented actors within the academic engagement of dancehall, and the various boundaries crossed by dancehall.

PERFORMING GEOGRAPHY IN KINGSTON'S DANCEHALL SPACES

THIS chapter summarizes research on the microspatialities of Kingston's dancehall performance. While it is generally acknowledged that the term "dancehall" derives from the space, hall or lawn in which dance events occur, little attention has been paid to the spatial nuance implied in the name. While early venues have been acknowledged (see White 1984 and Stolzoff 2000), no systematic investigation of venues, their locations and systems of use, has been attempted. I have therefore looked systematically at venues, their character, use and appropriation schemes, and the politics of their locations in relation to other sites and other practices. I have also looked at the kinds of events that characterize those venues (detailed in Chapter 4). My specific focus is on delineating a typology of urban venues and the centrality of specific urban locations to dancehall, in particular, the move away from venues in Central, East and West downtown Kingston to Halfway Tree as a contemporary dancehall "crossroads." The mapping of these performance spaces is one of the pillars on which the definition of performance geography is founded.

BLOCKING THE DANCEHALL STAGE

Like the slave ship and the plantations, the city had no provision for celebration. Kingston's English-style layout of residential squares left little by way of social spaces, in contrast to the Spanish-style plaza scheme that was also considered in the establishment and planning of Kingston as a city (see Bailey 1974). The social life of the enslaved was therefore built around abandoned or unoccupied spaces, streets, and other policed spaces that were appropriated for performance. Events were itinerant, and they evolved from the needs of the disenfranchised to ease their tensions, to give praise, to survive and to entertain. In most cases, earth was the floor, sometimes bounded by a metal fence along the perimeter. The earthen floor speaks to the lack of infrastructure, but also indicates a kind of veneration for, and connection, to the Earth that bears resemblance to African and Afro-Caribbean practices such as the enslaved kissing the earth when taking an oath of secrecy.

Ordinary spaces are transformed into dancehall performance spaces once the selector's turntable and speakers, the drink bar, and the patrons are in place. The organization of these elements defines spatial boundaries that are maintained through structures such as the systems of sound, dress, posture, gesture and other bodily actions. Bunny Goodison, the owner and operator of Soul Shack Disco, grew up in a yard on Orange Street, Kingston, and has observed the dance music scene closely since the 1950s: he says (2002) that it was "poor

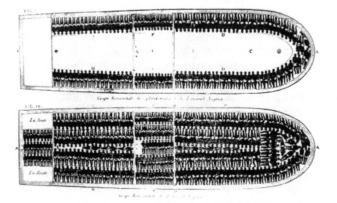

3.1 Plans of slave ship decks (Vessel Name: Brookes c. 1789)
Source: Courtesy of the National Library of Jamaica

people who went to dance halls" (see also White 1984). Indeed, it is clear from most of the interviews conducted throughout this research that dancehall is felt to be a "poor people" phenomenon. The dance provided physical, ideological and spiritual shelter for a generation of lower-class Jamaicans, particularly those who matured around the time the country achieved independence, in 1962, and the music style ska became popular. Dance venues were the spaces in which an ordinary sound system operator could achieve the fame of a prime minister by vying for the title of top sound system.

The typical venue then was a bare, mostly uncovered area. Winston Blake, owner of Merritone sound system, recalled (in Katz 2003, 4) that

> you had the most important part of the Jamaican scenario called lawns, like Jubilee Tile Gardens and Chocomo Lawn, big places that were either concrete slab or wire fence, and you'd have a dance in that area, either at the back of a house or the side of a building—a space where you could put up music.

Merritone was responsible for some of the events that began on a Friday and continued till Sunday evening, creating dances that occupied a space within, but outside the confines of, the state and its apparatuses for several hours. This is consistent with the historical accounts highlighted in Chapter 1. Many venues were marginal spaces such as gully banks or the Dungle, a virtual city dump, made popular in Orlando Patterson's novel *The Children of Sisyphus* (1964), but later destroyed.

3.2 A Typical Gully Bank along which many livelihoods are constructed
Source: Roy Sweetland

Today's equivalent, a residential landfill out of which people eke a living, is Riverton, now partially being transformed into the low-income
housing scheme of Riverton Meadows in the west-southwestern part
of the Kingston Metropolitan Area (KMA).

Dance events can be characterized as nomadic, in the sense that
they move from space to space. This peripatetic trend is particularly
characteristic of events in venues located above the geographical class
marker of Cross Roads. Events in that location were subject to complaints about noise pollution, which today attracts penalties under
the Noise Abatement Act 1997. This signals the contest with enforcers
of the law, who often deem the dancehall enterprise to be a disturbance
of the peace. Venues such as street corners, used mostly by communities below Cross Roads, exist outside the formal structures for lease
or rental and are appropriated at will until they outlive their spatial
capacity or welcome. (I discuss the street as a venue in detail below.)

The nomadism that characterizes the dance event parallels the way
in which after Emancipation the former slaves roamed the countryside and moved to urban areas in which markets were viable economic options. An important dimension of this nomadism is the policed
spaces the former slaves occupied. To evade the actions of the state,
which could include confiscation or destruction, slaves masked policed spaces and instruments in a variety of disguises. Broadly, the
power structure set by colonial slavemasters did not allocate spaces of
residence or entertainment for the majority slave population to freely

3.3 Four Grand Finalists (including The Blues Busters from St James & Hoola Hoop Dancers) in the All Jamaica Opportunity Hour Contest, Palace Theatre c. 27 August, 1959.
Source: Jamaica Gleaner Company

3.4 Performers in a Ska Contest held at Ritz Cinema, Maxfield Avenue, Kingston c. 29 July, 1964
Source: Jamaica Gleaner Company

occupy or own after Emancipation. Such regimes of power exist within the context of contemporary governments that reproduce the relations of power consistent with colonial rule. Squatting and related phenomena have existed and persisted as housing or even entertainment solutions for the peasantry and now the poor.

According to Bunny Goodison (2002), in the 1950s and 1960s many venues were lodge halls belonging to registered friendly societies or mutual benefit societies, of which a number were in the Beat Street area (White 1984, 56). Many venues were lawns, including Chocomo Lawn on Wellington Street, King's Lawn on North Street, Jubilee on King Street, Bull Head Lawn in Trench Town, Pioneer and Barrel O Tile Lawns in Jones Town, Dollars Lawn, Olive Lawn, Batchame Lawn and Skipper Lawn. Why were they called "lawns" when many of them did not boast the green grass which the word suggests? Conclusions can be drawn based on the location of these venues below the geographical class marker and the lack of grass. It is likely that "lawn" was applied to lend prestige to the venues, in the style of middle- and upper-class designations such as the "lawns of King's House," the Governor General's residence, on which many social events occur.

MORTIMO PLANNO'S EXPERIENCE AS A DANCE PROMOTER

The late Brother Mortimo Planno (1929–2006), Rastafari Elder and mentor of Bob Marley, lived on the Dungle until 1957 and organized events there, before moving to 18 Fifth Street and making that into a dance venue (see Derouet 2006). Though marginalized, the Rastafari too sought to celebrate in dance. I interviewed Planno in 2002 when he reminisced about the Kingston dance scene and supplied some of the history of the class boundaries around which dancehall was organized then and, to some extent, now.

From the 1950s to the 1970s the venues for "uptown top ranking" above Cross Roads included Silver Slipper, near the Carib Theatre; the Glass Bucket on Halfway Tree Road, which used to cater to uptowners; Pear Tree Grove, below the Hope Botanical Gardens on Hope Road; and Red Gal Ring in Stony Hill. Those below Cross Roads, or downtown, included Jubilee Tile Gardens at 155 King Street; Marcus Garvey's Liberty Hall at 76 King Street; Foresters Hall at 15 North Street, on the corner of Love Lane; King's Lawn, across the street from Foresters Hall; and Success Club, a lodge hall on Wildman Street. In Planno's memory, some of these were lodge halls that were rented in order to raise funds. Others were Mizpah; the Chinese-owned Commodore on East Street; the Bustamante Industrial Trade Union premises, rented to those who were politically aligned; and Doncaster Scout Headquarters on Windward Road. Dances used to be held at Bournemouth Club on Bournemouth Street.

Events were organized by Planno himself at the Dungle and the Bellevue Hospital, known then as Asylum. It was customary for Planno to advertise such events. For example, "Better Cali Coming ..." was one trailer than ran at the Carib Theatre in Cross Roads: Planno had paid twenty-nine pounds to have it put up on the big screen.

BECOMING A VENUE: TIME, SPACE AND LOCATION

There are rules of organization and rites of celebration that govern the use of a venue, and these are pronounced in the case of venues without the infrastructure found at clubs. In most cases there is only a boundary, usually a wall or a metal fence, which is sometimes constructed to enclose the event. The sound system, the bar and other vendors set up prior to an event. There is usually no designated location for any of these, except at more established venues such as Skateland, where the bar and sanitary facilities are permanent structures. The sound system and the bar are set up inside.

I use the terms inner court and outer court to distinguish between the interior and exterior regions of the venues respectively. It is important to highlight these, because to fully understand the dance venue these spaces and the activities within them need to be accounted for. Most vendors locate their stalls in the outer court and stay there, except for those selling peanuts, chewing gum and "weed" (marijuana), vendors who remain mobile.

Each event in any particular venue is likely to follow this general pattern, but the location of the speakers, the bar(s) and the central dance floor can also vary depending on the crowd size anticipated and the number of sound systems used. Another important but variable feature is the "pre-dance" period, when the selector arranges his music and tunes the sound equipment.

The dancehall is then the "primary profiling space," where vendors, dance patrons, cars and motorcycles, gaming tables and street youths abound (Stolzoff 2000, 200). "Profiling," which has to be understood as verb, adjective and noun, is one of the key cultural signifiers: people profile what is "in style", or profile to view the current style. "Style" in turn covers the music, the dance, clothing and hairstyles, as well as cars and whatever else constitutes the latest "hype."

Music signals the movement toward the "early out" period, the initiation of the dance event where "oldies" music is played. By this time the venue is sealed by plastic streamers or tarpaulin to conceal the number of patrons in the inner court where necessary. This is significant, because a small number of patrons inside the venue during the "early out" period could encourage potential patrons to think that the event will be unsuccessful. The venue is therefore sealed from view and entry is often managed using formal / informal security arrangements.

In the "early out" period the venue can remain virtually empty, except for early arrivals. The period varies in length and it is often used to determine whether the event will "flop" by failing to attract a sizeable audience. Knowing the appropriate arrival time is an important element. An early bird could be viewed not as a regular but as a "dance junkie" or a vagrant. These include persons on drugs, but it generally refers to those who attend every dance, trying to hustle or swindle someone. The outer court is where early arrivals position themselves while profiling and/or observing the number of patrons entering the venue.

The shift in musical tempo, especially away from the "oldies," is an important signal telling observers to enter the venue. The selector moves from playing "oldies" to playing more recent musics in order to signal that the dance event is progressing to a heightened level of participation. Where there is more than one sound system this duty is shared by each of them. The least popular sound system typically plays first, then the next in popularity, and so on.

The selector's table is generally situated in the front region of the inner court. Established sound systems such as Stone Love or Metro Media have at least three speaker towers, depending on the venue and the crowd size expected. These towers often form an arc whose ends are close to the selector's table. Another common shape is the triangle, which is popularly featured in street venues.

There is an unmarked but precise space in which dancing takes place, especially by accomplished dancers. Often this consumes the total space available in the front region, but it is sometimes noticeably divided into at least three locations. Depending on the venue, this might be found on different levels. For instance, the main dance floor at the New Little Copa Club in Bull Bay is on the ground floor, but, depending on where celebrities or other emerging dance sensations go, they attract the attention of the video light. No one enters this space in the early hours of a dance. Instead, patrons skirt the space, filling the back region and the total perimeter of the inner court throughout the night, until the DJ signals the call. Sometimes this is done with a popular tune.

There is also an observable space occupied by dons (area leaders), dancers, dancehall promoters, models, "faithfuls" and popular crews—all are celebrities of dancehall. These are the people who give the event its signature or character. Sometimes the space they occupy is located in front of the bar or a block of speakers. Some crew members designate their territory in a venue by consistently using a particular space.

The physical placement of people in the venue is sometimes determined by status, age, gender, dance skill or musical experience, but no space is in a real sense off limit as much as the circle where intense dancing takes place. A patron who is attending a dance for the first time is in no doubt that this space is not to be used until the appropriate time. Movement on the dance floor takes place in stages. There is a dormant phase, an active phase and a phase of rest, and the cycle may repeat itself throughout the event. These stages evidence a certain logic that is polyrythmic and outside the understanding of a mere neophyte. The logic is polyrhythmic and human-centred, building on communal ecstasy as well as individual interpretative capacity and skill. For example, the space for dancing often surpasses the designated dance area to take in other areas, such as a nearby roof, a car or a speaker tower, depending on the individual skills and interpretations of dancers.

Patrons and organizers alike have a "ram dance" conception of space, considering that no space is ever too small to stage an event, as the more persons there are bursting at the seams of the venue, the more successful the event is. This is a consistent theme in dancehall culture, signifying an inherent philosophy of space linked to notions of success, transcendence and collective ritualizing. In this spatial philosophy, an expansive view of space and the primacy of performance are evident. Bearing in mind the obvious difference in volitional agency between the enslaved and the inner-city dweller, it is important to highlight that, as I have already mentioned, enslaved Africans celebrated after crossing the Middle Passage with dances on the ship decks. Whether it is the ship decks, slave yards or streets, space is transformed into celebratory space. What dancehall performance represents is the culmination of slave ship dances such as limbo.

CALIFORNIA CALIFORNIA AT RAINBOW LAWN

In order to illustrate some of the norms and codes of the dancehall space, I shall use the example of the California California dance event held at Rainbow Lawn on August 9, 2003.

I entered the venue at 1:30 a.m. If I had been a novice, I might have thought that the event would flop. This is where faith takes over. In contrast to the days when U Roy reigned as King of the Dancehall, today's events warm up at 1:30 a.m. instead of 8:30 p.m.

This is a fifteenth-anniversary dance, a link-up event that sees patrons coming not only from different locations within Jamaica but, in this case, from California and possibly elsewhere in the United States. The dance is therefore likely to be heavily patronized. Famous DJs, sound system operators and dancers will "represent," because absence could mean disrespect.

Three sound systems were present, Metro Media, Stone Love and Rebel T. Customarily, the event began with "oldies," many of which set the tone for purifying the spirit and mind, releasing tensions, forgetting troubles, and washing away pain while dancing to music. The mood intensified with the "juggling" of various musical moods along a performance continuum toward the event's high point.

Around 2:00 a.m., and with Rebel T at the controls, patrons started to arrive, positioning themselves along the periphery as they entered. The famous Hotty Hotty Cherry, a longstanding dancehall celebrity in her own right and an avid Stone Love fan, arrived at 2:30 a.m. Songs hailed her and selectors acknowledged her presence. The video lights were switched on and the cameramen started to comb the venue so as to give the eventual viewers of the dancehall footage a glimpse of the event's commencement. By 3:00 a.m. there were far more patrons than there had been at 1:30 a.m., and Rory, the accomplished Stone Love musical selector, arrived. With the pace of the event merely warming, by 3:30 a.m., and with many more patrons, Stacey, Dancehall Queen 1999, arrived. By 3:45 a.m. the dancer John Hype and crew arrived, simultaneously with the DJ Beenie Man.

The dance was now in full swing, yet the unmarked dance floor was not being used. It was Metro Media's selector Sky Juice who gave the call to everyone to come forward. They had to be invited into this sacred spot. This is customary. The unwritten rule is that the space is for the dancehall aficionado; it is celebrity space and only after they have actually or symbolically baptized the space is it ready for use by other patrons. The patrons answered the call, which was also a signal that, with a celebrity DJ at the microphone, other celebrities could come forward because the show was about to begin. The movement of patrons from the back region, behind the speaker towers in this instance, to the front region, in front of the selectors' turntables, filled the dance floor, initiating the communal ecstasy or "congregational kinesis" (Brathwaite 1995, 46) that the event was meant to bring.

With the dance floor now filled, it needed to be "worked," and the repertoire of popular songs rained down for the audience's pleasure.

As the celebrity DJ and the dancers communicated, in typical call-and-response manner, the audience reached frenzied levels, closing in around the dance floor to observe or follow every move. As the selector played one popular dance tune after another, the audience, led by the famous dancers, responded appropriately. For example, as DJ Elephant Man's "Pon di River," "Signal di Plane" and "Blasé," Beenie Man's "Row Like a Boat" and "Dude," and Predator's "Nah Nuh Head" were played, the corresponding dance moves were expertly demonstrated by Stacey and John Hype with their separate crews, each commanding the attention of separate video cameras that recorded their every move. For the rest of the night, as the dancing progressed, the most vibrant dancing could be seen in different locations, propelled by the location of popular dancers, the exhibition of current dance moves and the location of the video cameras.

The rest of the celebrants could be separated into spectators and revellers. Some were dancing, others were observing the unfolding proceedings. Young men converged around the perimeter of the front region, especially in front of the selector's table, to get a view of the dancing or the selector's craft. Once in a while the camera focused on the veteran dancehall patron Medusa, so named because of her long blond locks, or, when Stacey and John Hype took a break, Hotty Hotty Cherry. At all other times it was Stacey and John Hype who captured the attention.

VENUES POLITICIZED: HIERARCHY, POLICING AND POLICY-MAKING

Venues can be understood within the context of a hierarchy. Clubs were and still are the most prestigious venues, catering to the big bands and the rich from the 1950s to the present. However, there have always been relatively few clubs, and the ubiquitous "subcultural dance" venues (see White 1984) outnumber them just as the poor outnumber the rich. The hierarchy is therefore to be understood as having two levels: on the one hand, the prestigious stage or commercial venues, with clubs as the most prestigious; and, on the other hand, the popular, street and community venues, considered the sphere of the inner-city dwellers. The poor might visit the clubs on special occasions, but for them the most accessible and most preferred entertainment scene is the street dance.

Dancehall reveals striking continuities in the emergence of clubs, their relative success and their decline, as their appeal wanes or dancehall activity retreats from uptown into its core habitus, sometimes because of high levels of violence. Clubs have been most popular during the high points of dancehall, when concessions such as "dancehall nights" or "ladies free nights" have been offered in the hope of increasing patronage. Their prestige remains muted for the lower class, as it is only on one or two nights a week that clubs capture popular patronage.

In general, venues retain their character, use and meaning over many years. They could be considered nomadic, occupying marginal domains, but the wellspring of venues never dries out, for these life-giving spaces are constantly created or refashioned. Even as they are peripheral to Jamaicans of "quality," they are central to the articulation of a sense of community and cultural identity among the lower class and those abroad, some of them in spaces of exile.

Venues may be perceived as being under siege because of frequent raids by the police. This perception may be heightened by political affiliations, real or perceived, which attract victimization, sometimes reinforced through the paramilitary tactics of the state. Since the 1960s dance venues have been raided with considerable frequency, and raids, or "locking down the dance," became such a feature of dancehall life that dance patrons came to expect them and film crews could even request their re-enactment. In 1994, for example, eighty persons were detained and one was arrested for murder at the House of Leo venue during a paramilitary operation by the Jamaica Constabulary Force that was filmed by the Cultural Production Training Centre and then shown on *Entertainment Report* (a show then on Jamaica Broadcasting Corporation, known since it was privatized in 1997 as Television Jamaica). This particular raid is thought to have been staged for a British film crew.

The DJ Buju Banton's song "Operation Ardent" (1993) details his experience of one such raid. The song opens with blaring sirens after which Buju asks,

> What's di motive? Why dem keep meddling around the poor people dem business? ...
> What more? What oonu want di massive fi do?
> Every dance wey wi keep oonu mek dem get curfew ...
> Wid helicopter inna air, bright light a shine a ground ...
> Mi see mattick an SLR gun, soldier corral di place from head to the ground ...
> Like a fire drill dem part di dance inna two ...
> while two officer up a di front one a search an one a screw.

There was a helicopter shining bright lights as people scattered—including the singer/DJ Terry Ganzy, who ran off, leaving his girlfriend behind—then the police, armed with high-powered weapons and searching for criminals, penned the venue and turned off the sound system, ending the dance. The patrons formed lines based on gender and were subjected to searches, which produced no weapons. They were just people trying to enjoy themselves by dancing and listening to music, feeling the bass pounding through to the bone. What does the state want the poor—who have no adequate space in which to live and enjoy recreation—to do, when every attempt at entertainment, especially through the dance, is curfewed?

Many more raids have occurred in dance venues than those that have received media coverage, as the DJ U Roy (2002) explained. In the early 1970s King Tubby's Hi Fi was the top sound system and people from all strata of society, and from as far away as St Thomas in the East, attended Tubby's dances. It acquired a bad reputation because it was believed that "rude boys" also attended. U Roy recalled that when the sound system was playing at the Up Park Camp a police officer told the DJ that he must control the crowd, but the DJ took no responsibility for doing so. Raids, beatings, lockdowns and arrests became common. On one occasion U Roy himself was so badly beaten that he required his girlfriend's help to move. His turntable was confiscated with the explanation that it created noise at night, and he was imprisoned.

U Roy also recalled sound systems being destroyed by the police as they were on the way to venues. On one occasion in the 1960s the system was destroyed when they were en route to a venue called the Gold Coast, but King Tubby, who was known for his mechanical genius, rebuilt it by the following day for an engagement at the Students' Union of the University of the West Indies (UWI) at Mona.

According to U Roy, politics did not play an important role in the raids. Intervention by the police tended to be invoked when "society people" (from the middle and upper classes) complained about the noise from sound systems playing in venues above Cross Roads. Police officers were also incensed by the playing of certain tunes. Whenever they played Max Ruby's show-stopping song with the line "Babylon likkie likkie and beggie beggie" (roughly, "The police are avaricious mendicants") the police would immediately appear to end the dance by ordering the selector to turn off the sound system. U Roy recalled that the police officer Joe Williams was especially known for harassing "rude boys," whom he defined and separated based on their khaki clothing and Clark's shoes.

Another informant, "Harry T" (2002), recalled that

police look for wanted man in the dance. I used to think Babylon don't want man enjoy themselves back then ... "Sound system waan turn down" was the constant warning at midnight. If they come back, it's trouble. Sometimes police mash up the dance. Sometimes the Black Maria van was there with the police, and after they line up everybody and search them, they would load the Black Maria. Some of this was just harassment.

In another interview, Foundation DJ King Stitt supported these statements by saying that, for the police, being a DJ was tantamount to committing a criminal offence such as smoking marijuana (and of course these two activities have often had close association).

One of the most remarkable clashes between police and dance patrons took place at La Roose, a venue in St Catherine, on January 27, 2003 (as mentioned in Chapter 1). Though the occasion was not intended as a raid, English's Birthday Bash was targeted by policemen who reportedly demanded money on their arrival. When they were confronted by resistance from patrons, a shooting incident ensued, leaving at least five persons injured. Other raids have also been tainted by the suggestion that police officers demanded money from dance promoters in exchange for allowing the event to continue.

These accusations have increased since the passing and subsequent enforcement of the Noise Abatement Act 1997 and the Places of Amusement Regulations 1999. The act regulates both public and private spaces and events, and is intended to allow the police to control noise from a number of public activities, from political and public meetings to dance events. It states that no person in a private or public setting may sing, play or sound noise-making or musical instruments, or use any loudspeaker, microphone or other means of amplifying sound to a level "reasonably capable" of annoying individuals, particularly residents, visitors or the infirm, beyond a range of 100 metres from the origin of the sound. Loudspeakers should not be operated at levels capable of annoyance beyond 11:00 p.m., in the case of public meetings; midnight, in the case of political meetings held during election campaigns; between 2:00 and 6:00 a.m. on a Saturday or Sunday; or between midnight and 6:00 a.m. on other days. Penalties for offences under these measures include fines not exceeding 20,000 Jamaican dollars or imprisonment for up to six months. The act requires that persons intending to stage an event capable of disturbing nearby residents must seek permission from the police up to ten days before the event.

The operation of the Noise Abatement Act is closely associated with the Places of Amusement Regulations issued in 1999 by the Kingston & St Andrew Corporation, and similar regulations issued by other parish councils. These define a "place of amusement" as any public place freely accessed by patrons, paying a fee or not, thus including cinemas, clubs, dance halls, open-air dance venues, festivals, disco-theques, roller discos, skating rinks and amusement arcades. Operators of such places are granted licences upon paying fees ranging from 2,000 to 10,000 Jamaican dollars. While the definition of amusement activities is not limited to the staging of dance events, and attempts to get disaggregated figures from the Kingston & St Andrew Corporation have proved futile, it is safe to say that a large number of these permits have been issued for dancehall events.

Despite the "zero tolerance" position adopted by the Jamaica Constabulary Force in relation to enforcement of the Noise Abatement Act, the numbers of permits granted have been rising steadily, from 4,383 in 2002 to 5,076 in 2004, 7,709 in 2006 and about 15,700 in 2008 (see Planning Institute of Jamaica 2003–08 and Jackson 2009). This figure for 2008 indicates a daily average total of about forty-three events (Jackson 2009). It has been suggested, though it cannot be substantiated, that there may well be, on average, more than 1,400 live events in Jamaica every day (see Laidley et al. 2009). This in turn suggests that registered parties, bar openings, stage shows and the like are outnumbered by illegal or informal dances held without permits.

Having a healthy culture of amusement and a significant portion of the country's population, Kingston presents an urgent case for the examination of policies that are sensitive to the history and form of entertainment practices. Suggestions regarding the zoning of entertainment, as well as the provision of proper venues for staging events, can be seriously explored to shift the popular stance from policing to policy-making, but it is up to policy-makers to look at the dilemmas created by police raids and the clashes that often ensue from them, in order to cultivate healthy entertainment practices around dancehall.

Meanwhile, entertainment promoters continue to complain about the double-edged sword that characterizes the production and consumption of dancehall, and its relationship to the state and its apparatuses. Due to the "zero tolerance" approach to noise abatement, promoters feel that dance events have been increasingly policed as a method of minimizing criminality. However, at the same time that the authorities are increasing surveillance, there is an increase in the number of events, the revenue they earn and the means by which they serve as a release valve for the many who are frustrated by daily "sufferation."

There is also confusion and controversy over the apparent double standard evidenced in the light policing of certain favoured commercial events in contrast to the heavy policing of many street events. In particular, carnival, imported from Trinidad & Tobago as commercially viable and safe entertainment for the middle class, has come to occupy a prestigious place as a non-indigenous performance, highlighting some of the tensions at work in postcolonial Kingston. In Trinidad & Tobago carnival has often received negative criticism and sanctions, but the same seasonal performance culture receives positive attention from the authorities in Jamaica and is usually given all the requisite permits. In 2002, for example, the Jamaica Carnival J'ouvert event in Halfway Tree went on until dawn, way past the official deadline of 2:00 a.m., and featured very loud music. Dancehall, on the other hand, suffers often because permits are either not applied for or not granted, except in the case of commercial events such as Hot Shots or Heineken Startime, which are promoted months in advance, ensuring enough lead time to acquire permits. Informal community events, or those held at regular semi-commercial playout venues, suffer the greatest degree of state control.

The political dimension of dance venues is also seen in the politics of their locations and the partisan affiliation of their owners. This political dimension is not unique to venues, but applies to sound systems as well. For example, Kilamanjaro was seen as a Jamaica Labour Party (JLP) sound because of its location in South Kingston. Anyone who is known to be affiliated to the People's National Party (PNP) would think twice about attending a dance in this area because of the potential to become involved in arguments or even violence, and not being aware of these realities could mean life or death. Sound system selectors such as "Bop Campbell" (Olanzo Hawk) or Señor Daley, owner of Klassique, have attested to this. Campbell (2003) says that politics has sometimes affected his playing music, over a period of forty-two years. He believes that he has managed to transcend political boundaries through music, as well as activities in football, but, he says, political rivalries "affect my playing ... it affect everyt'ing.... Where I come from they seh is a Labourite area an' mi know seh nuff nuff likkle tings wha coulda happen fi mi nuh happen through dat." Señor Daley ascribes the branding of Klassique as PNP to the fact that it is based in Rae Town, although when the sound system played regularly within JLP areas it was then branded as JLP. Characteristics of the political parties have affected the sound systems in other ways. For example, systems branded as "culture sound" were likely also to be branded as PNP, based, among other things, on the ways in which Michael Manley's election campaign in 1976 reflected an affinity with Rastafari-inspired themes of liberation, redemption and socio-cultural renewal.

Venues also tell stories about nation and national affiliations. One important dimension is the Spanish names of clubs, such as Ad Astra, Havana, Copa Cobana, Esperanza or Sombrero, mostly concentrated in East Kingston, from East Parade to Bull Bay. This arose from economic and ideological shifts in Jamaica that increased the presence of Cuban musicians, dancers and ships. For example, according to Timothy Chin (2004), his father, who owned Club Havana, brought the dancer Estella to Jamaica to headline weekend shows. According to Brian Meeks (in personal interviews), in the 1960s and 1970s these clubs drew patrons from uptown and downtown, with a significant pool of patrons from tertiary institutions such as the Mona Campus of the UWI.

The role of Chinese Jamaicans is also noteworthy, since they have been at the helm of technology, promotion and ownership in dancehall since its inception, starting with distribution of jukeboxes. Tom "The Great Sebastian" Wong was one of the leading sound system owners in the 1950s, and other Chinese Jamaicans have operated some of the most successful clubs featuring dancehall nights, including, in the early years, Commodore; later, Cactus, Mirage and Asylum; and, more recently, Quad, a four-storey club opened in 2003.

The role of women in the maintenance of dance events has also been noted (by, for example, L'Antoinette Stines), based on their management of pubs, corner bars and cookshops (small restaurants). Some of the most popular venues have been named after women—such as Nanny's One Spot, Dawn's HQ, Joyce's Hot Spot, Peggy's Place or Cherry's Bar—and many dance events, such as Rae Town, Frontline, Top Line or Super D, have had women at the helm, steering initiation, negotiation of space and reorganization.

THEORIZING AND SINGING THE STREET

Dancehall events have consistently occupied streets, and streets have been the most available and popular sites for dance events. In further defining the performance geography of Kingston through a classification of its venues, I would like first to draw particular attention to the street, while contextualizing it and naming its heritage of use.

A cursory search for references to the street in sociology and cultural studies—in particular, studies of popular culture—reveals references to street children, street people, street vendors, street markets, street youth, street workers, street justice, street dance, street trends, street corners, street culture, street credibility or reputation, being streetwise or having street sense, and street noise. There are also tropes of the street as place of apprenticeship, employment, socialization and competition, as giver of life, as a space in which to gain strength and courage, as the site of displacement and home/lessness, travelling/journeying, survival strategies, territoriality, gangsterism: in short, the street as a space with its attendant philosophies of use. Operating at many levels, then, the street is a physical, conceptual, symbolic and mythical construct (Forman 2002, 83–84).

Black popular culture is specially tied to the street. Dance acts and the sites of their performance allow us to theorize those locations. As the space that characterizes performances in the Black Atlantic, the street has featured in performance practices around the globe from time immemorial, in carnivals, parades, rituals and ceremonial commemorations.

Street performance is conventionally distinguished from what is staged, yet street performances themselves can be staged performances too: consider such forms as demonstrations and rallies, parades and pageants, carnivals, circuses and puppetry shows. Studies such as those anthologized by Jan Cohen-Cruz (1998) include expositions on street performances that agitate, serve as tools of witness, politicization and popularization, or reveal the imaginary of a citizenry. The street is an important signifier of lower-class ideals, space, aesthetics and aspirations. This is why the distinguishing features of street performance are widely understood as different from those associated with the stage, in the narrow sense of the staged performances associated, not with the street or the lower class, but with the trained or schooled middle and upper classes, and their "high" culture. Street performances have to be schooled before they can be staged in this sense. Further, while the stage is understood as the proscenium stage, with its three material walls and its crucial "fourth wall" separating the audience from the performers, the street is associated with ubiquity, for it has no walls, only fluid lines between performers and audiences.

Weekly dancehall events at or around bars or clubs on particular streets can be mapped within the lived city landscape. Street venues also live in the songs that mention their names, bringing into focus the citizens who occupy and make their lives in these streets. The majority of dancehall patrons do not own homes, buildings near these events or corporate entities. By virtue of these performances patrons can have a stake in what Regis (2001, 756) calls, in the context of jazz funerals, "collective ownership of the streets" (see also Harrison-Pepper 1990, Forman 2002 and Hannerz 2004). Street events do not stop or yield to traffic. When events impede the normal flow of traffic on communal streets during events such as Passa Passa on Spanish Town Road in Tivoli Gardens, West Kingston (see also Chapter 4), it says something about the transfer of authority, even if it is temporary, as this often happens in the presence of law enforcement officers. This presents interesting challenges for the conceptualization of public space as owned and regulated by a state that uses its apparatuses for ultimate control. However, as Michel de Certeau (1984) tells us, it is the use of space that creates meaning.

Dancehall culture and performances, as in hip hop, for example, inscribe a "spatial sensibility" bordering on a cartography of survival (see, again, Forman 2002). The street is foundational in this cartography, as it is a consistent site for dancehall practice. Where hip hop has block parties that dominate streets, dancehall has events that occupy streets and community squares, originating from pubs or other public spaces and spilling onto the street. The street is a physical/material space, but it is also a symbolic space. Its currency for the representation of particular identities is evident in musical and performance genres ranging from carnivals, the blues and hip hop to kwaito and reggaetón. Indeed, street performances have served to alter the public culture of many urban areas around the globe, where the drama of spectators and performers unfolds. Political and economic relations are built, severed and reinvented, while lives and identities metamorphose. Performances in the public city space have precipitated battles over the use of space, and interactions between the law and the "unlawful." In this sense, the street can be viewed as an exclusive space as well as an inclusive and disciplinary space, a site of a public order regulated and maintained by civil laws, street signs and other prescriptions supported by laws.

Ultimately, citizens claim space and identity in the urban street through their performances. Street performances, except in the relatively few cases in which permission is actually granted by the state and its apparatuses, involve claiming space that is planned. Contravening the prescribed use is, in a sense, an engineered conquest, if only momentarily, for many lower-class citizens of Jamaica.

The street often bears association with the ghetto, gully banks and other marginal communities, since the streets used for entertainment and performance by the masses are mostly within areas occupied by the poor and the marginalized. Narratives of the ghetto and their streets come in various forms, from DJs, ordinary citizens, scholars and politicians, at home and abroad, and Jamaican recording artists, from Bob Marley and the Wailers, Big Youth, Super Cat and John Holt to Baby Cham and Mavado, have documented various aspects of street life, and its multidimensional morphology, in particular ghetto life and "gangsta" life.

In "Dem Belly Full (But We Hungry)" (1976) Bob Marley encourages the poor to "forget their troubles and dance" in the face of hunger and the high cost of living. In "Johnny Was" (1976) he further elaborates the experience of the street through a description of the mothers who lose their sons and daughters to violence in the streets: "Woman hold her head and cry 'cause her son had been shot down in the street and died from a stray bullet ... just because of the system," the quintessential battle cry from the woman and the wider community who are constantly plagued by the ills of a poverty-ridden society. In "Talking Blues" (1976) Marley describes the conditions of ghetto living— "Cold ground was my bed last night and rock was my pillow too" —for a young boy who has just moved from the country to the urban centre within which he must engage with the reality of struggle, destitution, competition for scarce resources and survival strategies to overcome these, as he hones his musical skills.

John Holt's song "Ghetto Queen," first released in 1980 (and re-released in 2002) describes how

> She lives in the heart of the city
> Down there where there is no pity.
> She knows the root of the rootless,
> She lives among the baddest of the baddest.
> She is the queen of the ghetto ...
> She don't wear no fancy makeup,
> She don't wear no fancy dress,
> She is a natural natural beauty,
> Her heart is pure and clean.

Super Cat also added to the many ghetto stories that have been told by the poor and downtrodden with songs such as "Nuff Man a Die" (1992) and "Ghetto Red Hot" (1992), and so too does Red Rat in the single "Nuh Live Nuh Weh" (1997), which describes how the street is home because there is no other place to dwell. Indeed, many have resorted to the street for dwelling spaces, perhaps as many as those who seek the street for pleasure and celebration in dance events.

More recently, ghetto life has come to be increasingly associated or even equated with gangsta life, as numerous youths around the globe have responded to the themes of songs such as R. Kelly and Wyclef Jean's "Ghetto Religion" (2003):

> The ghetto is a part of my religion,
> The only thing my eyes can see.
> There ain't no man gonna stop the vision ...
> I'm a part of the ghetto,
> The ghetto is a part of me.

The lives of such youths are also represented by Akon in the single "Ghetto" (2004):

> These streets remind me of quicksand.
> When you're on it you'll keep goin' down....
> Gunshots every night in the ghetto,
> Crooked cops on site in the ghetto,
> Every day is a fight in the ghetto....
> That's the life when you're living in the ghetto.

In "Gully Sit'n" (2006) the DJ Assassin incisively takes up the duty of lauding the poor who live in marginal, vulnerable, often captured spaces such as gully banks, street corners and trenches, documenting their experiences and highlighting the injustice of their neglect by politicians who represent the state. He is speaking to those who live in tenement yards, to ghetto girls, taxi drivers and juveniles, to the poor who can't pay their utility bills or buy concrete blocks with which to build homes, to all working people who try to make ends meet. He speaks of the food they eat, where they reside and the community strategies for ending monthly utility payments:

> Well, poor people the system reject unu,
> A nuff a dem unu elect an dem neglect unu,
> All who fi serve an protect a dem a disrespect unu,
> But Assassin don't forget unu.
> Well, mi come fi big up every gully and mi big up every trench,
> Big up every base and every corner, every ends,
> Mi big up over Grants, Mi big up over McCooks,
> An mi big up over Cockburn, big up all the pens ...
> A ghetto, a ghetto, gully sit'n ...

Baby Cham's "Ghetto Story" (2006) could be considered a sort of anthem of ghetto "livity" (life energy, fullness of life, as expounded in the Rastafari movement). The chorus expresses the feeling of elation that ghetto youths share because they have the weaponry to defend themselves against those who would threaten the poor:

> This is my story, real ghetto story.
> I remember those days when Hell was my home,
> When me and mama bed was a big piece a foam ...
> When Mama gone a work me go street go roam ...
> I remember when Sunny Avenue tun inna warzone
> An' Mickey madda 'fly him out cau' she get a loan,

But Mickey go to foreign and go tu'n Al Capone,
Mek whole heap a money and send in our own.
Now a we a lock the city and that is well known.

Baby Cham further describes the type of society Jamaica was in the
1980s from the perspective of one who lived in the ghetto: evading
the officers who policed the streets; stealing food from the Chinese,
known for their longstanding tradition of shopkeeping in Jamaica;
making food available for Mama to cook a big meal for a change; and
dumping ballot boxes, engineered by political henchmen to secure
victory for their party. Gangsta, ghetto and street life in Jamaica are
represented as inherently linked to certain strategies of survival, including using political affiliation or patronage (particularly strong in
"garrison" communities) to gain access to, and control of, what are
considered scarce resources. It also involves competition, revenge,
"badmanship," loyalty and certain illicit activities, including theft
and extortion. The urban is tied to competition and gaining access to
power through control of certain resources and, increasingly, space.
The area leader or don, the man who controls the corner, has gained
prominence in the last twenty years as the person who has de facto
control over specific configurations of urban ghetto space. Inherently linked to the don, therefore, is the area that he controls. Therefore, when Baby Cham says, "Now we a lock the city and that is well
known," there is satisfaction in acknowledging the fact that he and
his crew are now the people in control, with the ability to wield and
bestow power.

In this context, Mavado's self-designation as a "gangsta for life" (the
title of his debut album, 2007) is the most forceful statement of ghetto
"livity" from a Jamaican DJ since the self-proclamations by the "rude
boys" of the 1960s and 1970s. It acknowledges his link to the ghetto
and the gangsta lifestyle characteristic of many contemporary ghettos. Mavado is from Cassava Piece, which has a name with overtones
of the agricultural plots characteristically found on many of Jamaica's
steep hills, overlooking rivers or their tributaries, although it is in fact
in the KMA. He has a barrage of tunes with lyrics about gangsta life.
His debut album can be seen as a treatise on gangsta epistemology,
pedagogy and ontology. There are questions about who the gangsta
is, principles to live and die by, respect, and money. Answering questions about his self-designation, Mavado responded in the following
way (Shore 2007):

Weh wi a come wid is a street vibe and people relate to me. Mi sing
fi the garrison, the gully and the trenches ... so when a yute inna

the gully see Mavado is like him a see himself. We represent fi every garrison ...

Mavado is one of several artists who have recorded what I refer to as letters from the gangsta's battlefield, revealing stories, strategies and spatial philosophies from the street. By the summer of 2007 dancehall was dominated by the line from one of his songs, "Di gangsta deh yah pon di gully side if yuh waan know weh fi find mi" ("The gangster is here on the gully side if you want to know where to find me"). It locates the DJ as having an umbilical link to the gully, where slime and refuse resides, and the poor take shelter on almost uninhabitable banks. Mavado defiantly claims the space of the gully: it is his current locale and has been forever in the representation of his cohorts who have lived in such spaces, it is where he and his navel string can be found, a space he symbolically and materially proclaims ownership of, referencing and claiming a marginal place within the community and the national identity. There is certitude in these proclamations. He is the gully gangsta for life.

The song also describes the ideological differences and feuding over dancehall "territory." Feuds have been common within dancehall, especially among DJs, such as Vybz Kartel, The Alliance more broadly involving Bounti Killa, Mavado, as well as Ninja Man, Lady Saw and Queen Paula. The longstanding feud between Beenie Man and Bounti Killa saw developments such as Beenie Man marrying Bounti Killa's former girlfriend, D'Angel. Yet Mavado's song implores ghetto street youths to keep the music clean and not turn it into a battlefield, a development for which hip hop and rap have become known since the deaths of Tupac Shakur in 1996 and of Biggy Smalls, The Notorious B.I.G., the following year. Mavado's music is materially and symbolically linked to the street, and therefore his calls to keep the music clean are also calls to keep the streets, and ultimately the nation, clean.

In "Don't Cry" (2007) Mavado addresses the badmindedness, censorship and feuding that come as part of life on the ghetto battlefield. He speaks to his mother of those who want to take the gangsta breath he breathes from the time of his birth in the gully to getting his "stripes" there and, of those who want to steal from him when he is trying to make a living for his family. In what sounds like a slightly uptempo dirge, akin to the singing within second lining in jazz funerals, Mavado brings the capital G, as signifier for gangsta "livity" as well as for his mother, into sharp focus. He implores his mother:

Mama, even if dem kill mi, don't cry,
Dem can neva take dis G from mi.

Mi ah prepare fi mi enemy,
Wey si mi wid mi things and waan try tek di key from mi.
Mama, even if dem kill mi, don't cry,
Mi know none of dem never build mi
Even if dem kill mi.

The lyrics speak to existence, for many who occupy tough urban land-scapes, on the edge, on the thin line between life and death. They also bring to mind questions of death and the afterlife posed by rappers. It was Tupac Shakur who raised questions about whether Heaven has a ghetto and concluded that Heaven has no shortage of gangstas. Mavado, explaining that he was born "from di gully" but never chose it, and has no financial success, only music, announces that he has to make a living for the sake of his family and would like to give his mother money too. In singing of his everyday experiences, he says that "they" have not seen the best of him, there is much more to come. They can't take the G (for "gangsta" and simultaneously for "gully") from him either.

Scholars have recognized that "'G' is a counterculture hero who embodies fierceness for youth all over America" (Regis 2001, 765; and see Forman 2002), as well as in the African Diaspora more generally. Judging from Mavado's popularity by the time of Reggae Sumfest in August 2007, when a record-breaking crowd was on hand just to see his performance, the G that Mavado wears is highly respected, not only because of his lyrical dexterity, but because such crowds believe that he is speaking of and to youth living at the edge, and beyond. There is an inextricable link between place, identity and status here. The ghetto, its streets and the everyday life that characterizes it gain a place in the performances of dancehall artists, who achieve status from the constituencies they build among the people in those spaces, the people they themselves come from.

CLASSIFYING AND MAPPING VENUES

Some venues, especially street venues, are numerous and ubiquitous, others are few in number and exclusive in style. Some venues are temporary, others have outlived the regular events that used to be staged in them. Then there are those venues that enjoy immense success and consistently attract the attention of law enforcement officers.

A survey of primary and secondary sources provides data about 159 venues that existed in the KMA between 1950 and 2004, revealing a great deal about the terrain and the spread of dancehall activity. The venues in this sample can be broadly divided into 109 community-based venues (street venues, gully banks, lodge halls, rented playout venues and sound system bases), fifty of them from before 1970 and fifty-nine from after that year; and fifty commercial venues (clubs, schoolrooms and theatres), of which twenty-three were active before 1970 and the other twenty-seven from 1970 to 2004.

Venues are generally classifiable in their order of historical development as well as their degree of commercialization.

(1) First comes the street corner or street side, as the most ubiquitous, most popular and available site. The use of the street as a stage was perfected by traditional Jonkonnu bands and Burru drummers, as well as street preachers and "itinerant songster–troubadours" (Witmer 1989, 13) such as Slim and Sam, who were active from the 1920s to the 1940s (see Taylor 1983). In Kingston from the early 20th century onward, such itinerant performers were increasingly superseded by sound systems, evolving from sound system bases or dance yards whose street addresses, both above and below Cross Roads, were dropped because they had become so popular. Apart from the "lawns" (discussed in Chapter 2 and earlier in this chapter), among the most important and influential of the street venues for sound systems were the corner of Luke Lane and Charles Street, where Tom "The Great Sebastian" Wong played; the corner of Rosemary Lane and Tower Street, used by Emperor Faith; and the corner of Dunrobin and Constant Spring Roads, the site of Jack Ruby's sound system (see Thompson 2002). A new sound system was likely to play on a street corner for some time until it gained enough experience and popularity to make the transition to a more established venue. Contemporary street venues include 66¾ Chisholm Avenue; the corner of Pink Lane and Charles Street; the corner of Beeston Street and Matthews Lane; and Fletcher's Land Square, where the Dutty Fridaze event takes over the entire space. These street venues are more common today in the downtown lanes, such as Pink Lane or Matthews Lane, than they are uptown, on Red Hills Road or Constant Spring Road. This could be attributed to the decline of dancehall activity on streets above Cross Roads, due to the enforcement of sanctions under the Noise Abatement Act, especially between dancehall high points. Even so, the street still factors into most venues, as events overflow onto streets, transcending boundaries set by walls or fences. Activities among spectators, such as vending and "profiling," contribute to the overflow.

(2) Gully banks around which shanty dwellings cluster were the sites of some of the earliest dances, as Bunny Goodison (2002) confirmed. People gathered to experience the music of established or emerging DJs, including those who lived in these shanties. Although gullies are

3.5 A Typical Dance Scene at the Dutty Fridaze event
Source: Sonjah Stanley Niaah

some of the most marginal sites, they have attracted large numbers of people. One contemporary example is the dance venue referred to by residents as Verena Banks, on Verne Avenue at the edge of the Sandy Gully, which drains the KMA. Another example is Gully Thursdays in Cassava Piece, whose gully has become famous since Mavado, who (as mentioned above) grew up in Cassava Piece, referred to it in songs such as "Gully Side" (2007).

(3) Lodge halls operated by fraternal societies, predominantly in downtown Kingston, were venues for quadrille and other historical dance forms until, as Bunny Goodison (2002) recalled, "subcultural" dance events began to be held in them during the late 1950s and into the 1960s. They included Foresters Hall, King's Lawn and Marcus Garvey's Liberty Hall. The sound systems that played within these spaces included Sir Coxsone's Downbeat and King Tubby's Hi Fi. Within the location known as "Beat Street" there were as many as seven sound systems vying for the title of "champion sound."

(4) Rented or regular playout venues below Cross Roads, often affiliated to or initiated by a bar, pub or cookshop in the area, are still common. Contemporary examples include Joyce's Hot Spot on Admiral Pen Road, Cherry's Bar on Baker's Street in Jones Town and Dawn's HQ near Cross Roads, which hosted Stone Love dance event in the early 1980s. The Backline events, on which the later Frontline and Top Line

events were modelled, took place at the corner of Beeston Street and Spanish Town Road in West Downtown. Frontline's regular venue was the Frontline Pub on Red Hills Road, while the Top Line events were held at Southdale Plaza on South Avenue.

(5) Sound system bases, which spread from the late 1950s onward, included Nanny's Hot Spot on Laws Street, where Studio One's Clement "Sir Coxsone" Dodd's Downbeat sound was the resident sound system; 33 Bond Street, where Duke Reid's The Trojan was first located; and Brotherton Avenue, where Doc's Thunderstorm was based. Although these were some of the earliest venues for listening to sound systems, they did not constitute commercial playout venues until the 1990s. Stone Love's base at Burlington Avenue is a current example, hosting events such as Wedy Wedy Wednesdays. This category also includes Grotto Swing on Hannah Street and Fire Links on Cling Cling Avenue.

(6) Rented or regular playout venues just outside the KMA were especially popular during the 1960s and 1970s. Sound systems travelled regularly to locations in other parishes, and venues such as Guava Ridge and Glengoffe in St Andrew, the Spanish Town Prison Oval in St Catherine, and the Bull Bay Quarry in St Thomas, to the East of the KMA, became popular. The sound system Stone Love had a regular playout in Glengoffe. Jamaica Gates hosted the Sunday night Super D dance, named after the sound system, during the early 1990s.

(7) Clubs in the 1960s included the Bournemouth, the Glass Bucket, the Silver Slipper, Club Havana, Copa Cobana, Baby Grand, Colony Club, Blue Mist, Sugar Hill and Ad Astra. At first they mainly accommodated big bands. They were the most prestigious venues in those years, especially among the middle classes. They boasted magnificent infrastructure, including permanent structures such as bars, sanitary facilities, stages and dance floors, and were outside the sphere of the poor, who could not afford to patronize them. In the 1990s the leading clubs were Cactus, Mirage and Asylum (now closed). By 2009, the Quad and Fiction emerged. Today clubs are more accessible to the lower classes. There have also been less exclusive clubs in working-class communities such as Molynes Road, including Sombrero, Road House and Trap.

(8) Rented or regular playout venues above Cross Roads or otherwise outside the inner city include Shady Grove, the Students' Union at the UWI in Mona, Red Gal Ring, House of Leo and Cargill Avenue, the site of the longstanding Thursday night Stone Love dance for more than ten years. Others include the Market Place, the Tavern Skating Ring, the Blue Mountain Inn, the Constant Spring Golf Club, the Caymanas Golf Club and Mass Camp. Still others include Chelsea Jerk Centre, Skateland, now renamed Rainbow Lawn, the Hermitage Community

Centre and the Appliance Traders Complex. Apart from clubs, these are the most commercial venues, with cover charges being applied. Large venues such as the Constant Spring Golf Club are reserved for stage shows, which attract thousands.

(9) Schoolrooms have been used for social events since the 19th century. Winston Blake, the owner of the Merritone sound system, recalled (Katz 2003, 4) that even in the 1960s "schoolrooms or church halls was where you had social functions."

(10) Theatres have been venues too. For example, the Palace Theatre was used for Vere John's popular talent show Opportunity Knocks, from which many talented singers gained exposure, and the Majestic Theatre was used for rehearsals by the sound system owner and producer Duke Reid.

A crude assessment suggests that, of the 159 venues in the sample, 85 were located downtown, below Cross Roads, 57 were uptown and 17 were at the edges of or outside the KMA. Their distribution across the city indicates concentrations of dance events in six main areas: Halfway Tree, Cross Roads, Jones Town, East Downtown (stretching to Rollington Town), West Downtown and Central Downtown. Between 1950 and 1970 there were more venues in the last four of these than in the first two, but between 1970 and 2004 Halfway Tree, East Downtown and Cross Roads were dominant, indicating a migration of venues due to the upsurge in inner-city violence and police raids, and the increasing commercialization of dance venues. However, West and Central Downtown have since been able to boast thriving new venues and events, such as Passa Passa, held in West Downtown since 2004, or Dutty Fridaze, taking place in Central Downtown since 2007.

Despite the loss of venues to Cross Roads and Halfway Tree, East Downtown continues to have vibrant dancehall enterprises, partly because of the continuation of oldies dance events spearheaded by pubs and corner shops, many around the Rose Garden area. On the other hand, Halfway Tree, where most venues between 1950 and 1970 were clubs, has seen the addition of many more venues as the popularity and commercialization of dancehall have intensified. While the volatility of some inner-city communities has contributed to the movement of events outward from the inner city, Halfway Tree has surged in popularity, particularly during dancehall high points, owing to the increased promotion of dance events. Venues that were active there between 1989 and 2004 included Skateland (now Rainbow Lawn), Southdale Plaza, the Countryside Club, Hagley Park Plaza, Baron's Plaza, Manalty Lane, House of Leo, Dumphries Road, Chelsea Jerk Centre, the Appliance Traders Complex, the Jamaica Broilers Sports Complex, Stone Love Headquarters and Market Place.

Half of the clubs that existed between 1950 and 1970 were located below Cross Roads, but these have since disappeared. Clubs continue to dominate above Cross Roads, largely because they are accessible to middle-class patrons who are more comfortable with such venues, and are prepared to pay the entrance and cover charges. Among downtown clubs, the Asylum nightclub, which celebrated its tenth anniversary in 2007, has maintained some longevity and was rivalled in popularity only by its predecessor Cactus, which closed in 1997.

Finally, a survey of commercial studios below Cross Roads suggests that there has been a similar shift away from downtown in music production as well as in dancehall venues. Between 1950 and 1980 65 percent of known studios were located below Cross Roads, but between 1980 and the present this declined to 11 percent, as much of the commercial recording industry moved to Central Downtown and West Kingston. Not only was there a remarkable shift from downtown to uptown, but there was far less clustering and a much wider spread across the KMA, beyond Central Downtown and West Kingston. Notably, both commercial and non-commercial home studios are now located in diverse areas across the KMA. The resources required for the purchase of equipment, and the renting or purchase of space to house and operate the equipment, suggests that studios by definition require financial backing. The phenomenon of the non-commercial studio in which pre-production recordings are done, whether by sound systems for dubplates or specials, or by musicians, singers and DJs, emerged in Jamaica in the 1990s, in the same way that kwaito stars in South Africa have begun owning and operating home studios. With production rates for the services of commercial studios as high as 4,000 Jamaican dollars an hour, it has become much more economical for artists to invest in computerized recording equipment for home use than to use these studios.

LOCATING HALFWAY TREE

The centrality of Halfway Tree as a site of continuous dance activity, if not of music production, raises questions as to its place as an entertainment crossroads. In a sense, it may be evocative of the spirit of the city for the Yoruba people of Nigeria, Benin and Ghana, for whom the city revolves around a wheel-like structure (Pelton 1980, 155), reflecting the centrality of the spiritual, political and lived experience of its people. The urban morphology of indigenous cities reflects the body and voice of its citizens in a way that colonial replica cities cannot. For example, street names, rivers, historical sites, shrines, prayer booths, and parks are important features. In Jamaica place and street names are often transplants from Britain, and there are few public sites that celebrate the spiritual, political and lived experience of Jamaicans. Today National Heroes Park and Emancipation Park, both in the KMA, stand as public sites of historical and cultural significance, with monuments established to past heroes, both free and enslaved. Arguably, these sites represent expressions of nationhood far removed from the lived experience of the folk who are underrepresented in hard locational indices.

Originating in Kingston's development as a marketplace, the tree that Halfway Tree is named after provided a shady halfway point for farmers and vendors from the Blue and John Crow foothills who used the route past the tree to transport their goods to the downtown market. Today it connects all the major roads within the city and continues to be a halfway point, accessible to both uptown and downtown, betwixt and between, a crossroads trafficked by vehicles and pedestrians, and also the site of significant events of celebration.

Skateland in Halfway Tree has operated as a meeting point for all classes and as a core around which other events spiral outward. The almost spontaneous street dancing initiated by Colo Colo and emerging Cadillac and other crew members in 2003, to show their skills and entice commuters, mostly secondary school students, on a Friday evening, directly evolved from Skateland where the crew established a base. Geographically, Halfway Tree, including Skateland, could be considered the centre of the KMA, and metaphorically, possibly the entertainment crossroads of a city whose plan did not include formal spatial allocations for popular entertainment.

The idea of Halfway Tree as an entertainment crossroads becomes less surprising when one considers Damian Marley's album *Halfway Tree*, which won the Grammy Award for Reggae in 2001. The cover of the album depicts him standing under the clock at Halfway Tree, presenting Damian Marley as an embodiment of Halfway Tree because of his parents' differing social origins (Cindy Breakspeare was from uptown and Bob Marley was from the ghetto). He is suggesting that, like the Halfway Tree itself, he stands at midpoint on the line between the uptown foothills of St Andrew and the downtown ghetto. Perhaps the title of the album is less responsible for its success than the quality of the recordings, but both are inextricably linked with a reality of nation embodied on the ground beyond and before song.

On the title track Marley sings of Halfway Tree as the site of a fight for musical turf, where DJs are defeated by the young reggae artist who intercepts the lineup at a stage show. The song is almost prophetic because, as it suggests, together with the rest of the album, it leapt past all others to win the coveted race and eventually the Grammy Award, which is based on sales and therefore popularity. Importantly, it is Halfway Tree where the race is staged and won, and it continues to take shape in the various venues of the area. As Damian Marley suggests, summarily dismissing those who still wish to contend but can't win the Halfway Tree race, DJs without intellect

> return to the venues
> you used to fill
> and return to the ends
> where you used to chill.

Like other crossroads around the world, with their guardians such as Eshu, the trickster god of the Yoruba people, Halfway Tree and its venues have operated as a kind of halfway point for the citizens of the inner city. It is accessible to the transport-poor, who find relief and solace from their daily troubles against a wall at the dance, or on the outer perimeter, sometimes just to pick up bottles to sell for tomorrow's dinner. Rituals of dance and worship take place there, as patron after patron honours the spirit of life that enables them to partake in the dance of the gods. Here they can leave hunger, indignity, violence, sick mothers, yard squabbles, gang feuds, babies or nothing in particular behind and step into another world. As rituals of the crossroads go, dancing, laughter, play, potentiality, paradox, exchange, transformation, reversal of status and order into disorder, thereby creating other kinds of orders (see Pelton 1980 and Chevannes 2001), relocate the dancehall, which originates from the margins, into a national centre, dancing in essence to its own beat. Halfway Tree embodies a neither-here-nor-there quality: it is a betwixt-and-between place, a halfway point, an *eshurita* (shrine of Eshu), which suggests a liminal space, in a geographical but also a ritual sense. It is fitting that Halfway Tree, this liminal space, is considered a crossroads because, it is said, Eshu dances to the beat of a pounding mortar if there are no drums (Pelton 1980, 132). By invoking the crossroads, then, I seek to highlight an embedded reality of performance at the crossroads, in this instance, not only in the god that dwells there, but for the patrons whose bodies perform their life stories night after night.

Events in and around Halfway Tree since the 1970s may be understood as the latest in a continuum of dance events beginning with the slave ship and culminating in sacred performance acts within Jamaica. Arguably, since the 1970s no other place in the island has pulsated with sound to the degree Halfway Tree has, and continues to. Whether dancehall events migrated to Halfway Tree because of its crossroads nature or because of the sacred texts underlying the enter-tainment practice of Kingston's citizens, which remain unlocked in the collective consciousness, is not clear.

There are plans to redevelop the inner city in order to stem some of the decay and encourage renewal. Halfway Tree holds important sites of memory for dancehall, and the migration of dancehall entertain-ment to this area reveals that something about the inner city has been virtually lost due to economic and social decay. A qualitative socio-poetics serves well to place Halfway Tree at the centre of Kingston's performance geography and ethos.

CONCLUSIONS

A mapping of Kingston's dancehall spaces, their history, evolution, character, use and classification, helps us to widen the angle from which we can interpret and analyze dancehall. Kingston's dancehall memory is bound up in these spaces, where histories, selves, and new modes of community and nation have evolved. The exposition of performance geography and the use of space as a holistic category to view performance allow for a delineation of microspatialities, lo-cal postcolonial spatial politics, and modes of creating space through performance for entertainment and memorializing.

Kingston has an established history of popular performance, and these spaces have rivalled and infected the performance culture and aesthetic of the upper class in no small way. It is virtually impossible to visit Kingston and not hear a sound system in the nightscape or notice the ubiquitous advertisements for the latest dancehall event. These events occur mostly in street venues appropriated for the night without lease or rental. They continue to emerge and flourish at the people's will, despite state sanctions.

I have viewed the street historically, relating its use and appropria-tion in Jamaican popular culture to local, national and transnation-al ontologies of the ghetto, gangsta "livity," and the Black Atlantic performance-scapes more broadly. Although dancehall street events constitute an autonomous zone, in the sense of eluding the strictures of state control even as it exists in a wider field of boundaries, dance patrons create and claim space by transcending designated spaces through the nature of their dance performances, whether by dancing on a roof or a car, or, more concretely, by appropriating planned space for unplanned uses. These mechanisms evidence the ways in which the dancehall citizenry opens spatial frontiers, even as the state ob-serves and waits to make its "lock down" move. Boundaries exist, but within a philosophy of boundarylessness held by key dancehall participants, by way of which the disenfranchised can be seen to use space as a strategy of power, dwelling within, and simultaneously evading, the discipline of urban planning with strategies that camouflage the contradictions of social production.

Dancehall culture has thus created several unbounded sites through everyday street events around music and dance. Where tactics of social control by the state have kept the poor outside the mainstream economy and political apparatuses, citizens carefully craft their undisciplining and unmasking within the urban performance sphere. Spatial arrangements, and the power evoked by such arrangements, are noisily displaced by the performing bodies that perpetually recreate the dancehall aesthetic and simultaneously reappropriate public space.

RITUAL SPACE, CELEBRATORY SPACE

ONE significant characteristic of the humanities and of interdisciplinary enterprises such as cultural studies is the need for thinking through a critical tradition that gives voice to absences around spirituality—the oneiric, metaphysical and esoteric—that occupies the everyday lives of peoples of the global South and their Diasporas. Ideas about the absence of a theorization of the spiritual or the sacred, within cultural studies generally and studies of dancehall specifically, have become mired in questions of the philosophy of religion, moral tensions around African and African-Diasporic embodied practices, including dancehall, and the dichotomy between sacred and secular. North Atlantic traditions in the humanities and, to some extent, the social sciences, include a longstanding philosophical tradition around established world religions, sacred practices, sacred sites and their place in human life. However, engagement with the sacred in the context of the African Diaspora largely remains linked to discussion and analysis of a few specific religions.

A major part of the intellectual work in this chapter comes from thinking about the methodology for writing absence into presence in the context of the sacred—the sacred that is both ordinary and extraordinary, both everyday and seasonal, both ephemeral and omnipresent. This chapter is concerned, therefore, with the ways in which the sacred is represented in the popular realm, at the intersection of the secularization of society and its inherent ideological, philosophical, existential and methodological crises. I see these questions as following from the social theory perspective in the tradition of Émile Durkheim (1915), but, also, and more critically, from a consideration of how the sacred and the secular are coterminous, symbiotically linked, and expressed in everyday actions. Where do the masses fit into the sacred constellation? Is it only in the realm of insurrection, or the "struggle for social meanings," that the sacred can be analyzed in the postcolonial context? How are sacred acts made manifest in everyday life, and where are their sites of improvisation (see Moten 2003), disruption or cohesion? I argue in this chapter that the power of the sacred in dancehall is an important site of engagement, as we seek to understand and document its charismatic and ritual foundations.

I have been thinking about the intersections between the popular secular and the sacred since the late 1990s, acknowledging that in that very intersection Jamaican popular culture has consistently produced, called into question and critiqued notions of being for many Jamaicans. Within this popular site—and I am privileging site over text—there is an inextricable presence but theoretical absence of the sacred. My reading tries to move away from a set of binaries to a holistic reading of the sacred in everyday life. This chapter interrogates dancehall culture using an understanding that the popular, especially in the Black Atlantic world, has been intertwined with the performance of ritual. The intention is therefore to highlight the underexplored bridge between the popular, performance and ritual.

What is the nature of dancehall performance? Cultural scholars have overlooked some of the permanent possibilities of everyday life that have been harnessed by urban innovators through performance. Life-cycle and seasonal events, including celebrations of birth, death, community, anniversary, victory and relationships, reveal the ritual significance of dancehall's performance practice, creating a map that may be read using Victor Turner's concepts of *communitas* and liminality (see Turner 1967 and 1969). The perspective in this chapter moves the discourse on dancehall beyond superficial understanding of "resistance" or "the carnivalesque"—analytical categories frequently used within cultural studies—to sacred geographies, in which events and lifestyles merge without undue focus on the body as merely a pleasure zone. Critical examination of dancehall events and their celebratory ethos reveals the power of those from the margins to perform, constitute new forms of community, entice international audiences, and transform self and identities through ritual.

Dancehall events constitute everyday life for their innovators and perpetuators. With no central organizing body, they are spontaneous celebrations that are heavily symbolic and ritualistic, performed in private, public, formal or informal settings, as well as at specific times and seasons. They are also spatially processualized, with urban as well as rural reach. What do such events celebrate? What do such celebrations entail? What is their import? Specifically, dancehall events celebrate the spectrum of life from birth to death, including birthday bashes, clashes and anniversaries. Events also celebrate oldies music, gangs, girls and queens, the return to school, and the memory of an individual. The more recent "link up" events celebrate Caribbean Diasporic and community networks, and wealth consumption. In these events are observable ritual elements closely tied to the power of the corner, the area or the local community. Events are also responsible for the revision/expansion of categories such as "community" and "area," as performance allows for their extension and metamorphosis into geographies larger than themselves.

There is a sense in which performance through dance in dancehall events constitutes a street drama of total aesthetic and psychic transformation. Dancehall events celebrates birth, victory, anniversary, death, relationships, memory and the norms accompanying these milestones, around music, food, drink, dance and spontaneity, constituting the rituals with which Afro-Jamaicans replaced lost African rituals (White 1984, 73). Katrina Hazzard-Gordon (1996) has pointed out that the adaptation of traditional West African patterns to new sociocultural environments involved the role of the sacred being transformed, as dance moved from its sacred ceremonial African context to the numerous secularized uses it acquired under slavery. However, I want to emphasize, even more than Garth White did, that an understanding of dancehall within a ritual schema creates space for reinterpreting its role.

A READING OF RITUAL

My aim is not to argue that ritual—understood, in the traditional sense, as that which is practised among many indigenous peoples—can be found in the dancehall. Ritual in the traditional sense has an important link with spirituality. It is the act of communicating with Spirit for healing at the level of the community/village, body and soul. Using particular spaces with planned and unplanned elements, ritual is not an everyday formality, but a call to Spirit, often including ancestors, for transformation and healing through reconnection with purpose. As Malidoma Somé puts it (1999, 146): "Ritual is a dance with Spirit, the soul's way of interacting with the Other World, the human psyche's opportunity to develop relationship with the symbols of this world and the spirits of the other."

The purposes of rituals—sets of actions with symbolic value, the performance of which at regular intervals is usually prescribed by a religion or by the traditions of a community—are varied, and may include compliance with religious obligations or ideals, satisfaction of spiritual or emotional needs of the practitioners, strengthening of social bonds, demonstration of respect or submission, obtaining social acceptance or approval for some event or, sometimes, ritual just for the pleasure of the ritual itself. Ritual actions revolve around the performance of special music, songs, dances, processions, gestures or words, the recitation of certain texts, or the manipulation of objects, special clothing, food or drink. Rituals can aid in creating a firm sense of group identity, fixing and reinforcing the shared values and beliefs of a society, or aiming at particular transformations, often conceived in cosmic terms. Even such common actions as shaking hands or saying hello can be analyzed as rituals. Essential features of ritual include the fact that actions and their symbolism are not arbitrarily chosen by the performers, but often are prescribed and imposed upon the performers by some external source or inherited from social traditions. It is the latter that constitutes the structure of the bridge that exists between the popular, performance and ritual in the Black Atlantic world.

My concern here is the everyday celebration of a continuum—God, self, life, death, anniversary—that dancehall presents within its calendar. Though Garth White's insight separates ritual in the traditional African sense from dancehall, dancehall performance can be read as ritual, that is "action wrapped in webs of significance" (Kertzer 1988, 9). In this sense, a more open interpretation of ritual needs to be claimed and explored. The experience of dance in this New World context has enabled the rereading of status, cosmos and sense of space, especially among dancers, and this is tantamount to a counterinvention of the self as a cultural and political strategy (Wynter 1977, 36). Through ritual events the self can connect to a deep-structured and pre-conscious origin. Through celebrations of life, death, anniversaries, victory and birth, conscious pacts with ancestors in traditional Jamaican dance forms such as Gerreh, Dinki Mini, Kumina or Jonkonnu, as well as contemporary forms, give way to techniques of freedom manifested through the body in an everyday context. Neither the state nor violence can deter the ritual, nor is it encumbered by denominational or moral branding, as in, for example, the Christian churches. As social commentators and creators, dancers and patrons make social, cultural and economic space in real terms.

Victor Turner's signature concept of *communitas* resonates in this reading of ritual (see Turner 1969). The concept is Turner's representation of how, in the negation of normal rites and social hierarchy, the bonds between people, which enable society to exist, can emerge in ritual contexts. Turner highlights the experience of heightened sociality, such as that found in the liminal phase of rites of passage, which crucially separates the dancehall event from any other event perceived as mere entertainment. Turner sees liminality as by far the most important phase of the ritual process. It involves a prolonged period where the participant is both literally and symbiotically marginalized. During liminality the status of the participant is vague, in order to ensure the distinctness of the ritual process from normal life. Turner argues that if this period of liminality is prolonged, it can lead to the development of a transcendental feeling of social togetherness. This interpretation is supported by the claims made by dancehall patrons I have interviewed about the psychological benefits and feelings of attachment they derive from dancehall events. It is this that the concept of *communitas* is aimed at capturing: the transcendence of social structure that brings the participant under the authority of the community, as the initiate submits to nothing less than the authority of the community. The popular DJ Bounti Killa (2003) puts this into sharp focus: "Poor people keep a dance, poor people gather, poor people spend money, poor people make money, we build each other. ... Poor people do these things for themselves." Ritual is therefore to be viewed as an everyday potential, seen in the liminal spaces through which entities can pass outside the realm of normal or dominant classificatory schemes that serve to ground them in particular cultural/symbolic ordering systems.

This new permanent possibility and place of the liminal in the analysis of New World performance highlights liminality as "an idiom of performance" (Austin-Broos 1997, 47). This performance is the way in which social beings reclaim lost rituals, create and recreate themselves and their way of being, and remember (Connerton 1989, 22). Significantly, performance rituals within commemorative ceremonies are "expressive acts" having "conspicuous regularity" of a formal, stereotyped, stylized and repetitive nature, and are important over time and space, and beyond the ritual itself, to "non-ritual actions, to the whole life of a community" (Connerton, 1989, 44–45).

The dance event, then, ultimately represents a celebration of community. There is a sense in which the dance typifies the sense of community that inner-city dwellers have had to negotiate through shared activities around yard and area life, or "livity," evidenced by the purpose, sociality and character of these events. Early events that epitomized this sense of community were the "welcome home" dances performed within the Burru drumming tradition during the 1930s to celebrate the return of a member of the community from prison (see White 1984 and Hebdige 1997). Sound systems such as Sir Coxsone's Downbeat continued such events, and today their meaning is expressed particularly in street events around the community corner shop, bar or domino tables.

A recent and unique example of community celebration is the major street event called Passa Passa, held on Wednesday nights since 2003 on Spanish Town Road in Tivoli Gardens, West Kingston, an area long controlled by the Jamaica Labour Party and therefore avoided by Kingstonians from areas affiliated with the People's National Party. Passa Passa was initially dominated by residents of Tivoli Gardens and surrounding areas, but it soon attracted persons from outside the community once it was declared safe to attend. Sponsorship followed, from corporations such as Jamaica's most popular mobile phone network, Digicel, and the image of the event among performers became immune from the perceptions of violence and instability that have plagued Tivoli Gardens. The community used to become a sort of ghost town after dark, but Passa Passa has transformed it, making it a convergence zone for a variety of patrons, local and international, rich and poor, uptown and downtown, mingling in the street dances. On Wednesday nights the community becomes an open border that can be crossed by residents of the community and surrounding areas, Asian and other tourists, businessmen and ordinary folk, even during periods of heightened tension. Passa Passa has helped to stimulate economic activity in Tivoli Gardens and the neighbouring community of Denham Town. It has also helped to shape a new community identity, as well as a spirit of community among residents and patrons.

There are many other examples of events that constitute celebrations of community, such as the weekly Backline event once held at the corner of Spanish Town Road and Beeston Street in West Kingston, or the popular Sunday vintage music event on Rae Street, known as Rae Town, in eastern Kingston. The occurrence, consistent emergence and impact of these celebrations make it impossible to ignore them.

NAMES, TIMES, THEMES AND PURPOSES

Dance events are fundamentally linked to economics, status and survival strategies, and there are structural elements that accompany their celebratory ethos. They have observable rituals of preparation and arrival, community, birth and death, victory, memorializing and anniversary, accession or ascension, transcendence and transformation, welcome, competition, and fertility (see Ryman 1980 and Cooper 2004a). In order to fully explain the importance attached to dancehall, its events and the formalities of its performance practice, I shall discuss the names, times, themes and purposes tied up with the ritualistic or commemorative aspects of dance events.

Dance events always have names. Their appeal and consequent power converge around the naming of this ritual of celebration, which usually takes the form of a reference to the latest dancehall tune or piece of inner-city lingua franca. This is crucial to attracting patrons. Names taken from songs (whether titles or lines within them) have included Bruck Out Bruck Out, Clean Up Yuh Heart an' Come, Fully Loaded, Gimme Di Light, Girl's Dem Bashment, Ol' Time Something Come Back Again, Rasta Jamboree, Raw and Rough, Survival Story, Real Ghetto Story, and Weh Di Gal Dem Want: Vitamin S-E-X.

Named events dot the nightscape almost every night throughout the year, in a kind of "liturgical calendar" that persists regardless of season, state power or sanctions. This presents a challenge to conceptualizations of popular dancehall culture as "carnivalesque" in the Bakhtinian sense, that is, as confined to specific carnival periods when everyday norms are relaxed. It is true that weekend and holiday events were the most frequent and popular in the 1950s and 1960s, but by the late 1980s a typical weekly calendar would be as follows:

MONDAY	Stone Love sound system at Tropic Club and Waltham Park Road
TUESDAY	Super D sound system at Top Line Bar (later Southdale Plaza)
WEDNESDAY	Backline event on Spanish Town Road, Metro Media sound system at Woodford Park
THURSDAY	Stone Love at House of Leo
FRIDAY & SATURDAY	standard weekend commercial and party events (usually several)
SUNDAY	Klassique sound system at Rae Street and Super D at Jamaica Gates

By 2004 Kingston's weekly dancehall calendar had expanded to take in several events, in a manner characteristic of a dancehall high point:

MONDAY	Early Monday (both at Waterford and Stand Pipe), Hot Monday
TUESDAY	Kool Tuesday, Asylum Ladies Night
WEDNESDAY	Asylum Oldies Night, Weddy Weddy Wednesday, Blazing Wednesday, Passa Passa
THURSDAY	Early Thursday, Asylum Dancehall Night, Sicky Sicky Thursday, Stress Free Thursday
FRIDAY	Jiggy Friday, Spooky Friday, Kidz Friday
SATURDAY	Crazy Saturday, along with numerous other commercial events

SUNDAY	Rae Town Oldies, Bad Mind Sunday, Asylum Vintage Night, along with popular events in West Kingston.

It should be noted that the emergence of "Early" events signals higher levels of coordination among promoters, who are successfully reclaiming the total hours during a given night. Three or more events a night are commonplace. Key patrons attend all events and can be observed moving from one to the other at precise times. This level of coordination is unprecedented. The protocol related to the placement of events within the weekly calendar is an area for further study.

A survey of the calendar in summer 2007 revealed the following additions:

MONDAY	Money Monday
TUESDAY	Dutty Tuesday, Month End Tuesday (every last Tuesday)
WEDNESDAY	Early Wednesday
THURSDAY	Bembe Thursday, Talent Thursday, Let Me Loose Thursday, Gully Thursday, Frontline Thursday
FRIDAY	Dutty Fridaze, Rebel T Friday, Energy Friday, Sell Off Friday, Spoogy Friday
SATURDAY	Cadillac Saturday
SUNDAY	Prendy's on the Beach, Spicy Sunday, Sunday Flava, Love Sundays

Characteristically, there are more events at the end of the week (from Thursday to Sunday), but, uncharacteristically, Fridays and Saturdays now feature regular events. This was not the case in the late 1980s and early 1990s, when weekends were customarily left free for staging income-generating events, such as commercial and corporate-sponsored stage shows.

What sustains such high levels of performance activity, in the face of seemingly diminishing economic and social capital, is the power of the ritual, the sustenance it affords, its democratic regimes, its tangible structure of norms and codes, alongside a highly developed

sense of meaning and identity tied to location among its key participants. In this light dancehall differs from carnival. Consequently, a full
understanding of dancehall would be negated by a reading of its liberatory potential based on Bakhtinian analysis of the carnivalesque.
Where a Bakhtinian analysis simply offers a liberatory potential, the
daily persistence of dancehall is liberation actualized, in the sense of
enacting a daily celebration of the everyday condition. Even while its
habitus is marginal, dancehall is a sacred space by virtue of the sense
in which souls continue to be sustained. Obviously, there is also the
matter of importing readings of culture that are decontextualized in
their wider application.

The timing of commencement and termination is a significant feature of any event. For dance events in Jamaica both times have varied
over the past fifty years. The significance of the dark for planning re-
volts, telling duppy and Anancy stories or performing dance activities
is well-known. Reminiscent of the secret slave meetings on the plantations when Massa was asleep, the 21st-century dance event of Kingston
warms up, on average, somewhere between 1:00 and 5:00 a.m., when
the rest of society is in a state of slumber. This time contrasts with 8:00
p.m., standard in the 1960s, and 11:00 p.m., standard in the 1990s.
However, not all events begin after dark. At the furthest extreme of
commercial dancehall practice, stage shows, particularly those on
beaches, often commence in the mid-afternoon to evening hours.

In the 1960s the average event lasted five hours, if it was not ended
prematurely by the police or other disruptive forces. This average duration has also applied in recent years, when the later starting time of
events has meant later ending times. Downtown community events
generally end at dawn, while events at uptown clubs tend to end earlier. Clubs observe strict ending times because of the terms of employment of their staff, their location within Kingston's business centre
and their potential for causing disruption to rush hour traffic.

The dance, then, is not just an event, it is a system of rules and codes,
an institution. Patrons are aware of the latest dance moves, the latest
songs, debates and artistes. There are salutations, tributes and paying
of respect. Validation is signalled in specific ways, by using cigarette
lighter flashes or gun salutes, or saying "Pram pram, "Bouyaka" or
"Bung bang." The audience participates in the fundamental themes
or moral codes that have been part of the dancehall scene, many of
them from its inception. These include celebrating the community or
local area; friendship and love versus animosity; the power and prowess of the rude boy or bad man; competition and struggle; sexuality,
and the morality of the penis and the vagina; celebrating the vagina,
women, mother, girls; celebrating the DJ and/or the sound system; the

authority and divinity of Haile Selassie (in Rastafari) or God (in Christianity); "the essential herb" (marijuana); colour and class identity; material culture; and the relationship between state institutions and the people. In truly ecological terms, codes are maintained through repeated performances, and those who do not adhere to the expected norms are closely monitored, tested and challenged or, eventually, humiliated and discouraged.

Key dancehall themes are apparent in the music and in the calls of selectors soliciting appropriate audience responses. Among other liturgical incantations, it is not uncommon to hear a selector calling his crowd to respond by showing their hands to comments such as "from a bwoy nuh badda dan you" (if you are the baddest), if you "have yu owna man" (if you have your own man), "if you hole no condemn" (if your vagina is not condemned), "from yuh neva dash weh belly" (if you have never had an abortion), "all who seh ganja fi bu'n" (all who say marijuana is to be smoked) or "if you a nuh batty man" (if you are not a homosexual). Similarly, a selector sometimes calls for a show of hands from those who love God, the audience responds and then a song that typifies the sentiment is played. There is a particular ritual of interaction being enacted here in the dynamic relationship between the patrons, the selector, the music and the dance.

Events also have norms and codes of dance, location, fashion and status. Women adorn themselves according to the dictates of the current dancehall fashion. From the 1960s to the 1980s women wore platform shoes, bellbottomed pants or dresses below the knees, long sleeves and high necklines, and afros, the trend by the 1990s moved through pieces of red or white, this or that, to extremes both of nakedness and of glamour. In the early 1990s gold braids, coloured wigs, gold cargo necklaces and earrings, mesh tops with one-inch holes, transparent low-cut blouses, transparent leggings or stockings, g-string panties, gloves, nail extensions and spectacles were common. More recently the trend has shifted to athletic jerseys and shoes from Tommy Hilfiger, Ralph Lauren, Fubu or Nike, and, by the summer of 2007, a range of both short and long dresses as well as scarves by 2009.. Yet, no matter the nationality, weight or reproductive status of an individual woman, she is welcomed in the dance and the same codes apply. Fat women, pregnant girls, Japanese women or patrons of Euro-American descent such as Medusa each have a place within dancehall's inclusivity.

Crews have always been part of the social scene that is amplified within dancehall. They are essentially social groupings, sometimes gangs, peer groups or persons defined, for example, by style, by performance skills or by residence in a particular area, as with the Standpipe crew or the Montego Bay crew. Crews are a significant part of the ritual of arrival, reminiscent of the shipmate bonds of the enslaved. They may be community, fashion or dancing crews, such as Ouch, Black Roses or Sample Six and Ravers Clavers, or a combination of these. Among crews I have observed such fashion statements as afro picks in young men's hair, distinctive headgear, school uniforms and tight shiny pants akin to those worn by pop stars in the 1980s. What is clear is that fashion is taken seriously by crews. Historically, not only has the crew been a sign of social relations, but it has served important functions such as maintaining security. Some patrons, especially men, attend dances with a crew only, depending on whether the dance is being held in a politically volatile area, whether the sound system is politically labelled, the existence of gang feuds or the possibility of police invasion. In such a space the crew remains alert and in close proximity to the perimeter or wall of the dance venue, which can be scaled in the case of gunfire or any other act that suggests the need for a quick exit. As my informant "Harry T" (2002) pointed out, a crew member who is aware of the security risks involved in attending an event that might prove volatile needs to be able to see the gate.

Once the event's tone and structural elements are set, purpose takes over. Events are organized around a purpose: a regular session for enjoyment, a commercial event such as a stage show or a celebration of older music such as an oldies party. Previously, dance events have been identified on the basis of how, why and by whom the music is played. For example, Norman Stolzoff (2000, 194) identifies two major types of sound system dances according to the mode of music being played: competitive or "clash" events and non-competitive or "juggling" events. He also distinguishes "performance modes" determined by the selector's performance, such as ritual and sacrifice (2000, 210–12). However, highlighting the music does not fully take account of the purpose of these events.

Because most dance events seek to celebrate an aspect of everyday life, they reveal a great deal about Kingston's society and culture, starting with Christmas dances, which dated back to the experience of enslaved Africans and was the antecedent of all contemporary dance events. Oral accounts reveal that people looked forward to a Christmas dance with great anticipation, as a chance to affirm, or "big up," their social identity and cultural experience. Yet by the early 1980s Christmas dances had disappeared. Marcia Davis, proprietor of the Frontline Pub, says (2002) that in the late 1980s her business partner started staging events to bring back the spirit that had faded with the decline of Christmas dances. Events around Christmas and New Year became more frequent once again, and in 2005, for example, they included Buzz 2005 at Skateland, the Pre-Xmas Link-up at Papine Jerk

Centre, and the Ghetto Story New Year's Eve Countdown at Sherlock Crescent. Sting, Pepsi Teensplash and Stone Love Anniversary dances also remain popular at this time of the year. Other events celebrate commonly marked holidays, such as Valentine's Day, Independence Day (on August 6) or National Heroes' Day (on the third Monday in October). There are also events dedicated to Rastafari culture, including the Jah Love sound system dances and, in 2003 for example, Melkam Liddet, a celebration of the Ethiopian Christmas at Rainbow Lawn on January 7, and the Rasta Jamboree at 2 Skibo Avenue on March 29.

Celebration of style is also crucial, with events in 2003, for example, including the Red and White Party at Rainbow Lawn on February 15, the Sports Wear and Jersey Dance at Breezy Castle on April 12, the British Fashion Party at Villa Ronai on April 24, and the Workforce Uniform Party at Market Place on August 5. Other celebrations focus on, and are named after, dance moves, such as Pon di River or Higher Level. Other events are dedicated to oldies music, such as Merritone Disco's Old Hits Party; Grooving on a Friday Afternoon at Venus Headquarters, 22¾ Waltham Park Road; or Heineken Startime and Good Times, two of the most popular commercial oldies events, which are staged at least twice yearly.

Ultimately, dance events facilitate changes in social, psychological and spatial states for the individual and the group. The dance hall is delineated as ritual space in the passage from home to the dance event, the passage during the event into other states—including from non-entity to legitimacy of purpose, especially among lower-class communicants such as the dancehall queens—and then the return home. The persistence of this nightly celebration merges the ritual with the everyday, blurring the boundaries to extend dancehall into daily existence, as a different world inside yet outside society. One could also argue, based on dancehall's mostly non-seasonal nature, that it exists within a kind of social limbo for key participants such as the dancehall queens (see Chapter 5). There is really never incorporation back into everyday life, since what is everyday becomes the entire ritual of preparation, communion, withdrawal and rest, then back to preparation all over again.

MAJOR TYPES OF DANCE EVENT

Without attempting a comprehensive typology of the various dance events in Jamaica, in this section I examine nine major types of dance event: birthday bashes, memorial dances, anniversary dances, girls' dances, celebrations of gangs or crews, stage shows and festivals, sound clashes, oldies dance events, and link-up dance events.

(1) The birthday bash, which is by far the most ceremonial of dance events, moves through important stages, including the cutting of the cake, as well as tributes to celebrated and specially featured artistes. For example, at the birthday bash for Stacey, Dancehall Queen 1999, held on December 8, 2001, at Mahoe Drive in her hometown of Cockburn Gardens (formerly and popularly known as Cockburn Pen), Beenie Man, Spragga Benz, Lukie D, Mad Anju and Cecile all performed at a street event, attracting no cover charge. To take another example, Bounti Killa's birthday bash, It's Tha Party, held at the Caymanas Polo Club on June 14, 2003, featured international acts, the entire Bounti Killa "Alliance" of recording artists and other friends, and girls dancing in cages, then a new feature for dance events in Kingston. Other birthday bashes that have attracted large crowds include those for the video producer Jack Sowah and John the Dancer, at the New Little Copa Club on May 22, 2002; the cosmetologist Sherene at the Wet 'n' Wild Roof club on July 7, 2002; the promoter Q45 at Stone Love's Burlington Avenue base on November 6, 2002; DYCR at Hellshire Beach on March 23, 2003; Elephant Man at Mass Camp Village on September 10, 2005; and Mavado at Temple Hall Estate on December 1, 2007. There are also generic birthday events, such as Taurus Hype: It's a Birthday Affair, held at the New Little Copa Club on May 8, 2002, held for all those born between April 21 and May 20.

(2) Memorial dances for popular figures typically involve family members, DJs, government officials and friends, in addition to regular patrons paying tribute. Observances such as moments of silence are common. This mode of celebration functions as collective memorializing, consistent with such older rituals as wakes, nine nights or "second lining" at jazz funerals (see Regis 2001). Communal memorializing claims city space, and voices individual and collective creativity and subjectivities, in a long tradition of black performance. Participants' daily lives become testimony to vulnerability and reduced agency in the face of the pain, violence and competition of urban inner-city life. Repeated participation in memorial dances stamps the deceased firmly in the minds of participants. It also bolsters civic pride, which is intensely reduced by area politics, gang warfare and poverty within the communities of many dancehall patrons. The landscape becomes engraved with the memory of those who have meant much to dancehall patrons.

There are standard expectations about when memorial events should commence and how long they should last. For example, it is widely believed that, if memorial events begin in the first year after a person's death, they must be staged every year after that, but if there is an interval of one year or more between the death and the first event, they can be held whenever it is convenient for the family. It is also widely believed that continuing memorial dances beyond ten years after the person's death might bring destruction on the family.

Prominent examples of memorial dances include those held to commemorate "dons" or area leaders, such as Lester "Jim Brown" Coke, whose life is usually commemorated every February, or Willy Haggart of the Black Roses Crew, who is commemorated every April along with Blacka Douge, a businessman who was killed at the same time as Haggart. Coke was one of two leaders of the West Kingston Shower Posse, which was charged with gun- and drug-related crimes both in Jamaica and in the United States (Gunst 1995, 42–43), and he and Haggart, like other dons, were reportedly involved in illicit activities. However, they were and are regarded by some as role models, with responsibility for giving financial aid to the less fortunate in the area or community they had de facto control over. Memorial dances are also held for dancehall celebrities such as Gerald "Bogle" Levy of the Black Roses Crew, who died in 2005. The Wacky Birthday Celebration for Gerald "Bogle" Levy, A Back to School Treat, took place at the Rebel T headquarters on Dumbarton Avenue on August 18, 2006, with major sound systems such as Stone Love and Rebel T providing music.

(3) Anniversary dances may celebrate a variety of significant dates. These include, for example, the founding of sound systems. Thus, the Jack Ruby sound system celebrated its twenty-eighth anniversary in 1987; Rebel T marked its ninth anniversary on August 20, 2004, and its twelfth anniversary on August 3, 2007; and the Fire Links sound system, which initiated the Hot Mondays event in 2003, celebrates its anniversary consistently, although not always on the same date, since one of its anniversary dances was at the New Little Copa Club on October 19, 2002, but another was on December 25, 2005, at the Market Place. Stone Love held special dance events to mark its twenty-first anniversary in 1993; its thirtieth, at the Market Place, on December 14, 2002; its thirty-first, again at the Market Place, on December 13, 2003; its thirty-fourth, at Mas Camp, on December 9, 2006; and its thirty-fifth, at Mas Camp again, on December 15, 2007. In each case there were Stone Love anniversary events during the first three weekends of December in addition to the main anniversary dance. The main dance included an early "juggling" session in which each of the sound systems and guest selectors present played in order of seniority or popularity, before musical selections by the star selectors signalled the move to a higher level of expertise and engagement, with the host sometimes

accommodating performance tributes from amateur and professional DJs at certain periods.

The anniversaries of dance events are also celebrated. For example, the first anniversary of Hot Mondays was the theme at Market Place on October 20, 2003, and Passa Passa marked its own first anniversary at 47 Spanish Town Road on February 25, 2004. Both Hot Mondays and Passa Passa have held similar anniversary dances every year since.

Anniversary dances can also celebrate the existence of a venue, such as the New Little Copa Club (May 25, 2002) or Asylum (ninth Anniversary Party, November 18, 2006, at Mas Camp); a newspaper, such as *X-News* (August 8, 2003); or tenure in a political office, as on March 10, 2002, when the Labour Party politician Edward Seaga, a former Prime Minister who was then Leader of the Opposition, celebrated forty years as Member of Parliament for the constituency of West Kingston with a dance at Tivoli Gardens, at which sound systems Swatch, Katarock and Stone Love delivered a musical feast.

(4) Girls' dances combine celebrations of fashion, dance moves and attitude in events totally dedicated to the women of dancehall. With names such as XXX Girls (August 14, 1994) Roll Out 2002 (July 21, 2002, bylined as "the girls' roll call") or Hot Girls Fiesta (August 2, 2003), they range from the relatively conservative to the X-rated. For example, Hot Sex, held at Charlton Plaza on October 27, 2006, was advertised with a picture of a naked woman holding her crotch and featured "dutty wine" dance contests modelled on the popular dance move of that name (discussed further in Chapter 5).

Among the many girls' dances that centre on the crowning of dancehall queens or sound system queens, one of the largest is the Red Label Wine International Dancehall Queen Contest. Although this event is always staged in Montego Bay, which is 84 miles away from Kingston and in the opposite (northwestern) corner of the island, more than 70 percent of the contestants at the sixth annual contest, on August 10, 2002, identified themselves as representing Kingston or the neighbouring parish of St Catherine, parts of which are included in the Kingston Metropolitan Area (KMA). People also travel from Kingston to attend the event. The show was initiated because of the popularity of the dancehall queen Carlene during the early dancehall high point between 1989 and 2004.

(5) Celebrations of gangs or crews form another important part of the calendar. The annual Original Spanglers Dance, celebrating the Spangler's posse, is an annual event, held, for example, at Rainbow Lawn on April 27, 2002 and April 26, 2003. This event is always a crowd-puller for those seeking to show their allegiance to the posse or their shared affiliation with the PNP, from DJs booked to perform or just

passing through, to regular patrons and large numbers of vendors. Such an event, unlike a street dance, attracts a cover charge, and its proceeds may be used for charity or to pay the DJs who are hired to perform.

(6) Stage shows and festivals, varying in size, duration and appeal, require more capital investment than any other dance events, but also offer greater potential profits. The largest among them are the annual festivals that have put dancehall on the performance map for members of the international community, including the now defunct Reggae Sunsplash, the Reggae Sumfest in Montego Bay, and Sting, which has been staged at the Jamworld entertainment complex on the outskirts of the KMA every Boxing Day (December 26) since 1984. In 2003 Sumfest attracted more than 25,000 people to its dancehall night and in 2007 more than 30,000 attended. Other festivals, such as Sashi, held on James Bond Beach for three days in 2002, have proved to be ephemeral.

One-off stage shows, such as Hot Shots, held at the Constant Spring Golf Club on December 21, 2002, and featuring Shaggy, Sean Paul, Damian Marley and Bounti Killa, among others, tend to attract cover charges that equate to the fee for one night at Sumfest. They generally have to attract a wide cross-section of Kingston's population in order to be commercially successful. DJs have their own brand of stage shows, including East Fest, promoted by Morgan's Heritage, Tony Rebel's Rebel Salute and Capleton's St Mary Mi Come From.

(7) Sound clashes have been popular since the inception of dancehall. Beginning with Sir Coxsone's Downbeat and Tom Wong's The Great Sebastian, sound systems have clashed several times, desperately vying for the position of top sound. This trend continued and intensified in the early 1990s. Sound systems travelled from Japan and Germany for clashes in Jamaica, and vice versa. Events with names such as Metro Media Versus Bodyguard or African Star Versus Crystal Disco became common. "Specials," DJ recordings honouring sound systems, were used as sonic weapons to ensure positive crowd response with dancehall's signature salutatory mechanisms, including salutes with guns, cigarette lighters or cellphones.

Clashing between sound systems has also entailed violence, which has plagued the dancehall tradition since its inception, but particularly during the first high point, between 1989 and 1994, when gun play, gun salutes and gang warfare peaked. Sound clashes coincided with matie wars, political and gang warfare, and DJ wars, and inspired violence among supporters. Certain tunes induced the blazing of guns and others brought on fights. Many events ended in violence or police raids. Winston "Wee Pow" Powell, the owner of Stone Love has recalled (2002) that in the early 1990s a sound clash between Stone Love and the rival Kilamanjaro sound system was widely anticipated. They met about five times, but each clash ended prematurely with no clear winner. Clashes were expensive, since the sound systems had to be in top shape, and "specials" had to be recorded and marketed. Ultimately sound clashes led to broken spirits, both for the patrons and for the sound system operators.

During the period 1995 to 2005 clashes declined in importance and became rare in Jamica. Perhaps this is because they produced more losses than gains locally, however they continue on the international scene, in Japan and Germany in particular. Recent sound system clashes have thus included Who Rule the Holy Mountain—War, It's War, War Tonight, involving the German sound system Sentinel, at Cactus Lawn in Middleton (rural St Andrew) on September 20, 2003; and World Clash, involving selectors from systems such as Mighty Crown (from Japan) and Bass Odyssey, as well as the veteran clash selector Rodigon, in Montego Bay on April 9, 2007. DJ wars, also called clashes, have remained a staple of the stage show scene. At the Sting festival in 2003, for example, the veteran DJ and clash master Ninja Man engaged with the emerging DJ Vybz Kartel in a war of words that ended in a fist fight. Clashes have ensued between DJs such as Bounti Killa and Beenie Man, Vybz Kartel and Mavado, and in the 1980s between Ninja Man and Shabba Ranks as the most noteworthy examples following on the trend set in the 1960s by Prince Buster and Derrick Morgan.

(8) Oldies dance events, also known as vintage dances, are different in approach, patronage, speed, appeal and popularity. They have held an increasingly strong position on the dancehall calendar because of their appeal to a distinct group that is expanding over time, as well as to persons from younger generations who do not appreciate typical contemporary dances.

Oldies dances are epitomized by community events such as the annual Rae Town street dance in East Kingston, but there are also commercial stage shows that celebrate oldies music, such as Heineken Star Time, Stars 'R' Us, and Good Times. Smaller events include Sunday Classics at the New Little Copa Club, Party Party at 18 Patrick Drive every March and Olanzo Hawk's Birthday Bash, held on September 5, 2003. Sound systems classified as "soul sounds," such as Soul Shack, Purple Love, the Mid Wheel Disco or Merritone, are the sonic specialists at these events, where the emphasis is on playing musical selections from genres such as R&B, soul, disco and reggae.

Kenneth "Bop" Campbell, who plays regularly on the Mid Wheel Disco, has said (2003) that the oldies event is about bringing back the love, the memory of how to love and respect, the family spirit/stability, and relationships among people of all ages. He attributes the lack of respect for life in Jamaica to the lack of love, and explains that at vintage dances people hug as they dance, a phenomenon which needs to return to dancehall.

(9) Link-up dance events are organized around the need for various constituencies or groups to link up or get together at a more organized and sophisticated level than the usual weekly, seasonal or round-robin events in the community. Constituencies may be as small as a taxi collective—as at the Taxi Link-up on Sarah Street in Central Kingston that I attended in 1999—or as large as a nation or a diaspora, with such events as the Miami Link-up at Arizon Inn, Port Henderson, on January 4, 2002; the New York/Jamaica/England Link-up at La Roose on April 6, 2002; the link-up for Jamaicans from Washington DC, Philadelphia, New Jersey, Canada and Britain at La Roose on May 11, 2003; the Baltimore link-up at Mas Camp on May 23, 2003; or the California link-up at Rainbow Lawn on August 9, 2003. The British Link-up is by far the most popular and takes the form of a season of events.

One of the most interesting variations of the link-up is the All-Deportee Friends and Family Link-Up, first held in 2008 and then at the Club View Roof on April 9, 2009, because of the way it celebrates persons who have been forcibly returned to Jamaica, mostly from the United States, after being convicted of charges ranging from murder to breaches of immigration law. Deportees have been revered as much as they have been disrespected, and the staging of dances to honour them is one part of the celebration of community and all its elements in the context of dance.

PASSA PASSA

It was Wednesday night and time to attend Passa Passa, the dance event on Spanish Town Road in Tivoli Gardens, initiated by Mile's Enterprise with the aim of celebrating community. The way in which this is manifested is the real miracle of Jamaica's dancehall, taking in clouds of smoke, cigarette lighter salutes, market trucks passing, the bright light of the Moon, the dancer Labba Labba, music pumping, children playing, male youth showing off their motorcycling skills, drinks galore, sugarcane and jerk chicken on sale, elders "dropping legs," Japanese tourists, the Guns and Roses Girls from Montego Bay, school uniforms, "batty riders," video cameras, Rastafari brethren, and gangsters.

I arrived at 12:40 a.m., got a drink from a barmaid modelling a glittering outfit, and at around 1:00 a.m. I settled on a bench beside the selector's table. There were a few cars on the road, an outside bar, chicken and soup vendors, young men and women almost invisible to the naked eye lining the wall at the edge of the sidewalk, and patrons ensconced in Mile's Bar. During this "early out" period (see Chapter 3) the selector was playing a heavy selection of dancehall music from the late 1980s, two boys aged about twelve and thirteen were running around, another two, and a little older, were riding motorcycles up and down the virtually empty street. Women and men were slowly arriving for the night's event, and one car after another lined the sidewalk across from the selector's table.

The cane vendor, a man in his late sixties, was dancing vigorously to the rhythm, which was infectious. Simultaneously, as if to signal the impending move from the pre-dance to the dance period, a woman about forty-five years old, wearing a dark T-shirt and skirt, and dancing intermittently to her favourite tunes, did something that at first was unfathomable. It seemed that she was attempting to put a large silver hoop into her eyebrow. This failing, she proceeded to remove her T-shirt, which she then wrapped around her head. With her brassiere now revealed, she untied the front of what I had thought was a skirt to reveal a black formal dress with puff sleeves. As she stood up, pulled the dress to its full height and placed the puff sleeves on her shoulders, she signalled that her dancehall outfit was not the mere T-shirt and skirt she had previously been wearing. She then turned the dress back to front and, leaving the top unzipped, revealed a pair of shorts, which were vital to the sartorial ensemble. This done, and with the music now moving to the tempo of the mid-1990s, she crossed the street and began to show her moves. Athletically, stylishly and with appropriate timing, she danced as she did her ritual crossing of the street, which was still virtually empty.

By 1:40 a.m. the video cameras had arrived. A Japanese crew and the area leader, whom one of the selectors that night called "the President [who] rules the residents," arrived in his 2002 Jaguar by 2:00 a.m. All had their drinks (libation) or the "holy herb" (fire) to help loosen their legs, hearts and minds. Buying out the bar is, of course, a sign of one's financial means, and the crates at some patrons' feet were evidence of this.

I moved to the sidewalk across the street to get a good view of what was becoming a swinging Passa Passa. The selectors called on their audience to participate in the usual declarations of moral codes, especially against abortion and against homosexuality, and led the feverish dance pitch that everyone had come to witness, but it was only the dancers who could manifest this pitch. The music played and they responded, and the video cameras followed them wherever they went.

This is the purpose of the Passa Passa event: a celebration of community, enjoyment and "bigging up" the self, with a central component being the video camera. As they danced, patrons sent greetings to their partners and friends, and hailed crews. Some poured out their heart's emotions and others just danced to express their moods.

The tempo of the dance is of central importance to the way in which the event proceeds. The art of "juggling," pioneered by older sound systems such as Stone Love, ushered oldies through to more contemporary selections as a warm-up mechanism for the dancing body and the senses. The rhythm-centred nature of the event is distinguished by the nexus between the music and the dancing bodies, including, in some instances, the selectors' and cameramen's bodies. Modes of musical selecting, such as dramatically playing small segments of a song in a repetitious sequence known as "hawl and pull up," serve to intensify the effect of the selection, which eventually moves the dance to trance proportions by using a sort of teasing mechanism. In other words, the dancing bodies move through varying states of arousal with each song played, starting with low, then increasing to high, while observing rests.

The street appropriated for the night's event was officially transformed from the "ghost town" that is typical for the early hours of the morning into a performance space lined by patrons. The street remained permeable, inviting and hospitable to uptown, downtown, around-town and "outernational" (Jamaicanism for "international") crews from, for example, the United States and Japan. In the front region of the venue was the selector's table directly outside the bar of Mile's Enterprise, as well as the sidewalk to the right and left of the selector's table, lined by patrons on both sides. Dancing took place on the sidewalk and the cameramen could be seen moving through the crowd on the sidewalk as well as the street. Immediately in front of Mile's bar was the hot spot where the Guns and Roses Girls took their positions. At the end of the sidewalk on either side could be found a speaker tower. The third speaker tower completing the sound triangle was located directly across the road facing the selector's table. These speakers formed the main boundaries within which dancing took place.

For approximately 100 feet the street was lined by cars parked at the edge of the sidewalk. Immediately in front of the cars a corridor about twelve feet wide filled up when the high point of the dancing was reached. At other moments, when the pace slowed, the dance area became empty. This ebb and flow went on throughout the event, depending on the tempo of the music. There were moments when the dance area separated into two or three main areas because of the video cameras present. Each of the two cameras filmed two separate sites within the dance area and this propelled the dancing to further heights.

To the south of the main corridor or dance area was the second largest expanse of space, demarcating the back region where most of the spectators were located. Vendors and patrons could be seen moving forward to the main dance area, or back to the sidewalk for a rest when the musical pace slowed. The main dance area stayed open to those who were not celebrity dancers, but were moved occasionally to participate in the heightened dance fever. The sidewalk immediately behind the cars to the South, which was filled with patrons and vendors, was bounded by a wall behind which other patrons stood. They could hardly be seen, except for the flicker in their eyes depending on the location of the video camera's light, but they were very much part of the proceedings. The event lasted until dawn and all were satisfied after engineering freedom to celebrate community in the streets.

At the playing of the appropriate tune the dancing crews or societies rolled out, taking centre stage in the street, which by this point was occupied for a distance of at least 100 feet. (For me they were reminiscent of the "mulatto does" of late-18th-century Suriname, where the small numbers of free Blacks and Coloureds developed dance groups or societies known as "does," including "gold doe," "silver doe," "amber doe," "fashion doe" and "love doe," as observed by Stedman 1992, 332.) They were dancing to Elephant Man's tracks "Blasé" and "Pon di River, Pon di Bank," running up and "down the flank" in accordance with his commands in the latter song. In perfect unison with each other and the environment, they performed the generic bubble or "wining" (hip-rotating) dance, with variations such as the "tick tock wine," characterized by start–stop movements. Further embodied interpretations of song lyrics, demanded by the rhythm or the music selector, appeared in such dances as the pop di collar, the screetchie, the zip it up, the wave, the internet, the zagga zow, the give them a run, the propeller, the chaplin, the fan dem off, the hand cart, the wine pon it, the sidung pon it, the float and the back stroke. In some respects the role of the selector as clash artist (see above) has been superseded by his role as dance maestro, as he guides his audience through the various moves. With so many different moves available, the selector in command of his selections serves as a memory bank.

It was not unusual for the selector to play latin, hip hop, disco or rock and roll, among other musics, including songs such as Madonna's "Like a Virgin" (1984) and Gwen Guthrie's "Ain't Nothin' Goin' On But the Rent" (1986). Of course, these constituted hit songs in their respective genres (pop and R&B), and their popularity catapulted them into the Jamaican dance scene, where they were absorbed into the dancehall aesthetic and practice, or "dancehallified," especially through dance styles such as the bubble. The directions from the selector continued in the typical dancehall style until dawn, when the event ended.

In spite of all the dancing, space was made throughout the event for passing cars and for trucks coming in from rural Jamaica with provisions for the start of the market weekend early on the Thursday morning. As if all elements of the city's life were integral components of the event, united in choreography, vibration and execution, no one was bothered. At least one car was inducted into formal Passa Passa membership by a dancer who decided to "wine" down on its hood, as if it had trespassed on consecrated ground.

Events such as Passa Passa have created new entry strategies for communities that have been seen, accurately or not, as volatile—especially those, like Tivoli Gardens, with a history of affiliation to one or other political party—and written off by many who occupy Kingston's nightscape. Such events have maintained their appeal precisely because of the often self-imposed taboos that prevent ordinary persons from entering such "garrison" communities. It is the order precariously maintained by area leaders that explains the open invitation to locals and international guests to attend Passa Passa, and the sustainability of peace, if only temporarily, for the weekly event. Today Passa Passa receives corporate endorsements, in addition to being used as a springboard for launching various corporate and other products and events.

BEMBE THURSDAY

The dancehall calendar has changed and so have the days of the week. According to those responsible for the change, the days are now Monday, Tuesday, Wednesday, Bembe.

Richie "Feelings" Bailey and the Bembe Squad initiated Bembe Thursdays on October 12, 2006, with the aim of bringing back the spirit of early dancehall events (see Bailey 2007 and Taylor 2007). The Squad includes Raz and Biggy, a selector duo; Rolex and Jigsy (a.k.a. Angry Bembe) from the Danga Zone sound system; and Tony Matterhorn. Because of the formation of this selector alliance, Bembe also makes use of other known selectors, such as from Swatch International of Passa Passa fame, Ricky Trooper and Z. J. Liquid. Selectors are a key part of the event. Indicating his deep understanding of the role of the selector, Tony Matterhorn (2007) likens it to that of a therapist (see also Hohn 2007):

A selector is like a psychologist. Most selectors don't know because them just see music and play.... We tell people about their problems temporarily so they have to come back the next night, or they can go to one dance and don't need to come back any more. It's like you're going to therapy, because we talk about so many topics and issues that even the radio would never talk about.

There are other examples of "early events," such as Early Mondays and Early Tuesdays, designed to bring patrons out long before the very fashionable starting time of 4:00 a.m., when celebrity dancing crews, DJs and selectors arrive for what can accurately be dubbed "dawn events." The reason for this late starting time is unclear, while the early start of an event such as Bembe Thursday is undoubtedly influenced by the Noise Abatement Act, which stipulates that events end at 2:00 a.m., and the likelihood that residents will report excessive noise produced by the event. Various acts of infringement have been met with sanctions. Vendors of illegal substances such as marijuana have either been arrested or had their products seized, and on March 29, 2007, for example, in an operation involving the Kingston & St Andrew Corporation and the Jamaica Constabulary Force, vehicles that were parked illegally on the street were confiscated. A significant point is that such operations do not occur at Passa Passa.

Bembe Thursday was given its name by Richie Feelings, who considers himself to be a large man, resembling the "bembe," the name of largest marble in the packs sold to children. "Bembe," then, simultaneously represents that which is large and stands out, and that which can roll over everyone, though not in the sense of competing with other events. The word resonates with cognate terms elsewhere in the African Diaspora, including the bemba or bembe drum of Trinidad & Tobago, and the *bembé* in Cuba, a semi-private event involving ritual drumming, singing, dancing and feasting, a party for the deities associated with the Santería religion derived from the traditions of the Yoruba people of Nigeria, Benin and Ghana. This resonance gives some insight into the ritual significance of dancehall. In many ways dancehall activity has served many of its adherents in the same way as such sacred activities as attending church, or taking part in Kumina Duties or Revival Tables. It constitutes a New World ritual for many.

Bembe Thursday takes place at Weekenz, a venue in the Halfway Tree area above the geographical class divide. Weekenz is a rented venue with infrastructure such as a stage, a parking lot, bars, sanitary conveniences, and electricity supply, amenities deemed necessary for the middle- and upper-class citizenry, who are well represented. In contrast to the downtown Passa Passa event, the numbers of selectors with uptown roots and of patrons arriving in cars solidifies Bembe Thursday as an uptown event. Many patrons of Passa Passa come on foot from communities neighbouring Tivoli Gardens, but many patrons travel from across the KMA to attend Bembe Thursday. Passa Passa is a community event, but Bembe Thursday is not. Where Bembe Thursday benefited from immediate corporate sponsorship or endorsement from Magnum Tonic Wine, Passa Passa gained such recognition only later in its existence, from companies such as Digicel. The Bembe event and its DJ squad have become brand names in dancehall, and are active beyond Bembe Thursday itself, playing in such shows as Orientation: The Ultimate School Uniform Party on June 22, 2007, also at the Weekenz venue.

On March 29, 2007, Raz and Biggy were the celebrity selectors, replacing the early "juggler" who was in command of the turntable when I arrived. As the event warmed up, around midnight, dancehall notables such as the dancers Medusa, John Hype and Dance Expressionz, a group comprising formally trained dancers such as the dance educator and performer Orville Hall, could be seen arriving for a night of dancehall "niceness." Characteristically, the event ended at around 2:00 a.m. after receiving its share of police presence and patrols into the venue, while patrons engineered their intended escape into a performance world filled with dance and song, in a way reminiscent of what Tarrus Riley and his father Jimmy Riley document in the single "Pull Up Selector" (2007):

> Music is all we got, now we must defend it
> Dancehall don't need no war
> Man and a woman a par
> Everyone is a star, King Alpha and Mama Omega
> Dancehall the people's church, yes, it's where
> Where everyone is gathering, need no bothering,
> A just love.
> Everyone, everyone, must come together
> Everyone, everyone, join in the pleasure
> Everyone, everyone, music forever
> The sweetest relief, dancehall sweet, dancehall sweet ...
> Everyone come to express themselves,
> They dress to impress,
> One black love and one African-ness

BRITISH LINK-UP EVENTS

The British link-up events (already mentioned above) illustrate the continuing tangibility of the Jamaican diaspora based on perform-ance practice. The British dance, featuring the "nicest" girls, the best dancers, the most prominent dancehall stars, and the most expensive clothes, automobiles and beverages, has come to epitomize the no-tions of "bashment," "bling bling" and "ghetto fabulous," interrelat-ed terms referring, respectively, to excitement, hyped possessions and the manifestation of lower-class prosperity.

The British link-up events, which began in 1990, are highly antici-pated and well known for spectacle and pageantry. Every year Jamai-cans residing in Britain and their descendants come to the island, sometimes on chartered flights, for a "British" welcome in dancehall style. These events are commonly designated as "big dance," having a character and appeal rivalling stage shows. The dancehall commun-ity looks forward to the British events in Jamaica, around Easter and Christmas, and in London, around Jamaica's Independence Day on August 6, as well as in Canada and the United States. The Easter events constitute a season that includes a bus ride, a pool party, a beach bash, a school uniform party and a final British link-up dance, though there have been additional events such as the British Fashion Party held at the Villa Ronai in Stony Hill on April 24, 2003, and the British Sport Swimwear Affair on the Urban Development Corporation's beach in Montego Bay on April 26, 2003. Here I highlight the British Pool Party and the closing British Dance held in 2002, and then the British School Uniform Party held in 2003.

At the British Pool Party in 2002 female patrons wore the latest ath-letic or full-cut bikinis, covered with pieces of silk and mesh, while male patrons opted for jeans, T-shirts and caps, leaving the females to display skin in the customary dancehall way. One informant reported that she was disappointed by the scene, because police officers were manning the gate as well as collecting tickets, and the music was at a low volume on police orders. There was just one intense moment when the music became loud again and the police came to assert their inten-tion to turn off the sound if there was no compliance with the regula-tions. This significantly interfered with the vibe of the link-up event, which epitomizes the most hype. Police's presence was a result of the venue being in a residential neighbourhood from which complaints had allegedly come. The imposition of state control on this and other events reduces breaches of the Noise Abatement Act, and may deter or prevent criminal and other unwanted acts, but it simultaneously affects the mood of the event.

The British Dance held at La Roose on March 27, 2002, ended pre-maturely. After the sound system had completed its early selections an armed detachment of police ordered them to stop playing under the provisions of the Noise Abatement Act, even though La Roose is located beyond the immediate proximity of the residential areas in Port Henderson. Millions spent in preparation for the event were lost; vendors, as well as car dealerships and rental agencies, lost revenue too; and thousands of patrons taking trips built around the British link-up dance calendar were disappointed. To compensate for the disappointment the organizers staged a "continuation dance" at the New Little Copa Club. An awards ceremony for dancehall promoters, selectors and DJs, among others, was incorporated into the proceedings. The former heavyweight boxing champion Lennox Lewis was present at this event (and has been sighted at others, such as the International Dancehall Queen Competition that year). The continuation dance progressed until dawn and a successful extension was mounted at Club EQ in London later that year.

The genesis of the "uniform party" is sketchy, but the British School Uniform Party, held in 2002 and 2003, was preceded by the Mavia School Party in Stony Hill in 2000 and followed by the Workforce Uniform Party at Market Place on August 5, 2003. This type of event, a masquerade that parodies, as it temporarily overturns, the order within educational and other state apparatuses, features various uniforms such as those for high school students or nurses, or professorial gowns, as worn by Beenie Man, a.k.a. The Doctor. In 2003 the British School Uniform Party featured uniforms modified to suit the dancehall aesthetic and to facilitate ease of movement. Females' skirts and shorts were revealing, and included "batty rider" or buttock-hugging shorts. Tiny knapsacks or "matie bags" replaced regular knapsacks. Female blouses stopped at the diaphragm and shirt-tails were tied across the midriff. Males wore khaki pants and white shirts with loosened ties. Other school signifiers employed include the "Stop! Children Crossing" sign carried by school traffic wardens. The event was patronized by members of the British Crew, celebrities such as the selector Sky Juice from the sound system Metro Media, dancers Keiva and John Hype, the DJ Beenie Man, and Pinkie, one of the dancing icons of the first wave in dancehall and the star of the British television documentary *Dancehall Queens* (see Beckwith 2000), who was wearing her pink school uniform. Pinkie, who now lives in the United Kingdom, travels to Jamaica at least once each year for the British link-up events.

Selectors from Stone Love and Stereo Passion took turns playing the latest tunes to entice the patrons. The selector from Stereo Passion announced, "Bare movie star t'ing straight back till morning," as he saluted the British Crew, who received regular "big ups," as did the other dancehall celebrities present. The salutes, concretizing the moral ethos of dancehall culture were most apparent in such participatory calls as "All batty man [homosexuals] put your hand in your pockets," offering an opportunity for all the "girl's man" (heterosexuals) to put their hands in the air.

The ceremony began at around 4:00 a.m., when the number of patrons peaked with the introduction of each member of the British Crew standing in the dancing circle. Spirits of choice were sipped by each crew member as well as by many patrons, sometimes in salute. The event emphasized new dance movements as the quintessential expression of sound and body magic. The selector's call initiated demonstrations of the latest moves as a sign of the participatory nature of the event. It was Stacey who stole the show, however, with her signature climb onto the top of the speaker tower, where she displayed moves such as the head top (winding the waist while positioned vertically on the head). Then she sought to attach herself to the nearby roof as a spider is attached to its web. Hanging from the roof by both hands and both feet, she proceeded to show the crowd the "body basics of dancehall," confirming her position as a popular dancehall queen.

Such school uniform parties reveal interesting psychological dimensions, and should be distinguished from uniform parties featuring a variety of costumes. Even though the effect of the school uniform party is superficially benign, there are other readings that need to be taken into account. Arguably, this event enacts a sort of subversion of school rules, since in Jamaica uniformed students are not supposed to be seen on the streets after dusk. Yet it also takes us into the area of school students' fantasies about playing grown-up games, either at school or after school, or even the possibility of perversions related to dating schoolgirls, as pristine representations of womanhood, even if only subconsciously. This association cannot be overlooked in light of the disciplinary measures, and the corresponding failures, of many schools seeking to prevent students from roaming the streets after dark and becoming susceptible to inappropriate relationships. The increasing associations between child molestation and operators of public passenger vehicles, licensed or unlicensed, cannot be ignored. This is an area for further research, given increasing concern about the effect of dancehall culture on adolescents in particular.

In 2004, following the imprisonment of Owen "Roy Fowl" Clarke after a trial in England, the annual British dance events fell dormant. They returned, however, on April 7, 2007, with the staging of British Link-Up: The Rebirth, marked by the revival of lavish displays of the best in fashion, automobiles, alcoholic beverages, sound systems, DJs and selectors. I arrived at La Roose at about 2:20 a.m., bought my ticket and walked a torch-lit red carpet, under a canopy of red, white and blue balloons, before reaching the main venue. Red, white and blue, the colours of the British Union Jack flag, were the theme colours for the event. The two-tiered site had multiple sections and significant permanent infrastructure, with sanitary conveniences, a covered stage with the DJ's sound station, and balconies and bars where the dancehall celebrities assumed their positions. The celebrities present included Winston Powell, Bounti Killa, Lexus, members of the British Crew, Dancehall Queen Stacey, dancing crews, media personalities, videographers and selectors. Sponsorship for the event, an arrangement that is now normal rather than non-existent as in past years, was received from the popular hip-hop drink Pimpjuice.

By 3:30 a.m. three video cameras had started to capture images of the red-carpet rebirth of British link-ups. Patrons from Canada, Jamaica, Britain and the United States were attired in dancehall regalia of a semi-formal or formal nature, including gowns and suits, often adorned with glitter and expensive jewellery. As the event heightened in intensity, around 4:30 a.m., video cameras could be seen tracking the dancers, who were performing popular moves such as the tek weh yu self. By the time Stacey and male dancers such as Sadiki arrived, at around 5:00 a.m., the musical tempo had changed to more hard-core dancehall hits from Mavado, Bounti Killa, Mr. Vegas, Beenie Man and Buju Banton, among others. The male dancing crews included "Kaution Roll Out" from Seaview Gardens area in the Western KMA, in which the average age is thirteen, all wearing shirts with the words "Kaution Roll Out" on them. Located at the centre of the action within the main venue, they captured a fair amount of attention from the video cameras as they performed.

Donna Hope (2004) has argued that the activities of the British Link-up Crew go beyond sartorial and material exhibition to constitute the articulation and creation of transgressive selfhood in the competitive Jamaican terrain. Each event, she suggests, represents a multilayered politics of consumption and trans-identity on a "capitalist stage," punctuated in no small way by the ritual(ized) implications of the events being staged at significant intersections of the Christian and national calendar, since Easter, Christmas and Jamaica's Independence are imbued with ritual celebrations around fasting and feasting. While this analysis is consistent with my argument about the ritual significance of dancehall, because of the celebratory ethos, Hope does not situate the Crew historically and therefore leaves important cultural antecedents to be explored.

The ritual celebration of self-presentation and financial independence, associated with unique appearance and the consumption of brand-name products, has existed since the 1960s, if not earlier, and thus long before the current emphasis on Versace, Armani, Dolce & Gabbana, Moschina, Gucci, Tommy Hilfiger, DKNY or the like. Early dancehall patrons, DJs and musicians created—to take only the most notable example—the "rudie" aesthetic of dark hazard glasses, Clarks shoes from England or big-heeled suede boots, "bell foot" (bellbottomed) pants, calico shirts and CB-200 motorcycles as the transport of choice in the 1970s. In 1986 Super Cat's song "Trash an' Ready," a classic salute to dancehall's celebration of the outward signs of financial liquidity, namechecked the Arcade, Firehouse, Webster, Brooklyn and Brixton Posses, and celebrated the ability of DJs and the masses, local and global, to be "trash" (dapper), that is, to wear the best clothes, such as Clarks shoes, Kangol hats and diamond-pattern socks. Super Cat also admonished girls fighting for "old bruk" (old clothes) or wearing their friends' clothes, calling them "mascot" or "old bruk clean up." Closely paralleling the discourse of being "trash an' ready," there has also long been an emphasis on remaining "fresh," by bathing regularly, smelling, looking and feeling fresh, and eating fresh food. The belief that "woman nuh want nuh man if him 'fraid a water" (women don't want men who are afraid of water) helps to explain such emphases. There are also variants such as "Nuh frowsy arm" (no foul smelling armpits). In some ways the discourse of the body is an overarching theme, as the healthy, "fabulous," "blinging" body is promoted over and above the anorexic or otherwise undesirable body. It is important to acknowledge these antecedents in order to place activities viewed during dancehall high points as having continuities with, even if they may be exaggerations of, activities already in existence, rather than being new manifestations. Even more critical is the fact that scholarly attention to dancehall should not be limited to an understanding only of its high points.

CONCLUSIONS

In this chapter I have expanded the definition and historicization of dancehall as a whole culture through greater exposition of its institutional frameworks, systems, codes and ethics, most importantly its reclamation and reinterpretation of ritual, and its manifestation of New World rituals. This approach enlarges the scope of dancehall beyond being just one more example of a carnivalesque space of seasonal, fleshly and "escapist" liberatory potential, and grants its citizenry a fuller and richer status than that of playing the allotted role of a worthless, unsophisticated, passive underclass.

Dancehall events expose a performance geography imbued with ritual acts across the dancehall populace at home and abroad. By viewing rituals performed through the spectrum of events celebrating death, birth, life, anniversary, victory and memory, I hope to contribute to new ways of understanding both dance and community. Deeply marked by Eurocentric interpretations within both dance research and sociology, "dance" and "community" can be deceptive conceptual categories, to the extent that they mask a complex performative system, on the one hand, and the sociocultural system on the other. Through dance, performers define, project and re-engineer their identities, contesting prescribed categories, and delegitimating, expanding, reinventing or absorbing them as desired. There are firmly held systems of maintenance and renewal in the social imprint of morality, the codified norms and values that are manifested in rituals. The consumption of lyrics in dancehall through bodily movement and around specific themes reveals potent modes of community throughout history, signalling developed forms of commentary, problem-solving and memorializing.

Dancehall provides another space, process and means of connecting to a higher self, that which is elevated beyond the drudgery of survival. It also provides a means through which patrons, especially marginalized youth within the Jamaican lower class, can connect with their communities. Dancehall represents an open-ended enactment of self and community or area. It is about the stylization of everyday life, a performance through the actions of the body. I rearticulate here that the dancehall citizenry and their practice straddle the Old World and the New World, as they exist at the edge of society yet continue to make space and imprint themselves on the national identity. This is elaborated more fully through the concept of limbo and, by extension, liminality. I propose that liminality is expressed as context (space, place, location), as consciousness, history, method and identity between here and there, East and West, centre and margin. In this liminal space dancehall has been criticized and predictions of its demise have increasingly been publicized. Yet it is the liminal that occasions its possibilities of articulation and rearticulation through ritual celebrations.

GEOGRAPHIES OF EMBODIMENT—DANCE, STATUS, STYLE

KID HAROLD, Baskin, Pam Pam, Persian the Cat, Labba Labba, Bogle, Carlene, Stacey, Keiva, Craigy Dread, Mad Michelle, Sample Six, Ravers Clavers, Ice, Colo Colo, Shelly Belly and Black Blingers have all made indelible marks on the repertoire and performance style of popular dance in Jamaica, from the dance events at Marcus Garvey's Edelweiss Park in the 1930s to the contemporary dancehall events such as Passa Passa in West Kingston. Creators of dance moves such as the gully creepa (David "Ice" Smith), the no linga (Marlon "Overmars" Hardy the Above a Dem Crew and formerly of Ravers Clavers) and the dutty wine (Attitude Girls), these individuals continue the task of dancing their way into local, regional and global performance histories.

The dance is a distinguishing feature of the dancehall space. In dancehall dancers and other patrons take on the toil of ridding their mind of daily troubles, becoming enslaved devotees, not (solely) in a capitalist (post)modernity that disenfranchises, but in a somatic and kinaesthetic sense. As if each was a "slave to the rhythm" that beats around them and inside them amid the social ills of everyday Jamaica, in the way Grace Jones (1985) suggested in her song of that title, the exerting body on the contemporary dance floors of Jamaica literally and symbolically replaces those on the plantations that preceded them. This reading is sharpened when one considers Saidiya V. Hartman's analysis of dance throughout slavery and on the popular stage, which acknowledges that terror and violence were "perpetrated under the rubric of pleasure" (Hartman 1997, 4), and that slavery and freedom are inextricably linked in mechanisms of law, identity and liberties. Here is the body that, through contestation, exploitation, discrimination and oppression, has preserved itself in performance to tell the tales of history, while dance venues become delocalized for just a moment when they transcend time and produce the inevitable "congregational kinesis" (Brathwaite 1995, p. 46). The dance space is therefore linked to old and new ways of toiling for freedom, creating space through rhythm.

A terrain of boundaries, dance reveals boundedness and unboundedness in the gender, temporal, and local and global nuances present in the ways in which people make and link spaces through their creations. It is notable that dance styles have been patterned from R&B moves of the 1950s, jazz, Afro-Cuban and Afro-Brazilian styles, as well as from traditional Jamaican forms such as mento or gereh and the dances of folk religions such as Kumina. Such movement patterns propelled the creation of indigenous moves that coexist with popular moves brought from the United States. The modelling of dances from feature films, performed by the likes of Kid Harold (c. 1911–1985) (White 1984, 72), has existed alongside purely "blues moves" such as "legs."

5.1 Colo Colo and the crew displaying their moves
Source: Roy Sweetland

(It is worth mentioning that Kid Harold was a dancer and much more (see Hamilton 1988, 87–111). He was part of one of Jamaica's top show groups, the comedy team Harold and Trim, and also led the Butterfly Troupe of dancers. Known for his tap dancing, he was personally recruited by Marcus Garvey to perform at Edelweiss Park and to assist Gerardo Leon, the dance trainer/coordinator on its staff. Kid Harold also appeared in plays at Edelweiss Park written and produced by Ranny Williams. Other local moves include the shake-a-leg, going to town and, later, rocksteady and reggae (White 1984, 74). Famous dancers from the ghetto have included Needle, Clifford Strokes, Persian the Cat, Bop (Mr. Legs), Sparkie, Pam Pam and Baskin, who appeared at major dance events and stage shows. Garth White (1984, 72–73) proposes that such practitioners should be considered "culture heroes" for creating a celebratory ethos, facilitating the development and tempo of Jamaica's popular music industry and performance practice.

Much public debate about dancehall moves has revolved around evaluative judgments. This chapter examines some of the central and, arguably, underexposed creators of dance moves, and, by extension, their personhood within the dancehall and everyday life. Their voices are mostly mediated through those of DJs, selectors of music and singers, but dancers have not been silent. Their expressions are mostly through movement as a tool of celebration. With the body as their instrument, they have made their marks on Jamaican history, politics and nationhood, as well as the world. The discussion of dance moves here is based primarily on discussions with the dancers as key informants and the observation of movement as key texts. This chapter highlights the general character of dance movement and their proliferation, as well as gender demarcations, kinaesthetic mapping and recruitment patterns. Ultimately, this chapter is intended to establish the central place of the dancer within dancehall through the presentation, translation and interpretation of their own language, with emphasis placed on the dancer's practice and space.

"OL' TIME SOMET'ING COME BACK AGAIN": AFRICAN AND OTHER CONTINUITIES

Kariamu Welsh-Asante (1985) argues that the commonalities in contemporary dances of the African Diaspora have a connection to ancestral Africa "through epic memory and oral tradition, even though these dances represent different languages, people, geographies and cultures" (1985, 71). Following from this, she identifies seven foundations or senses in African dance: polyrhythm, polycentrism, curvilinearity, multidimensionality, epic memory, repetition and holism. All of these are evident in contemporary dancehall moves.

Following from the understanding of continuities, specific aesthetic qualities have been isolated. Dancehall moves display features also documented in various African dance patterns, such as the emphasis on the beat, and the "natural bends" of elbow, head, pelvis, torso and knee (see Dagan 1997). Other characteristics such as grounding of the body rather than lifts, rhythmic complexity and parallel feet have also been well documented. Cheryl Ryman (2003, 170–71), in discussing the connection to ancestral rhythms, draws attention to the characteristic "wining" (rotating) of the hips, the bounce facilitated by natural knee bends, and the S-shaped stance in both male and female dances. The S-90 skank of the 1970s, mimicking the actions of the "rude boy" on his motorcycle, is one example of this pattern, but it is also to be seen in traditional Jamaican movement forms such as Revival, Gereh and mento. Ryman (1980, 4) discusses the seeming preoccupation with hip-centred and thus sexually charged movements within the context of African principles:

If we understand that procreation was/is considered vital to the Africans' survival in life and death, in Africa as well as the Diaspora, then we can perhaps understand their apparent preoccupation with "sexual" movements. Further, it is not unusual, as in Jonkonnu, for the traditional treatment within the context of the dance to be such as to allow for what the folk themselves define as "sexual play." It is simply a representation in dance movement.

These characteristics pervade traditional and contemporary movement, and have utility outside the dance. Pelvic agility, for example, helps with uphill walks, especially with heavy loads on the head, and in this sense the hip acts as a "shock absorber" (Eskamp and de Geus 1993, p. 56). Dance moves such as the yanga (mento dance), the yank and the jerk show similar grounding in everyday life by evoking domestic activities (washing clothes, bathing), recreation (horse racing, cricket) or anything else that appeals to the ska dancer (Reckord 1997, 6–7). These moves in turn were the antecedents of popular dancehall moves such as the butterfly, the log on and the dutty wine. So are moves such as legs, performed by such famous dancers as Pam Pam and Baskin in the early years (White 1984, 72), as well as the chucky and the horseman scabby.

Another form of continuity appears in the debates that erupt from time to time about the supposed dangers of certain dances. The dutty wine dance, for example, was created and popularized by Dyema Attitude, who herself suggested (2006) that the dance, which was designed to exhibit the rotation of hair extensions with a characteristic simultaneous rotation of the head and the buttocks, was not being performed with enough caution. It was further popularized during 2006 by the DJ/selector Tony Matterhorn with his hit song "Dutty Wine." He explained in a television interview (2006) that, because "the girls weren't getting involved" and "the dances are created by men for a good period of time now," it was time for girls to return to centre stage. Then, in the *Daily Gleaner* on October 30, 2006, Rasbert Turner reported that the death of a dancer named Tanisha Henry at a school uniform party in the parish of St Catherine was due to injuries she had allegedly sustained while performing the dance. Coverage of this incident in the mass media included commentary from medical doctors, academics, dancers and others, giving their opinions on the cause of the incident as well as making calls for banning the dutty wine. However, two years later it was concluded that Tanisha Henry's death had been caused by heart problems (see "Dutty Wine Didn't Kill Girl").

However, the debate about the dutty wine dance between 2006 and 2008 centred not only on the physical danger it was said to pose, especially to the dancer's neck, but also on the supposed association of the pelvic moves in the dance with lewd, licentious, devilish behaviour.

Interviews and archival research confirm that there were similar debates in the 1960s about the alleged physical and moral dangers of dance moves such as the yank, the jerk and the twist. For example, the yank, a "dangerous" dance that emphasized jerky movements of the hips, was said to have led to performers' hips being "yanked out," causing them to collapse.

THE ROLE OF THE DANCER

The role of dance and dancers in the dance halls is paramount. The experienced dancer was and still is like a god, and anyone who could

5.2 Dancer Chi Ching Ching at Passa Passa
Source: Sonjah Stanley Niaah

not dance was and still is definitely seen as a lesser being. The ability to execute movements is an indication of one's class membership (White 1984, 75).

The portrayal of dancehall as only or mainly a matter of music misses the important role that dance movement plays, not only in the playing of sounds but in playing on sound. The norms and power of certain dance styles become evident in this description by Garth White (1984, 74) of dance moves at a typical blues dance:

> Two "legsman" may trade moves.... A group of adolescents may be in a circle, creating new amalgams; a man and a woman may be doing the "boogie-woogie".... Another couple may be dancing slowly, closely ... sometimes almost motionless, openly sexual.... One youth may be all by himself, shuffling or ... just "rocking." He probably pays no attention to women that night, being quite satisfied to rock, self-sufficient and wrapped up in the music.

Interviewed in 2003, Stacey, Dancehall Queen 1999, was clear about the role of the dancer in the dancehall: "The dance can't happen without dancers. They are the crowd pleasers; if the music has nothing to vibrate on, the dance can't be nice." Discussing the trend in dancehall with the increased proliferation of new dance moves (1999–2007), Stacey highlighted a special synergy between the dancer and the DJ, the young and the old, the friend and the enemy: "I have seen dancehall taking out old people; dancehall never so nice in the history of dancehall ... because it is not modelling, not hype again, just enjoyment and everybody together uniting, everybody." Stacey acknowledged that the proliferation of dance moves creates a synergy between dancers and DJs because there is always a new dance for the DJs to sing about.

GERALD "BOGLE" LEVY (1966–2005)

I want to focus here on one male dancer who embodies the conception of cultural icon, but who up until the time of his death was never proclaimed as such. Media coverage after Bogle was tragically slain by gunmen in January 2005 centred on whether he had been an icon or not, and even those media entities, such as the *Sunday Gleaner*, that concluded that he had been did so only after his death (see "Dancers' Duel"). After all, citizens from the underclass, despite their achievements, and their contributions to national identity and development, have historically had difficulty in being proclaimed official icons or heroes. The debate about Bogle as a cultural icon resembles the earlier debate about whether Bob Marley was a national hero, although no one would disagree that, on the one hand, Bogle had created more dancehall dance moves than any other figure, and on the other, Marley catapulted Jamaica to worldwide fame through his music.

An icon was originally a holy image, long before the term came to be used in relation to symbols on computers or in cultural studies, where the connection with a famous person or thing considered to represent a set of beliefs or a way of life persists, as in such examples as Elvis Presley, Marilyn Monroe or the skyscraper. Despite the lack of consensus about Bogle's status as an icon, his death allowed for important reflections on his place as a dancehall celebrity, dancer and choreographer, and his role in the creation and proliferation of dancehall culture. The title of "dancehall king" was reserved, however, for the "legsman" of yesteryear.

Bogle was born in 1966 in Trench Town, West Kingston. He recalled that he and his mother lived in a semi-permanent wooden structure until they moved to a concrete housing development in the 1970s. Although he grew up in the area referred to by residents as Jungle, he said that he never carried "the jungle" with him. His secondary education started at Charlie Smith All Age, after which he spent a short time at St George's College. Bogle explained that while he was growing up he had thoughts of becoming a lawyer, a doctor, a teacher or a civil servant as these were the respected professions, but being unable to take full advantage of the education system, he decided to go with what God seemed to be telling him: "You are star." He explained, "All of my life, a dancing me know 'bout ... or else me woulda mix up," even though he had received a copious number of floggings from his mother, who had no faith in his vocation. He started early. By the 1970s he was appearing on Louise Bennett's Saturday morning show *Ring Ding* on the Jamaica Broadcasting Corporation and in the 1980s he danced on the Saturday evening programme *Where It's At* on the same station (now known as Television Jamaica). By the early 1990s Bogle and his Black Roses Crew from the Roses Corner, later designated by Bogle as the Dancehall Dimension, formed a prominent dancehall phenomenon, successfully shaping and changing the image of popular Jamaican dance.

Bogle pointed out that, while the then-popular Carlene Smith had become a dancehall queen without creating a single dance, he had never been named a dancehall king, even though no other person has been credited with creating and popularizing as many dance moves as Bogle has. His moves included the zip it up, the log on, the L. O. Y., the pelpa, the pop the collar, the pick it off, the genie, the gwanie gwanie, the Mission Impossible, the hot 97, the erkel, the flip, the butterfly (Carlene also claims to have originated this dance), the world dance, the imitation bogle, the bogle, the wave, the row like a boat, the jiggy and the back to basics. Bogle often released the dances to the media before exposing them on the dancehall stage. He was also present at many events promoting the moves, sometimes dancing, sometimes on a microphone given him by a selector to entertain the audience.

Bogle had given thought to becoming a DJ, but did not pursue this idea until shortly before his death, when he released the single "All Dem Deh" (2005) and proclaimed to newspaper reporters that he would be spending a lot of time at the recording studio, where he had already recorded four songs that were shortly to be released. These have not materialized. Instead Bogle's sojourn in the studio comes across forcefully in the recordings about him that constitute proclamations of his place in dancehall. Even before Bogle's death Buju Banton declared in "Bogle Dance" (1992),

> Bogle a di order fi di day
> Di wickedest dancer from outa JA

Similarly, in "Row Like a Boat" (2004) Beenie Man sang,

> Black Roses time
> Well yuh dun know,
> A di return of di greatest dancer of all time,
> Fadda Bogle.

The praise has continued, as in 2008, when Elephant Man sang of Bogle and his Black Roses Crew:

> Mr. Wacky a di teacher ...
> Roses have di flow dem' ...
> Wacky set di trend fi dem

Stacey (2003) has also praised Bogle's contribution: "Bogle set the trend, Bogle a elder, Bogle a di real ting."

Dancing was Bogle's forte however, and his motto "Dance or die" was borne out in the amount of time he dedicated to his career and the number of dance moves he created. In his words, "a mus dance alone mi think bout all these years to create so many dance. Mi couldn't think about nothing else.... What else could I think about? The dance wouldn't come good. The dance wouldn't come clean!" Bogle suggested that he embodied the very essence of dancehall: "Because of me ... everybody wanna dance! Everybody wanna dance right now."

5.3 Members of the Group Voicemail at Dutty Fridaze
Source: Sonjah Stanley Niaah

In his opinion, the "dance don't change until Bogle come.... You never see any difference in the dance until Bogle come." He was confident about his ability to allow any DJ to reap success from a song if only Bogle created a dance for it. Bogle thus took credit for the success of such DJs as Beenie Man, Bounti Killa, Buju Banton and Junior Reid, all of whom have songs describing Bogle's dance styles or built on Bogle's lyrical suggestions. There are phrases such as "Mr. Mention," used by Buju Banton for his album and single of the same title (1990), that sprang from Bogle's fountain of creativity. These went largely unacknowledged, however, and Bogle was very concerned about the way his intellectual property was being used without appropriate recognition or royalties. Apart from DJs who used his phrases in their song lyrics, others forgot to mention or pay tribute to his creativity by acknowledging his place as a dance creator. For example, in his single "Log On" (2001) Elephant Man credited the dance of that name, not to Bogle, but to the dancer Keiva who purportedly has a "dancing school" to which she should take those in need of tutelage. (Elephant Man has built his career on recording songs about dance moves, from the log on to the online, the signal di plane, the pon di river pon di bank, the chaka chaka, the hot w/fuk, the willie bounce, the gangsta rock, the nuh linga and the gully creepa.)

Bogle's contribution did gain some significant international exposure. One of his dances, the wave, was created during a period of self-imposed exile in the United States. Bogle explained that "it is not easy to create a dance in America" and that "only Michael Jackson"could do it, so he created the wave and other dances, and "FedExed them out to Jamaica." Bogle's style had been to 'bus' or release the dances in Jamaica and 'fedex' (short for the worldwide courier Federal Express) or courier them to the world, in particular the USA. In the case of the wave he reversed the process, releasing it first in the United States, where it became popular, first as the wave in Miami and then, under the name the Super Bowl, in New York City.

Perhaps the most visible international platform precipitating increased popularity for Bogle was the music video. Beyond their appearances in locally made and distributed videos, a range of artists from Jamaica have gained international exposure through rotation of their videos on cable channels, in particular Tempo TV, which can be seen all over the Caribbean, and BET (Black Entertainment Television) in the United States. Bogle's appearances in music videos by international acts such as Foxy Brown were just one manifestation of the rewards for his hard work. Another was his transition from dancing to acting in films such as Hype Williams's *Belly* (1998).

Bogle's words "Jamaica caan pay me fi dance" specifically referred to the importance of his role within dancehall culture internationally, especially after his return to Jamaica in 2002 and his appearance in the Sashi stage show as an act in his own right. He made it clear that he wanted "some big open land to start teach people fi dance" and that, in his view, the problem was that there are "so many products in Jamaica," but Jamaicans "don't know how to put them in play." He believed that Jamaica doesn't understand how to honour his status as an international dancer, evidenced by his appearances with Stone Love at Disney World, his performances at various locations across the Caribbean and beyond it, and his appearances in music videos, films and television shows. His moves have also circulated within the more prestigious dance theatre companies of Jamaica, although Rex Nettleford, former Artistic Director and Choreographer of the National Dance Theatre Company, who acknowledges the common genealogy of folk dances and those within the contemporary dancehall space, has observed (2001, 11) that "new dances are hard to study because they disappear as soon as they appear in the dancehalls." Bogle felt that he had contributed immensely to the dance and music industries, but did not reap commensurate rewards or recognition. He was especially concerned about the treatment he received because he was a resident of a lower-class community. People responded with surprise on hearing him speak, because of their prejudice that citizens from lower-class backgrounds would not be able to speak Standard English fluently. Bogle summarized his position by concluding that "people always check where you are from, not where you are going."

Class identity and its link to political identity have created barriers to dancehall performance that are highlighted through Bogle's experience. Being a citizen of Jungle, an area affiliated with the People's National Party (PNP), and mostly residing in the PNP-affiliated Arnett Gardens, Bogle was seen as a PNP supporter. Added to this, his support for the sound system Stone Love, branded as a PNP sound because of its connections with PNP-affiliated communities such as Jones Town, inadvertently created spatial and political boundaries for Bogle, who did not attend, for example, the initial Passa Passa dance events staged in Tivoli Gardens, a "garrison" of the Jamaica Labour Party. He did not feel that he could step into that space without permission from its area leader. Anything might have happened and he was not willing to put the future at risk for the sake of past events. (In April 2004, however, I saw Bogle at Passa Passa and he informed me that he was making an impact there.) Bogle remained a resident of Arnett Gardens, in spite of the boundaries that placed on the otherwise boundless enjoyment that could be experienced within the performance practice.

Because of Bogle's presence in the dance there has been an increase in the number of popular male dancers, including John Hype, who received a contract with the promoters Shocking Vibes, former managers of the DJ Beenie Man; Blazay, the dancer who developed the dance of that name; other individuals, such as Shelly Belly, Ding Dong, Craigy Dread, Shortman, Spongebob and Ice; as well as male dance crews such as Cadillac, Sample Six, Ravers Clavers, Black Blingers, Colo Squad, and Sadiki and the Crew. These dancers have risen to prominence at a time when the stage had already been set for appreciation of dancehall dance, and have become popular features not just at stage shows and dance events, but also on platforms such as the national Independence Day celebrations in August 2008, or the homecoming celebrations in (October 2008) to honour outstanding Jamaican athletes after their success at the Beijing Olympic Games. These dancers also gain international exposure through the songs that highlight their names, as well as their show appearances. Most importantly, Bogle opened the door for others from places marred by political violence who, because of their performance practice, can be singled out in dancehall anthems rather than as statistics on the evening news. These dancers too have testified to dancehall's life-saving role.

REAPING REWARDS FROM DANCEHALL

The dancehall constitutes a space in which various rewards are reaped. For dancers these are often public and communal, but they may also be personal and private: the sheer pleasure of the dance itself, which is not to be overlooked; the satisfaction gained from attending dance events and receiving the crowd's approval; the gratification of receiving attention or cash from an admirer who later becomes a partner. One male dancer acknowledged that he had met all his girlfriends and "baby mothers" at dance events. Rewards for the dancehall queens such as Carlene included, by her own account, the ability to step into another part of herself. It was this that she eagerly wanted to develop, the sexy persona that the entire world wanted to see and through which she felt fully ignited. On the other hand, there are those who gain purpose, a space in which they are anonymous yet well-known and appreciated for their style. Most importantly, dancehall offers a means of escape from real hardships: as we have seen, Bogle was not alone in recognizing that dancehall had kept him out of a life of "badness" and disrepute.

Rewards can operate at both conscious and unconscious levels, for there is another site that is worthy of attention: the dancers' psyche. As Garth White (1984, 74) suggests, drawing on the work of Pamela O'Gorman, the reggae dancer is one who "can maintain a kind of introverted private relationship with the piece of Earth on which he dances alone." Throughout my research, dancers I have interviewed have made repeated references to feelings of becoming or assuming another persona or self. One dancehall queen explained that dressing in her dancehall regalia allows her to become a different person and that this helps her to deal with the public part of her existence. Another dancer admitted that she loves "wining" her hips because when she does it feels like renewing energy radiating through her body, and when these "vibes" take over she steps out of her self.

Dancers have also commented on the way in which dancehall provides an escape from their daily problems into a sort of heavenly world, in which people don't care where you come from or who you are. For the poor in Jamaica dancehall provides another space, process and means of connecting to a higher self as well as the community, outside the everyday routine of survival. Dancers report both having an ability to perfect dance moves while asleep and dreaming, and feeling as if they were in a dream world while awake and dancing. This intense blurring of dream with reality, and the ease with which a dancer steps outside his or her physical reality to enter an ethereal one, are consistent with the outcomes of many traditional performance practices in

5.4 Dancer Doctor Bird performs at a video shoot in Kingston
Source: Roy Sweetland

which varying states of possession are experienced (see Ryman 1980). Dance allows the dancer a particular kind of flight, the possibility of permanent and instant elevation in daily life, beyond sadness, pain and injustice.

In addition to high levels of satisfaction, dancehall constitutes a means of survival. Dancers report receiving financial returns from their skills in addition to such benefits as United States visas and work permits. Patrons who like the dancers or their moves sometimes give them money, and dancers have been able to obtain work and pay from performances elsewhere in the Caribbean, as well as in Africa, Europe and the United States.

Perhaps the most important reward, which has not been fully investigated, is a social one. In Chapter 2 I commented on the "geography of refuge" that underlies dancehall activity because of the perceived correlation between performance and social cohesion, and the inverse relationship between dancehall and social tension. The high points of dance creation and dance events, and their proliferation, have been periods in which there were no major social upheavals due to excessive violence, around general elections for example. This correlation is also suggested by the survey of about 150 dance moves that forms the basis of the preliminary chronology in the final section of this chapter. Apart from the increase in the number of moves created with each passing year, the decline in periods leading up to general elections, such as in 1990–91 and 2002–03, is noteworthy. This issue requires more detailed exploration, but what is clear is that dancehall's contribution to social cohesion is widely underestimated, especially by those who charge dancehall with playing a role in what they perceive as social decay. In the context of shortages of assets and capital investment for the masses who create and maintain this performance practice, dancehall continues to provide a space of multiple rewards for its adherents. Thus, the very spaces created for the consumption and production of cultural forms, and for access to pleasure, constitute sites of financial and political opportunity for that practice and its creators. While many exist just above or just below the poverty line, and are left to self-destruct in the quagmire of barely habitable conditions within Kingston's ghettos, they mock that context by surviving beyond its limitations.

MASKING (THE BODY) IN THE DANCE

The dance event invokes other sides of the self, other roles that are enacted, and the wearing of masks is important for the transition to these other selves and other roles. Masking in the dancehall is defined by the dress, hairstyles (wigs, braids) and behaviours (language, "profile") adopted in the milieu of social celebration. The masks are aggrandizing tools for the self, in a tradition that has its roots in "fancy dress" and related forms of masking in Jamaica. Indeed, as Rex Nettleford has remarked (1993, 1D),

Jamaican masquerade (Jonkonnu) flourishes today not only in dance hall, but also in the masquerade the ladies and gentlemen of quality in upper St Andrew and Mandeville have adopted via Byron Lee's enterprises.... Among the "people from below" the device of "masking" (in fancy dress) persists with a vengeance.... The ambush of a less than just society under the cover of festive masquerades has been one way of experiencing control, if only a temporary one.... The actual dress is important. For the costume is a mask helping to transform the persona to do wild and uninhibited things.

In addition to impression-management schemes embodied within such practices as dress (new outfit and hairstyle), the wearing of a different mask at each dancehall event ensures readiness for the video light, which signifies the eventual broadcast of not just a self, but a visual product (see Chapter 6).

I would like to link this discussion of masking to style, as both are characterized by adornment, transformation and the construction of identity. Dancehall style revolves around, and is expressed by, the body, which becomes a crucial site of articulation for the individual and the group. I want to associate the importance of style in popular culture with Dick Hebdige's vision of style as a means of communication through symbols, revealing distinctiveness, meaning and identity (Hebdige 2005, 130–42). Hebdige argues that subcultures—as groups basically delineated by their shared practices and interests, using "noise" to dislocate official codes and define their difference—have lifecycles of distinct separation and incorporation. Style is their signifying practice: it functions as an indicator or sign of larger discourses in the cultural, political and economic landscapes. For example, a particular garment may be chosen on the basis of price or taste, but at the same time it distinguishes one from another. The messages are sometimes intentional and sometimes not. These messages are numerous, and vary around status, beauty and taste.

The subject and its agency through style, in a ritual of self-fashioning, have been explained by different knowledge systems, including critical theory, cultural theory, anthropology, psychoanalysis and philosophy, by authors such as Louis Althusser, Michel Foucault, Stuart Hall, Arnold van Gennep and others. Judith Butler (2000, 30–37) takes a multidisciplinary cultural studies approach to her discussion of Hall's interpretation of Foucault's work on the subject's inner terrain, and the place of aesthetics in the constitution and agency of the subject, and uncovers useful terrain for the discussion of style. She writes of the "limit" (pain, non-identity) inherent in such conditions as the tensions between sexuality, status, laws and cities. This limit is the very condition for a possibility of transcendence rather than a static end. Similarly, George Lamming (1992, 34) makes use of the notion of style in his tribute to the Guyanese novelist Edgar Mittelholzer (1909–1965):

> It has to do with style. Nothing matters more than a man's discovery of his *style*, a discovery which is also part of his own creation, and *style*—not *a* style, but *style*—as the aura and essence, the recognized example of being, in which and out of which a man's life assumes its shape. The flavour of his thinking, the furious silences that fill his heart, and finally his function, the work that chooses him and for which there is no alternative: no other instruments he can select to fulfil that choice: these constitute the style of a man.

Lamming concretizes the point that style is to some degree synonymous with the core of one's being and sense of identity.

Whether at the individual level or the collective level, dancehall embodies this certain style, this deliberate stylization of everyday life and, within this stylization, a certain agency that provides avenues for the production and reproduction of selves. In tension with the status quo by virtue of its "limit" in Butler's sense, dancehall's style is far less familiar to those embedded within the middle-class status quo and aspirations. One example of this style is expressed in the fashion of inner-city citizens, which contests and rewrites historically biased religious, sexual and class scripts (see Bakare-Yusuf 2006). Indeed, Zora Neale Hurston (1933, 293–97), in her summary of the expressive practices of Afro-Americans in her own time, the early 1930s, reminds us of the place of adornment in Black cultures. The fantastic, the fabulous, the spectacular self operates as an excess of well-known characteristics of African expression such as "drama" and the "will to adorn." These are not just overinflated expressions of selves, but rather expressions of power, as Lamming conceives it: the power to create and recreate one's own essence. The average working-class person conforms by wearing conservatively tailored clothes to her place of work and to her place of worship, but reserves revealing and highly creative designs for night outings.

However, it is not uncommon to see women at funerals in the inner city wearing the same revealing or creative designs that they would wear to the dance. Such a fashion statement is indicative of a different regard for the rules governing attire and the presentation of self, as well as distinctly different interpretations of mourning. The dancehall aesthetic routinely transcends the norms of the middle and upper classes regarding "appropriate" adornment, dress and conduct. The female modelling crews that popularized the public display of the body, especially the Naked Posse led by Carlene around 1992, have set a trend for dancehall patrons. When mourners appeared scantily clad in revealing dresses at the funeral of Willy Haggart, a former area leader of inner-city Kingston, it was only the "men and women of quality" from the middle and upper classes who acknowledged the great sartorial divide in their comments about "ghetto aesthetics."

The dancehall aesthetic is also reflected in the techniques used to maintain the dancehall self as reflected in hairstyles, which show continuity with practices in African societies. The importance of hairstyle among slaves in Suriname in the late 18th century was noted by Stedman (1992, 95), who described the "seasoning" of the enslaved on their arrival in the New World: on the deck of the slave ship they prepared themselves for being shown off to the bidders, including by shaving parts of their heads, "which they generally do the one to the other, having no razor, by the help of a broken bottle and without soap." Proving the point that the ordeal of the Middle Passage did not obliterate culture, the hairstyle described by Stedman and depicted in one of the plates illustrating his book resembles hairstyles found in the Ashanti tradition, such as Gyawu Atiko or Nkotimsefo Mpua (Willis 1998, 112–13 and 142–43), which form part of the functional and symbolic cultural aspects of Akan culture in modern Ghana and Côte d'Ivoire.

Many men and women also believe that if they do not bleach their skins they are not in style. Winston, a member of the bleaching community, explained the practice in a television interview (2003): "It mek yuh look like yuh come inna di light." It is a style whose benefits increase under the light of spectatorship. It is not uncommon to bleach in advance of a dance event.

At the individual level, Stacey, Dancehall Queen 1999, has a definitive dance style. Her best hour is from 5:00 a.m. to 6:00 a.m., when she can be seen mounting the ground, a tower of speakers or a nearby roof. She has perfected the head top dance and performs it on the surface of her choice. In her best acts Stacey can be seen making space in between and outside the conventions of dance movement and the circle or designated dance space, as she pushes the boundary of what is considered "normal," especially as the level of skill and display that are normal for a dancehall queen are not typical for most dancehall patrons, or for citizens of the middle and upper classes. Stacey (2003) has admitted that in order to replicate her moves "one has to be real fit to do them" —and, I would add, one also has to shed enough of the puritanical morality to be able to conceive of what Stacey does as other than "slackness" or vulgarity.

Omofolabo Ajayi (1998, 2–4) discusses the "disembodied body" as the Western opposite of the more holistic verbal/non-verbal communication system where the body, as one such system of communication, is valued, or even regarded as sacred. Ajayi explains that for the Yoruba people of Nigeria, Benin and Ghana, perceiving "the body that dances with spiritual and pious fervour in worshipping God" and that same body dancing "with sensual pleasure and delight on social and courtship occasions" evokes no contradiction. She suggests that there are far-reaching consequences of the disregard for non-verbal communication that has its roots in Judeo-Christian traditions.

5.5 Illustration of Fat Women in Dancehall
Source: The Jamaica Gleaner Company

Dancehall is used as a space to resist the "other" by revalorizing aspects of the body that are censored in the wider social sphere, including shape, size, age, definitions of structure, social utility and symbolic value. These vary from place to place, and within social classes, races, age groups and genders, all of which have corresponding histories. For example, one remarkable aspect of dancehall culture is the valorization of the steatopygous female, the "buffer zone" (visibly plump pudenda, also known as the "buffalous" or "buff bay"), the "mampy" (fat woman) and "marky marky belly" (a stomach with stretch marks on it), especially as these are exposed through revealing figure-hugging or transparent garments. Based on practices within the space, a dancehall dancer or patron is not restricted to general social ideals of age (all ages are present) or body size (fatness is appreciated). The marky marky belly becomes a sign of fertility, while the steatopygous female and the mampy signal health. Therefore, the dancehall body exists within a different value system. Dancehall maps itself onto the dancing body in particular ways and these bodies have their own maps.

In this milieu, skill is crucial. All the dancers I interviewed described how they learned to dance and to assess a good dancer. Most admitted to being self-taught, learning the dance primarily through observation. (Stacey and Bogle are exceptional in the distinctiveness of their creations and trends in movement, and they saw themselves as having natural talent.) One dancer explained her standards for judging a good dancer as "If the hip nah move, yuh nah move" and, further, "If nobody paying yuh any mind, [it is] like yuh nah do not'ing." For her, excellence is reflected in the acrobatic movement of the waistline and in knowledge of all the dance moves, current and past. According to the dancehall celebrity Pinkie: "You have to know all the up to date dances; people hope to learn from you. That's what a dancehall queen is." She acknowledged pedagogical responsibilities, in relation to those who hope to learn the moves, as part of the role of the dancehall queen. Spandex highlighted specific attributes such as the ability to convey mood and emotions while dancing, and the ability to elicit crowd response with exciting, frisky, and neat movements. In a similar vein, Stacey (2003) offered that the dancer must make an impression with appearance, creativity, attitude, confidence and movement. The dancer's unique appearance should be accented with an attitude of self-confidence that conveys the movement effectively to his or her crowd.

Interviewees also made a distinction between dancing and "mogelling" (modelling), the latter being a display without real ability or talent. However, they acknowledged that the act of dressing up has its own appeal, which, in turn, enhances the appeal of the dance arena. Modelling and "profiling" are seen as secondary to dancing, yet essential.

DANCEHALL QUEENS

The phenomenon of the dancehall queen is yet another aspect of dancehall that has deep historical roots, invoking the status and symbolism of great African queens and queen mothers, such as Yaa Asantewa (c. 1840–1921), Queen Mother of Ejisu, whose war against the British in 1900 is still recalled in West Africa, or Menen Asfaw (1889–1962), wife of Haile Selassie and Empress of Ethiopia (see Edgerton 1995), as well as traditional forms in the Diaspora, both religious—including the Mother or chief spiritual arbiter in Revival, Mother Lundy in Burru and the Kumina Queens, such as Mrs. Imogene "Queenie" Kennedy, in the Congo-derived Afro-Jamaican religion Kumina—and secular, notably carnival queens across the Caribbean and beyond (see Murray 2000,

105–06, and Scher 2003). The idea of the queen reveals the consistently elevated place of women as key counterparts of "kings," formal or informal, named or unnamed. The pervasive elevation of a central female persona is consistent with African popular and sacred traditions, as well as with kinship patterns that are matrilineal and/or matriarchal in character.

Dancehall queens emerged as informal community celebrities in the 1970s, but in recent years Carlene Smith, proclaimed a dancehall queen by the media in 1992, and Stacey, winner of the International Dancehall Queen Contest in 1999, have contributed the most to the rise of the image, style and appeal of such queens of dancehall, who are expected to demonstrate certain attributes of attitude and style as well as dancing skill. Ironically, Carlene was not considered a great dancer, but her modelling sense, her fashion designs, her fair complexion and her voluptuous figure won the hearts of many, and propelled her into an unusually long reign that lasted about ten years (Edmondson 2003, 1–16). She was out on a precarious limb that proved stronger than critics imagined. Stacey was popular from 1999 until about 2003, and continues to command respect for her dancing skill and the consistency of her representation at dance events, both locally and internationally.

Cheryl Ryman (1993, 2) has observed that the would-be kings of dancehall, successors to the "legsman" of yesteryear's dance sessions, have been displaced by a marked female ascendancy. Yet Carlene, Stacey and their successors have presided over an uneasy kingdom, in which their displays of natural attributes (the bigger, the better) and their dominance of the dance arena are muted by the exploitative role of the male DJs, counterbalanced only by the vessel-like role they play in facilitating the undisputed dominance of the queens on the dance floor. The shift to a space of female appeal has been attributed to a number of factors, but the most relevant may well be the maturation of Jamaican cultural expression in the years after independence was gained, in 1962, and the increased independence of women in the context of dancehall and other kinds of "independence projects," including feminism.

For the dancer, and the queen in particular, dancehall is a stage, an institution that bestows a status outside the social constrictions of everyday life, a space in which to emerge and maintain stardom on the basis of physical attributes and/or dancing ability. It is also a platform on which women can define the terms and conditions of success, style and contestation, creating place and space for other women (see Skelton 1995 and 1998). For example, while Carlene was a media-proclaimed queen and Stacey won her crown by dancing for it, but since then the standards for assessing good dancing have been sharpened. Additionally, Carlene and Stacey created a dance aesthetic that is available to Jamaica and the world, perfected through training by the Japanese dancer Junko Kudo (known in Japan, where the family name comes first, as Kudo Junko), who won the International Dancehall Queen Contest in 2002.

A recent development is the transition from "queen" to "diva," instantiated by Stacey after her reign had ended. Interviewed in 2003, she explained,

> As a dancehall queen—not even a dancehall queen, mi a dancehall diva—mi top the class as a queen. Yeh, I'm a dancehall diva! Yuh si, diva is weh everybody—the queen dem, everybody—look up to, everybody waan beee you, everybody dance like you, everybody try fi dress like you, everybody always a try portray your image, so that means yuh separated from the rest. You coulda never be a queen with the person who waan fi be you. So everything weh di dancehall queen have done, mi do that already, so mi an dem coulda neva be inna the same league, neva.... Mi travel more than them internationally. No disrespect to Carlene, [but] internationally, mi name a di most ringed name inna dancehall as a female. Every dance mi go a foreign, mi lock dat. Mi go a dance wid Junko [Dancehall Queen 2002], Junko become the audience. Mi an' Junko deh pon a show an' Junko stop, and become audience and start watch mi. When mi deh pon a stage wid her she fret, a mi haffi a work wid her and say, wa'appen to you —mi nuh deh pon no clash ting [competition] wid you.... So mi separate myself.... Even the queen dem demself who win, the girl name Michelle [McKoy, Dancehall Queen 2003] weh win, a mi groom her.

In defining a diva Stacey distances herself from other titles based on dance skills, regional and international travel and exposure, style, hard work, and seniority in the business. The diva, in this view, sets the trends even for the queens. The diva is not a backup dancer accentuating a DJ's performance but a translocal actor in her own right, an individual hired in her capacity as a dancer for local events, such as Lady Saw's Grammy Party on April 23, 2004, as well as for international events. Stacey has also used her distinctive, even definitive style in mentoring dancing aspirants as well as in training future queens. These factors are evidence of her contribution to the definition and maintenance of a dancing tradition in which she has progressed to new categories of achievement.

In particular, Stacey's performance at her own birthday bash in 2001 incorporated the use of diverse spaces for dancing, including passing vehicles, which she danced on top of or even entered to "wine" on the male drivers and passengers. This act seemed to be a signal to passing cars that they had encroached on ritual space and could not be allowed to pass until they had been properly inducted. The extension of dancing off the dance floor to vehicles is an interesting dimension of dancehall, reflected in music videos that portray dancing in cars or on top of them and in lyrics that compare women to cars, as in "Remind mi of mi Benz, mi Lexus an' mi Bimmer" (Bounti Killa), "Woman haffi drive di Benz till it crash" (Spragga Benz) or "Gimme di Benz punany mek mi gwaan drive it out" (Little Lenny). Such references, which also come from female DJs, are used in general to refer to male and female prowess and power. In spite of sections of public opinion that deplore the supposedly excessive consumption and incorporation of Western symbols of materialism within dancehall, the philosophy of space here is evident. As mentioned earlier, dancehall patrons generally do not view space in terms of its limitations, and a dancer at the level of a queen, with superior dancing abilities, can challenge limits that are unattainable by others. Just as patrons consider the success of a dance event to be contingent on how many patrons are bursting at the seams of the venue, the dancer, overtaken by the power of the event, can climb or mount any space for the purpose of staging a dance. In these instances the philosophy of limitless space allows its reclamation, its multiplication, even its transcendence. Further, the way in which female dancers' performances capture the attention of patrons at any event confirms that women have successfully used the dancehall as a stage on which to create space beyond male control, within what remains a predominantly patriarchal ethos.

GENDER DEMARCATIONS AND NEGOTIATIONS IN DANCE

During the 1990s, around the time when Bogle rose to popularity, dance practice in dancehall stood outside the boundaries of scrutiny by the "regulators" of gender identity, its display and its possibilities for transgression in Jamaica. There was thus no explicit anxiety about males in what had become a female-dominated practice, nor was any contradiction perceived between "feminine" display of dancing male bodies and the standards of macho, aggressive, tough masculinity prescribed by the Jamaican social context. To a large extent, Bogle and those inspired by him expressed a brand of masculinity within dancehall akin to that of the "legsman" of the 1960s. This included a non-aggressive mode of being, centred on the improvisational nature of the individual's and, increasingly, the group's creative dance process. Males danced with males, females with females, males with females, within groups (crews) and as couples. Arguably, there was less emphasis on sexuality, and more on expanding the space and performance of dance styles. This does not mean that macho masculinities were not also performed by dancers, but they were always less visible in male dancers' performances, in contrast to the pronounced, aggressive masculinity expected of male DJs.

An important dynamic in the dance scene after 2000 was that women were noticeably attending events on their own and there was less emphasis on partner dancing than there had been during the 1990s. One factor contributing to this shift was, arguably, the degree of independence that some women have achieved as a result of economic activities such as "higglering" (vending). One dancer observed when interviewed that, in the late 1980s and early 1990s, "girl just give you a dance and any amount a dance," because, among other reasons, they felt secure enough to do so. Another dancer revealed, "If dance a keep, wi go to get a girl." In an acknowledgement of the shift that has occurred since, female dancers admitted that they did not attend dance events with male partners but rather with girlfriends, because attending the event with one's partner reduced the degree of freedom the dancer could exercise in choice of dance moves and dance partners. The 1990s, then, could be said to have ushered in an element of free play among women in particular as new levels of economic and social independence were reached.

While male and female heterosexual identities are visible in partner dancing, through amorous display and sexually provocative or explicit dance styles that in many cases simulate sexual intercourse, perceptions of males dancing in crews began to gain visibility when associations were made with homosexuality. Anxiety about male dancing surfaced in dancehall around 2003, when male dancers and dancing crews began to proliferate and to upstage female dancers in visible competition for the stage, the street and the video spotlight. Male dancers adopted fashion trends consistent with a feminine aesthetic, and reminiscent of the styles adopted by performers such as Prince or Michael Jackson when they were reigning supreme over the disco during the 1980s. Such trends include tight pants, pink and/ or pastel-coloured clothing, accessories such as scarves, plucked or shaped eyebrows and make-up that goes against the grain for men in Western cultures. Associations with homosexuality or transsexuality find no comfortable dwelling place in the minds of some Jamaicans, who have contributed to the construction of the image of Jamaica as homophobic, arguably even one of the most homophobic societies in the world. Entertainers have been explicit not only about their intolerance of homosexuality but also about the ways in which, in their view, the "feminine" character of the dance, fashion and attitude of some males have overshadowed the female presence in dancehall. For example, the DJ/selector Tony Matterhorn of the Bembe Thursdays DJ Squad emphasized (2007) that the event was initiated to bring back females to dancehall and the dance arena generally. Males were thought to be dominating the dance floor, male dance moves overshadowed those created by females and the dancehall was overrun by a new male aesthetic that ran counter to normative social constructions of gender identity. It was not "gender appropriate" for men to upstage women on the dance floor. Statements by other DJs have revolved around sentiments such as "Tight pants a woman supp'n' [something]" or "Bad man nuh dress like girl."

It is important to note, however, that some dancehall actors enjoy the ability to transgress modes of dress, action, and perceptions about normative gender roles and expectations. For example, there are perceptions about the DJ Elephant Man's embodiment of a queer aesthetic, with an emphasis on his characteristically extravagant sartorial creations bordering on transvestism, including hair extensions, hair dye, scarves and shaped eyebrows. However, his song lyrics often belie his presentation of self, emphasizing the gangsta/badman lifestyle, and during his career so far there have been no public clashes about his fashion choices or his sexuality.

Dance and gender are also intertwined in the kinaesthetic emphasis that inadvertently invites classification according to the gender of performers. In discussing his creations, Bogle acknowledged that the bogle dance move was really for men, while the butterfly was created with women in mind (Reyes 1993, 48). While many dances have been performed by women, those such as the one foot skank, the legs, the cool an' deadly, the get flat, and, more recently, the chaplin, the bad man forward and the gangsta rock have been performed mostly by men. Even so, a larger number of dance moves have been performed by both men and women, including the world dance, the bogle, the tatti, the screetchie, the angel, the tall up tall up, the higher level, the curfew, the log on, the row like a boat, the wave, the parachute, the blazay, the signal di plane, the tek weh yu self and the gully creepa. Classically, female dances are generally those in which the essential point of articulation is the rotation or thrust of the pelvic girdle; male dances emphasize complex and coordinated movements of the hands and the legs and moves performed by both sexes are multidimensional in nature, not centred on the pelvic girdle, the hands or the legs, but emphasizing individual memory rather than dance skills. The entire community can execute these moves, and thus maintain the characteristic sociality of dancehall culture in which everyone can participate.

A PRELIMINARY CHRONOLOGY

Some of the major dance moves throughout the period 1986–2007 are highlighted in the preliminary chronology that is at the centre of this section (see Table 5.1). This chronology has been developed on the basis of the production years of songs about the moves, the memories of informants, mass media coverage, especially in the *Daily* and *Sunday Gleaner*, the *Daily* and *Weekend Star*, and the *Jamaica Observer*, and other secondary sources.

The dance moves presented here by no means represent the full extent of creations within the dancehall space. There are dance moves that have no names, such as the variations of the generic "bubbling" or rotation of the hips done mostly by women. In addition, not all dance moves have become popular beyond a specific community or corner.

TABLE 5.1

Chronology of Major Dance Moves, 1986–2009

1986–89	coolan' deadly, rocking dolly, water pumpee, horseman scabby, heel an' toe, bubble, pedal an' wheel, body move, shoulder move, bounce, duck, jump an' spread out, stuck, wine an' go down, get flat, bubble, one foot skank, della move
1990–91	crab, head top, prang, poco man jam
1991–92	bike back, big it up, roun' di worl', santa barbara, bogle
1992–93	imitation bogle, butterfly, armstrong, bruk wine
1993–94	worl' dance, tatti, soca bogle, position, limbo, kung fu
1994–95	mock di dread, body basics, a capella
1995–96	erkle, go go wine, ol' dog

1996–97	sketel
1997–98	mister bean, pelpa, the flip
1998–99	jerry springer
2000–01	angel, screechy
2001–02	l.o.y. (lords of yard), zip it up, log on
2002–03	online, drive-by, curfew (taliban), tall up tall up, higher level, party dance, wave, karate or martial art, blazay, row like a boat, pon di river pon di bank, signal di plane, chaplin, parachute, fan dem off, propellar, hand cart, shake dem off, elbow dem, rock away, nah nuh head
2003–04	shelly belly, internet, gallop, crazy hype, jiggy, thunderclap, fall the rain, hop the ferry, scooby doo, shankle dip
2004–05	chaka chaka, chaka belly, sesame street, wacky dip, out an' bad, willy bounce, summer bounce, spongebob, back to basics
2005–06	bad man forward, gangsta rock, tick tock, swing i' weh, ova di wall, stookie
2006–07	mad a road, live red, craigy bounce, bounty/killa walk, killa swing, swing song, prezi bounce, spread out, march out, dutty wine, hoola hoop, beyoncé wine, hot f/wuk, raging bull
2007–08	tek weh yu self, drunkin' dance, drop dead, rollercoaster, helicopter, earthquake, statue of liberty, energy, rum ram, no linga, sweep, gully creeper, 90s rock
2008–09	daggering, nuh behaviour, summer bounce, skip to ma lou

Dance moves are created overnight and can disappear just as quickly. In spite of power plays within the dancehall space and from external forces, the moves exist on every street corner and are accessible to each citizen, among them, according to Beenie Man in his song "World Dance" (1994), "the blind, the dumb, the deaf, and the cripple." That song itself, according to Beenie Man, was inspired by a new dance he had seen being performed on the streets, lanes and corners, that is, everywhere, and by or for everyone.

Among other things, the list illustrates the dynamic nature of dance creation and naming, especially throughout 1990–94 and again from 2001 to 2007. Just as musical rhythms have maintained their resonant and evocative names—such as punawny, taxi, sleng ting, rampage, old dawg, dewali, fiesta, wicked, nine night, tai chi, military, red bull and guinness, or anger management—so dance moves too have names that tell stories, stories of cross-fertilization, identification with characters, "vibes," phenomena, globalization, contemporary and historical Jamaican and African traditional forms, body parts, and the valorization of local culture.

Dance moves such as the head top, the body basics, the sketel, the bike back, the position and the various "wines"—the wine an' go down from the 1980s, the bruk wine from 1992–93, the go go wine from 1995–96, and the dutty wine and the beyoncé wine, both from 2006–07—have been created by and for women. Here what is central is the skill of "wining," winding the waist in a smooth, generic "bubble" or rotation of the hips, "wining" like a go-go dancer or "wining" on the head top. There are various songs that encourage wining and the development of wining skill. In "Go Go Wine" (1996) Captain Barkey sings of the dancers wining their waistlines, their chests and their rumps because they have no problems: they have fed their children and they are hotter than the competition. Elephant Man's "Wining Queen" (2002) asks who is going to be the next wining queen, the next wining machine, while his "Fan Dem Off" (2003) encourages the dancer to "don't stop wine up your body like a snake in the vine, wine it up 'cause you inna you prime." Patra's "Bruk Wine," Early Black's "Stuck" and Shabba Ranks's "Girls Wine" are all similar incantations to the dancer.

A crucial component of the wining capacity that dancers must have is control of the buttocks. In various body positions the dancer's buttocks can shimmy, thrust, rotate, release and contract, push, press and pump, in a light, heavy, frantic, sharp, fluid or jerky manner. Moves such as the bike back, the position and the sidung pon it are examples: not only do they require fluid movement of the hips, they also feature a particular aesthetic of the buttock. The large derriere which is celebrated in dancehall and more widely in Jamaican culture matters in such a move. A dancer with a posterior that can be manipulated will command attention, and the larger and more flexible the derriere, the better. Johnny P's recording "Bike Back" (1991) captures the bike back move and the importance of the derriere. He explains that, as the dancer hoisted her derriere, with bent knees facilitating rotating and flashing movements, perfect balance and control were mastered and maintained on the highly fashionable Kawasaki motorbike, so much so that she upstaged the competition and passers-by.

There are also explicit spiritual themes in dancehall dance. The poco man jam (1990–91) highlights the movement of a dancer belonging to the Pocomania and / or Pukkumina movement, closely related to the Revival religious group, who is possessed or on the verge of possession. The head, hands and feet are the central points of articulation. The dancer's head moves from side to side with sharp, jerky movements, and sometimes erratically, while the body is propelled forward with thrusts on the right foot and rhythmic thrusts of the right hand. This movement pattern, also associated with Revival religious groups, has been described as the "trumping" step (see Simpson 1956, 354, Baxter 1970, 142, and Carty 1988, 68–74).

In the butterfly, the most popular dance in 1992–93, the form of a butterfly is depicted with legs and arms outspread as the dancer moves with knees bent—a characteristic feature of African and Diasporic movement patterns—and feet flat to support the dynamic displacement of the hips, shoulder girdle and legs. The knees, which open and close fluidly on a horizontal axis, mimic the flapping of the butterfly's wings in flight. While the butterfly has clear connections with its North Atlantic cousin the charleston, which has roots in an Ashanti ancestor dance (Baraka 1968, 17, and Eskamp and de Geus 1993, 60), there are differences. For example, the forward and backward thrust of the hip that supports the opening and closing of the legs allows for increased degrees of variation on the movement style.

The jerry springer (1998–99) presents an interesting example for an analysis of dancehall in relation to television characters originating from the United States. Jerry Springer's explosive talk show is renowned for its high levels of controversy, and its public displays of interpersonal feuding and physical fights. Its reimagining within the bodily movement repertoire of the Jamaican space says something about the identities within both spaces, and the kinds of practices that they produce. At least one other dance is named after a character from American television: the erkle (from 1995–96) honours a nerd in the series *Family Matters*.

The angel (from 2000–01) is another dance with a spiritual theme, characterized by a side shuffle that moves the body to the left and to the right. In Harry Toddler's single "Dance the Angel" (2002a) the dancer is instructed to "dance the Angel, hail up Moses ... move to left, move to the right," in what Toddler (2002b) has described as a salute to the angels: "If you are not saluting the angels, you are up with the devil angels."

Information technology has introduced concepts that are reflected in the dances called the log on (2001–02) and the internet (2003–04), although the movement of the log on and its description in song are not strictly related to the act of initiating access to a computer. The lyrics by Elephant Man (2001) instruct the dancer to "log on an' step pon chi chi man, dance we a dance an' a burn out a freakie man" with a lift of the leg followed by a twist to the side before stepping down.

Everyday acts can also become more visible and take on new expressive proportions through dance, as in the row like a boat and the fan dem off (both from 2002–03), or the thunderclap and the fall the rain (both from 2003–04). As has been said of the blues, dancehall movement goes back "to the individual, to his completely personal life and death" for its "impetus and emotional meaning" (Baraka 1968, 67).

The messages to be read from dance moves may include tangible sociocultural and anatomical scripts. For example, dances such as the curfew and the drive-by (both from 2002–03) comment on social ills. The movement in curfew represents policemen carrying guns while searching for criminal elements in inner-city communities that come under pressure because of warfare between gangs or political factions. With the characteristic bent knees, sometimes to a very low level resembling the *grand plié*, the dancer walks in a forward motion, with hands mimicking the shape of a rifle, while looking forward and backwards. The get flat dance, popularized by the Bloodfire Posse in the 1980s, through their song of the same name was a forerunner of the curfew. As for the drive-by, while the term first came into common usage in Jamaica after criminals began imitating the drive-by shootings seen on the streets of the United States, and in its films and television shows, the dance itself has more to do with the influx of reconditioned cars in the late 1990s, which gave the middle and lower classes in Jamaica increased access to motor vehicles. The dance moves through a sequence of actions, such as steering, gearing down, turning left, indicating, braking and parking, but not shooting. One can even argue that the drive-by represents the coming of age of car culture in Jamaica.

Since the early 1990s the documentation of these moves has primarily been undertaken, consciously or unconsciously, by videographers. This section has contributed to that documentation with a preliminary record of the dynamic creation of dance moves within a cultural system of embodied elocution that holds dance to be a sixth sense. It is through this sixth sense that many key participants articulate their likes, dislikes, loves, burdens, prejudices and, ultimately, identities. As Elephant Man (2003) eloquently put it, "Dancing is Jamaica's middle name." With this sixth sense Jamaicans distinguish themselves and their culture of embodiment, with its hard locational indices tied to inner-city communities such as Cockburn Pen, Waterhouse, Trench Town and Greenwich Farm. A highly developed urban-centred geography of embodiment, dating as far back as the 1930s with the likes of Kid Harold, has been nurtured in the often voiceless and nameless communities that speak eloquently through their performances. The freedom to move in the dance, to create and maintain spaces of production and consumption simultaneously, constitutes an effective move beyond history, to transform the local present while making an impact on the global. It is this global context that is explored in Chapters 6 and 7.

PERFORMING BOUNDARYLESSNESS

THIS chapter discusses the celebratory ethos of dancehall performance and the way in which it signals an inherent relationship to boundaries. Whether it is the rockaway dance in a music video by Usher, the sampling of a tune by Sean Paul in one of Verizon's advertisement campaigns, the phenomenon of the Japanese dancehall queen, the Danish winner of the inaugural Irie FM Big DJ Break contest in 2006, or the appearance of Passa Passa events in the Eastern Caribbean, there are numerous examples of how aspects of dancehall practice have travelled outside Jamaica.

There is a story here about the place of dancehall and its progenitor, reggae, in popular consciousness and world musicscapes generally. As a contribution to that story, I would like to focus here on three ways in which dancehall evinces boundarylessness. These are dancehall's peregrinations within Jamaica, traversing and transcending class, temporal and spatial boundaries; its migrations outside Jamaica, especially through tours by prominent performers; and the standards and categories created and transcended by key participants. While it is obvious that dancehall's creative home is in the depressed, volatile poverty traps of Kingston's inner cities, it is not obvious how these communities sustain and continually recreate megapopular performance practices such as dancehall. What is even less obvious is the way in which this phenomenon that emerged from the margins has traversed boundaries of the street, the area or community, the nation and the Jamaican Diaspora to occupy global sound- and dancescapes.

BOUNDARYLESSNESS AND BOUNDEDNESS

On Thursday August 31, 2006, a feature on RE TV (Reggae Entertainment Television) opened with cameras in Yokohama, Japan, capturing the fifteenth-anniversary celebrations of Mighty Crown, the top dancehall sound system in that country. Jamaican performers took the stage to mark the event along with notable Japanese DJs Ackee and Saltfish, and Fireball, waving Jamaican and Ethiopian (Rastafari) flags.

The popularity and consumption of Rastafari and dancehall in Japan, documented by Marvin Dale Sterling (2000), were confirmed in this celebration of Mighty Crown's anniversary, which signalled the achievements of uncompromising dancehall perpetuators in Japan and the maturity of Japanese engagement with a globalized dancehall performance culture through its solid fan base, supporting its own clubs, sound systems, dancehall tunes, selectors, clashes, festivals, contests, and DJs (male and female). The commemoration was also linked with, and marked by, the launch of a new line of athletic shoes from Nike, a sign of successful negotiation for corporate sponsorship the likes of which Jamaican dancehall culture has yet to see. Thousands of Japanese patrons turned out to share in the anniversary commemoration, which was observed in Jamaica with an island-wide tour. The consumption and proliferation of dancehall beyond national boundaries, and the return of such images to the Jamaican market, confirm that dancehall circulates simultaneously within local and international spheres, signalling a symbiotic relationship that fuels and maintains the popularity of the practice.

In that same year a DVD titled *It's All About Dancing: A Jamaican Dance-U-Mentary* (Williams 2006), featuring dancehall celebrities such as Ding Dong, John Hype, Sadiki, Latisha, Elephant Man and Beenie Man, was launched by Penalty Recordings and Fine Gold Productions in the United States. A review of this DVD proclaimed that it does for dancehall what David LaChappelle's acclaimed film *Rize* does for krump dancing in Los Angeles. Images of Jamaican dancers, DJs, dance events and celebrations circulate in other ways, formal and informal, that have served to maintain a foundation for cultural consumption beyond Jamaica's borders. One only has to consider the upsurge in the numbers of dancehall songs appearing on the U. S. *Billboard* music charts and their British equivalents since 2000, or the early impact and international fame of DJs such as U Roy, Big Youth or Shine Head. Reggae and, by extension, its progeny, dancehall, form one of the most popular world musics, even, some would argue, the first world music, as evidenced by, among other things, the special place it holds in distinct reggae music racks within record and other music stores around the world. Its popularity is in no small way evidenced by its influence on other music forms such as kwaito in South Africa, hip hop in the United States, trip hop and jungle in Britain, reggaetón in Puerto Rico, makossa in Cameroon and the Democratic Republic of the Congo (formerly Zaïre), or fuji and afrobeat in Nigeria.

Given these developments, there is a strong degree to which "boundarylessness" could be used to classify the dancehall phenomenon. The concept of boundarylessness has been used in the context of organizational culture (see for, example, Halley 1998) and systems research (see, for example, Dempster 2002). Boundary theorists have also emerged within economics, mathematics, law, philosophy, political geography, political science, public administration and psychology, among other disciplines, to establish an interdisciplinary framework. However, I would like to expand "boundarylessness," beyond its use in organizational theory to refer to the blurring of "turf distinctions and established territories or cultures" (Halley 2004, p. 6), to incorporate an expanded conception of boundaries. There are categories, hierarchies, walls, styles, states and borders that create boundaries in specific ways. Such boundaries are created or inherited. Their transcendence is evidenced in the ways in which especially categories and hierarchies are pushed beyond the ordinary to new levels of style, prestige and value.

In acknowledging all this, however, I do not mean to ignore the complex ways in which dancehall's material and cultural production exists in varying states of "boundedness." Several factors converge in dancehall: the centrality of Kingston as the capital city of Jamaica; the geopolitical and aesthetic marginality of dancehall's creative ethos within Kingston's poverty traps and, in many cases, almost uninhabitable spaces; and dancehall's simultaneous centrality to Jamaican national identity. When Barbara Browning's analysis of African Diasporic performance cultures (highlighted in Chapter 1) is applied to dancehall, we can appreciate that it is a "war zone" as much as a party, with "infectious rhythms" and "contagious dances, often characterized as dangerous" (Browning 1998, 1–6). Browning explains that "the conflation of economic, spiritual and sexual exchange ... has allowed for the characterization of Diasporic culture as a chaotic or uncontrolled force, which can only be countered by military or police violence" (Browning 1998, 7). Thus she highlights "chaotic," "erotic" and "volatile" spaces, but also "policed" spaces. Numerous raids on dance events since the 1960s, alongside "sufferation" traps, political banditry, the "donmanship" of area leaders, gangs and the constant struggle to articulate identity, as part of the psychoscape, highlight the level of state policing and its futility within the bounded urban experience. This boundedness, then, is a consideration not just of place, but of psychic, natural, and social space.

Browning's analysis constitutes one part of the profile, especially when considering patrons' encounters with police brutality and violence. However, dancehall has evolved and maintained itself outside the state apparatus even while in tension with it. Its locus of creativity simultaneously announces the very marginality of its citizenry. This betwixt-and-between location, this liminality, is the source of its power. I do not wish to dwell on this liminality, however, except to highlight the point that an appreciation of dancehall necessitates understanding its multiple spaces and relationships, its marginality as well as its centrality. In other words, there is no place/space erasure here, no "cartographic non-existence."

Geographies of dancehall, then, have their articulation at the level of the streets that sound systems, selectors and performing artists traverse to enter the dancehall stage in the processes of production and consumption. To a large extent dancehall practice is transformed in the movement from street (community) to staged (commercial) events inside Jamaica, and transformed once again on international tours. Although international tours employ much the same commercial mode of performance as that which is visible at the local level in stage shows, these do not represent core practices in dancehall culture. In community events the emphasis is on the sound system and the playing of recorded music, but on tour the emphasis shifts to a one-dimensional focus on the live artist. In some senses, then, tours constitute a return to the roots of dancehall practice, before technological and commercial advances precipitated the recordings that have largely replaced live performances in dance halls. One important difference is in the spaces used and in related issues such as the scale of events, with all its effects on patterns of land use and infrastructural development.

On the other hand, there are important dimensions of community events that cannot enter the arena of stage shows or tours, where the focus is on the proscenium stage and the emphasis is on the recording artists billed to perform. In street events the emphasis is much more diverse and, significantly, it is delinked from the recording artist's presence. In this sense, international tours do not facilitate the performance of some aspects of the dancehall space as it exists in inner-city Kingston and in Jamaica more broadly. These include aspects that have become critical to the practice, such as dance and other elements involved in the preparation, performance and disengagement processes around events (highlighted in Chapters 4 and 5).

BUJU BANTON ON TOUR

Touring by dancehall performers offers one example of the way in which boundarylessness is manifested in dancehall, that is, the way in which it mediates local, regional and global zones in a variety of ways. Buju Banton's role as a translocal and transnational actor within the performance geography of dancehall offers an example of how artists contribute to the maintenance and proliferation of dancehall practice inside but, more critically, beyond national borders.

Buju Banton (2007) has acknowledged the local beginnings of touring. In an interview on Irie FM about his early experiences in dancehall he recalled the days of riding all night on the trucks that transported the sound system's boom boxes, and sleeping among them before and after performances, which may or may not have provided the highly anticipated career break on the popular dancehall microphone for the aspiring DJ. Trucks such as those mentioned were the means by which many early DJs such as U Roy and King Stitt toured throughout Jamaica, making the micro-journey of apprenticeship in preparation for the macro-journey of international touring.

My own personal journey with Buju Banton began to take shape in 1994 at the Superjam event in Kingston. I was so impressed by this DJ, whom I had been listening for more than five years, and so captivated by the performance that I sought to meet the man behind the awesome talent. Later, in October 1995, on a sojourn of my own in the United States, I met Buju again in Washington, DC, where he had arrived on a promotional tour for his album *Til Shiloh*. I was able to participate by travelling to and from the performance site at Howard University with Buju's entourage, and I experienced the performance from the vantage point of the stage.

The experience lingered with me and, through reflection, I developed an interest in the experience of touring for the artist and his (or her) team.

According to Donovan Germain, Managing Director of Penthouse Records, and Buju Banton's manager from 1990 to 2008, a tour typically lasts longer than one week, during which the artist and his team perform for patrons in specified locations outside their home country. A manager such as Germain typically starts the tour, stays for two weeks, departs, depending on the locations, and then returns in the final two weeks. The manager's role is to organize, oversee operations, collect money and ensure that contractual obligations are met. The road manager is the person in charge of the tour. In Buju Banton's case his team on tour can comprise fourteen persons, including the management and support personnel such as a chef, technical staff, backup singers, dancers and band members.

Buju started touring with the release of his first album *Mr. Mention* (1990) and has continued extensive touring with the release of his subsequent albums, taking in the United States, Europe, Israel, Zimbabwe, Ghana, Kenya and South Africa. Beyond the initial entry into a country by air, movement into various cities is mostly in self-contained recreational buses that are equipped with essential amenities. A tour within the United States alone can take two months, and it is not unusual for a tour to cover between seventeen and thirty-two of the fifty states, and up to fifty cities in total, as shown in the schedules for two of Buju's tours (see Tables 6.1 and 6.2). Tours within Europe also make financial sense, because there are major concentrations of reggae and dancehall fans in such countries as Germany, France, Italy and Sweden. A European tour can thus cover up to thirty cities or other sites in ten or more countries (see Table 6.3).

TABLE 6.1
Schedule for Buju Banton's Friends for Life Tour, United States, 2003

March 13	Hammerstein Ballroom, New York City
March 14	West Indian Club, Hartford, CT
March 15	The Trocadero, Philadelphia, PA
March 16	Club Conduit, Trenton, NJ
March 18	Lupos, Providence, RI
March 19	Higher Ground, Winooski, VT
March 20	The Chance, Poughkeepsie, NY
March 21	Club Eclipse, Newark, NJ
March 22	Crossroads, Bladensburg, MD
March 23	AT&T Amphitheater, Miami, FL
March 25	The Odeon, Cleveland, OH
March 26	Brickyard, Columbus, OH
March 27	Bluebird Theater, Bloomington, IN
March 28	Bogarts, Cincinnati, OH
March 29	House of Blues, Chicago, IL
March 30	First Avenue, Minneapolis, MN
April 1	Aggie Theater, Fort Collins, CO
April 2	Fox Theater, Boulder, CO
April 3	Port'o'call, Salt Lake City, UT
April 4	Crystal Ballroom, Portland, OR
April 5	Commodore Ballroom, Vancouver, BC
April 7	The Firehouse, Seattle, WA
April 8	McDonald Theater, Eugene, OR
April 10	Mateel Center, Redway, CA
April 11	The Avalon, San Francisco, CA
April 12	Catalyst, Santa Cruz, CA
April 13	House of Blues, Los Angeles, CA
April 15	Belly Up Tavern, Solana Beach, CA
April 16	Bash on Ash, Tempe, AZ
April 17	Sunshine Theater, Albuquerque, NM
April 18	Palm Beach, Dallas, TX
April 19	Club Negril, Houston, TX
April 20	Flamingo Cantina, Austin, TX
April 21	House of Blues, New Orleans, LA
April 23	TBA, Tallahassee, FL
April 24	Plush, Jacksonville, FL
April 25	Fuel, Tampa, FL
April 26	The Tabernacle, Atlanta, GA
April 27	Hard Rock Café, Orlando, FL

April 29	Music Farm, Charleston, SC
April 30	Lincoln Theater or Cats, Carrboro, NC
May 1	Tremont Music Hall, Charlotte, NC
May 2	Norva Theater, Norfolk, VA
May 3	DC Live, Washington, DC
May 4	The Palladium, New Rochelle, NY
May 5	Toads Place, New Haven, CT
May 7	Downtown, Farmingdale, NY
May 8	Ponash Ballroom, Springfield, MA
May 9	Water Street Music Hall, Rochester, NY
May 10	WBLI Show

Source: Penthouse Records

TABLE 6.2
Schedule for Buju Banton's Too Bad Tour, United States, 2006

September 12	Blind Pig, Ann Arbor, MI
September 13	House of Blues, Chicago
September 14	Bluebird Theater, Bloomington, IN
September 15	Annie's, Cincinnati, OH
September 16	Alrosa Villa, Columbus, OH
September 17	First Avenue, Minneapolis, MN
September 20	Fox Theater, Boulder, CO
September 21	Belly Up Tavern, Aspen, CO
September 22	Suede, Park City, UT
September 25	Crystal Ballroom, Portland, OR
September 26	Nightlight, Bellingham, WA
September 27	Neumos, Seattle, WA
September 28	Wow Hall, Eugene, OR
September 29	Mateel Community Center, Redway, CA
September 30	Mezzanine, San Francisco, CA
October 1	The Catalyst, Santa Cruz, CA
October 2	Slo Brewing, San Luis Obispo, CA
October 3	Century Club, Los Angeles, CA
October 4	4th & B, San Diego, CA
October 6	Sunshine Theater, Albuquerque, NM
October 7	Palm Beach, Dallas, TX
October 8	Matrix, Houston, TX
October 10	House of Blues, New Orleans

October 11	Floyd's Music Store, Tallahassee, FL
October 12	Plush, Jacksonville, FL
October 14	Music Farm, Charleston, SC
October 15	Lincoln Theater, Raleigh, NC
October 16	Ziggy's, Winston–Salem, NC
October 17	Starr Hill Music Hall, Charlottesville, VA
October 19	Sonar, Baltimore, MD
October 20	Terrace Ballroom, Newark, NJ
October 25	B. B. King's Blues Club, New York City

Source: Gargamel Music

TABLE 6.3
Schedule of Buju Banton's Rasta Got Soul Tour, Europe, 2009

June 16	La Vapeur, Dijon, France
June 17	Rock School Barbey, Bordeaux, France
June 18	Vooruit, Ghent, Belgium
June 19	Demand Night Club, Coventry, United Kingdom
June 20	Club Society, Huddersfield, United Kingdom
June 21	Stratford Rex, London
June 23	Demode Club, Bari, Italy
June 25	Live Club, Milan, Italy
June 26	Volkshaus Zürich, Zürich, Switzerland
June 27	Real Beat Festival, Česka Lipa, Czech Republic
June 28	A38 Ship, Budapest, Hungary
June 30	Rockstore, Montpellier, France
July 1	Joy Eslava, Madrid, Spain
July 2	Apolo, Barcelona, Spain
July 3	Festival Delta Tejo, Lisbon, Portugal
July 4	Summer Jam, Cologne, Germany
July 5	Melkweg, Amsterdam, The Netherlands
July 6	Pard Van Troje, The Hague, The Netherlands
July 8	Rototom Sunsplash, Udine, Italy
July 9	Tribuhne Kireau, Vienna, Austria
July 10	Backstage, Munich, Germany
July 11	Vistula River Open Air, Płock, Poland
July 12	Open Air Festival, London
July 13	Salle Robien, St.-Brieuc, France
July 14	Elysée Montmartre, Paris, France
July 16	Theatre Antique de Vienne, Vienne, France

July 17	Open Air Festival, Bournezeau, France
July 18	Stade de La Paguette, St.-Julien-en-Genevois, France
July 19	Dour Festival, Dour, Belgium
July 21	Île du Gaou, Six-Fours-les-Plages, France
July 23	Kafe Antzokia, Bilbao, Spain
July 24	TBA, Cartagena, Spain
July 25	Estadio Municipal de Futbol, Marbella, Spain
August 7	WaMu Theater at Madison Square Garden, New York City

Source: Buju Banton's MySpace page

In particular, tour schedules reveal the crucial role of festivals in the promotion and consumption of Jamaican music. For example, Buju's tour of Europe in 2009 took in the Rototom Sunsplash in Udine, Italy, which is a direct spin-off from the Reggae Sunsplash festivals staged in Jamaica from 1978 to 1999 and revived in 2006. The spread of reggae festivals has effectively broadened the market for entertainers by increasing the number of engagements they can secure abroad: more than 153 festivals are listed in the *Reggae Festival Guide* for 2009.

In response to questions about the process of preparing for international tours, Buju Banton cited Psalm 27, verse 1: "The Lord is my light and my salvation, whom shall I fear?" Such spiritual guidance may sustain self-empowerment at the personal level, but touring represents a physically demanding means of crossing local, national and transnational performance boundaries. International touring has also posed important challenges for Buju Banton's understanding of performance and spiritual wellbeing.

One important shift came during his tour of Europe in 1993–94 when, fresh out of Jamaica and bringing lyrics pregnant with sexuality, he witnessed the expectant crowd's appreciation of exemplary reggae performers such as Burning Spear, Lee "Scratch" Perry and Bim Sherman. On one occasion Bim Sherman's crowd appeal left Buju feeling so befuddled that he began to question his own musical prowess and lyrical potency. It was only after experiencing several more challenging incidents and receiving advice from Perry that he cemented his goal to be as compelling a performer as the likes of Burning Spear. Then, as he was focusing on improving his musical product with content that had what Perry called "a humanistic approach," another enduring shift began to take shape after he experienced head and knee injuries that he ascribed to spiritual wickedness in the world. On the occasion of the launch of his album *Rasta Got Soul* at the Mona Campus of the University of the West Indies on April 22, 2009, he explained,

> Bible? We never even into that, we go a road go play music and no know seh spiritual wickedness out there a wait on we, but this was my first confrontation out there, 'cause we no do nobody nutten. Things just a happen to me, me head bus', me foot swell big, unexplained!"

Twelve Bibles were requested from affiliates in New York and issued to the team on tour. Not only did Buju himself experience challenges, but so did members of his entourage, who were hospitalized with mysterious occurrences such as the heart condition experienced by a keyboard player while in Paris. Buju also recalls being booked for a performance on the Champs Elysée in Paris when the group was housed in a hotel next to a cemetery. Later, when he was performing at Elysée Montmartre, a most unusual occurrence took him by surprise. According to Buju (1999), his body became weak after he was touched by what seemed to be an apparition after strong mediations for spiritual centring—"a powerful chant"—before the performance. The product of these trials and the process of overcoming them was the song "Til Shiloh," the title track on Buju Banton's third and most popular album. It is clear that, after Buju did not receive the crowd response he desired in Europe in 1993–94, he made up for it in subsequent tours built around the moulding and delivery of a solid musical product with international appeal.

One tangible dimension of the translocal feature of dancehall performance on tour is the composition of the audiences that Jamaican DJs perform for. The producer–manager Donovan Germain reports that the composition of audiences at venues in the United States varies significantly from region to region: audiences in a Midwestern state such as Idaho may be 90 percent white, but audiences in New York City tend to be 90 percent black and those in New Mexico 90 percent Indian (Native American). Artists such as Buju Banton understand that, regardless of audience composition, touring maintains the artist's career in the same way that a recording can. Bob Marley and The Wailers were almost constantly on tour until only shortly before his death in 1980, laying the foundations for the enduring popularity of his music. It is apparent from the tour schedules shown here that popular Jamaican acts still have to maintain a balance between local and foreign appearances, with tours allowing immersion in contact with foreign audiences over relatively short periods.

STONE LOVE AND TONY MATTERHORN

In order to capture some of the central issues discussed above and to further emphasize the experience of space, I shall use the examples of the development of the sound system Stone Love and the experiences of the selector Tony Matterhorn, not in a music-centred analysis but in a spatiocentric one, based on interviews with Winston Powell (2002), Señor Daley of the Klassique sound system (2003) and Tony Matterhorn (2007), in addition to secondary sources and participant observation.

Stone Love spans the development of some critical aspects of dancehall: the centrality of downtown venues; the re-emergence of street venues in uptown Kingston; the movement of the DJ from dance halls to recording studios, television shows and music videos, and thus the international arena; and the shift from street dances to "big dances" with corporate sponsorship and commercial success surpassed only by that of large stage shows such as Reggae Sumfest. Stone Love began as a small-scale sound system playing at parties and had to ground itself within the downtown space in order to attract a large following, because Winston Powell always had ambitions for making it big. Jones Town was where they made their breakthrough from being branded as centred on American R&B to being known as a community-centred sound system. Improved technology, the skill of a new selector, and the groundings at Joyce's Hot Spot and Cherry's Bar, near and within Jones Town respectively, were important factors in this breakthrough. Jones Town is demographically illustrative of an inner-city community, a space in which the trappings of a metropolitan musical sense had to be shed for the sound system to gain local and later wider international appeal.

Once Powell's sound system had acquired a following, new opportunities materialized at playout venues with increased demand for the sound. As their popularity grew, however, so did police intervention, because dance events spilled onto the street, inviting attention and complaints. Moving through venues from Jones Town to Cross Roads, New Kingston and Halfway Tree, Stone Love climbed to "champion sound" status when it settled into a longstanding Thursday night playout at House of Leo in the Halfway Tree area in the mid-1980s. With a weekly local calendar, Stone Love was in demand. With more staff, kilowattage of sound, boxes, a playing style that was different from other sound systems, and links uptown and downtown, Stone Love changed the face of dancehall, simply by capitalizing on the ghetto and technology as vehicles to propel its capacity beyond that of other systems by the early 1990s. Eventually its sound capacity called one and all to join its dancehall calendar and be baptized into the fullness of its love. This baptismal resonance is confirmed by the late dancer Bogle, for whom church and school were replaced by dancehall: "He had to go every day to mark present" (Reyes 1993, 71).

It was in 1988 that Stone Love earned a commitment to play in Canada, on the first of its many forays outside Jamaica. Since then Stone Love has advanced the image and popularity of dancehall internationally, moving it outside the local realm to an international and transnational one. As Louis Chude-Sokei (1997) suggests, dancehall has negotiated a trans-Atlantic Diasporic space in which the celebration of the local has surpassed, if only superficially, the appeal of an African past and present reified in the culture-centred music of Rastafari and Rastafari-influenced reggae artists. The movement of Stone Love's equipment, audio and (eventually video) recordings, fans, specials and dub plates, and personnel from uptown to downtown, then out of town and internationally, has solidified its high levels of appeal.

Stone Love's space in the dancehall is also a political one, in the sense that they operate within and across certain borders that have to be carefully negotiated because they can mean life or death for a sound system. In the early 1990s Stone Love took the decision not to play tunes that incited gang feuds or "matie fights" (fights between women over men) or promoted gun talk. In addition, Stone Love has helped to maintain the standards set by the Sound System Association of Jamaica for democratizing the business. This has resulted in appearances at venues stipulated by the Association to break the monopoly of some systems over particular venues, in some instances within volatile areas.

One of the crucial lessons Winston Powell learned early within the sound system business was about the need to keep one's past firmly in the conscious present. This necessitates the capacity to accept invitations to play for and to promoters and fans who were there at Stone Love's inception. They cannot be left behind, because they were crucial to the establishment of the sound system from the start. Stone Love therefore acquired and established a new oldies sound system to navigate old and new spaces at the same time. This has a bearing on the partisan political trends in the business as well, since running different units under the name Stone Love has allowed the sound system to play at different venues in one night, sometimes for warring factions.

Stone Love's basic development reveals the depth and breadth of dancehall space, in addition to the ways in which dancehall perpetuators continuously negotiate and navigate a variety of spaces, policed and contested, old and new, local and transnational. Theirs is a significant achievement, which helps to solidify the sound system's honorary title, "The Immortal Stone Love." This "immortality" is inextricably linked to dancehall's identity and its rubric of multiple spatialities.

Beyond sound systems such as Stone Love, there are freelance selectors, with reputations rivalling those of sound systems, through whom dancehall performance has also toured. One such selector is Tony Matterhorn, a recording artist in his own right who has won four world championships for clashing, and is highly respected both locally and internationally. His travels have taken him to all the islands of the Caribbean, as well as Britain, the United States and Japan, a country that he has characterized (2007) as an intense dancehall site. He often travels solo by train or bus on arrival in metropolitan centres. Matterhorn's brand of the dancehall performance aesthetic is embodied and mobile, with large components being in the realm of attitude, personality and skill. The place of selectors such as Tony Matterhorn within the globalized dancehall performance geography—as intermediaries through whom dancehall increases its capital base for reinvestment into communities of adherents far removed from the locations being toured—has to be appropriately acknowledged.

DANCEHALL QUEENS BEYOND NATIONAL BOUNDARIES

There is another dimension to the unboundedness of the dancehall phenomenon. Jamaican dancehall queens such as Stacey and Carlene have made an impression on the wider world through their translocal practice. The dancehall space, while localized in focus and character, continues to shift scenes in the context of touring, for example, but, more importantly, it continues to attract international attention and participation on home soil through dance. Dancehall queen contests have gained popularity in Jamaica since the first annual International Dancehall Queen Contest was staged by Big Head Promotions at Montego Bay in 1996, and the phenomenon has transcended national boundaries. Corporate sponsorship since 2004 has given the contest financial injections that have helped to secure its place and popularity among dancers around the world. By 2002 it was clear that a local phenomenon had been transformed into a transnational one when (as mentioned in Chapter 5) the competition was won by a Japanese contestant. Jamaicans no longer held a monopoly on the practice that they had invented and popularized. By 2006 contestants were coming from the United States, Canada and Europe, as well as from Japan and from other nations in the Caribbean, while the eleventh contest,

6.1 Swedish Dancehall fans at Passa Passa
Source: Sonjah Stanley Niaah

staged on July 28, 2007, also attracted entrants from Austria, Estonia and Germany, and was won by a Canadian, Maude "Moo Moo" Francato from Quebec City, on her third attempt at the title and amid some controversy (see Wright 2007).

This international event has also spawned contests in the countries that the contestants come from, many of which have an established presence on the web, with, for example, MySpace pages. A recent survey of the international scene revealed dancehall queen contests in at least six locations in the United States (Atlanta, Brooklyn, Charlotte, Chicago, Detroit and Florida) and in four countries in Europe (Italy, Germany, Belgium and Poland), as well as in Australia and Japan. The Australian Dancehall Queen Contest is a national event featuring heats in Melbourne, Sydney, Perth, Brisbane and Adelaide before the national finals.

DANCEHALL IN JAPAN

Perhaps the most interesting variation on the dancehall queen phenomenon is the Japanese representation of Jamaican dancehall. There is a groundswell of Japanese interest in Jamaican dancehall that began in the early 1990s (see Sterling 2000 and Minako Kurasawa's documentary film *Born in JAHpan* from 2007). Girls in Japan are seen to depart from traditional roles when they choose to study and perform reggae dancing or dancehall moves. Some take the skill of reggae dancing seriously enough to teach it in dance studios, such as Groove Foundation or Body Beat, to perform in clubs, such as Club Es, Club Unity and Okadayo in Tokyo, or to enter dancehall queen contests, both in Japan and in Jamaica.

Reggae dancing became popular in Japan after dancehall music and documentary videos about it began entering the country in the early 1990s. The dance style is seen by many Japanese as a tool for enjoyment, freedom, courtship, releasing the shackles of tradition and expressing power, particularly sexual power, where this is mostly lacking for Japanese women. In 2006 five experienced Japanese reggae dancers entered the International Dancehall Queen Competition, of whom one was placed in the top three and the others returned home, disappointed but vowing to train harder for their return to the dancehall Mecca. In 2008 the competition had representation from six Japanese contestants. Their coordinator, Miyoko Walcott, could be seen with the list of contestants, following the progress of her entrants with a keen eye. So popular is her role in the contest that a regular attendee, Lennox Lewis, was seen greeting her and the team. Years of investment reaped significant dividends in 2008 when Walcott's entrant

6.2 Japanese Dancehall fans at Passa Passa
Source: Sonjah Stanley Niaah

Nami Crissy Kerisu gained third place on her fourth attempt. She was once again overtaken, however, this time by two American contestants, Michelle Young from Boston and Moika Stapley from Los Angeles, who took the titles of Queen and first runner-up respectively.

Ordinary Japanese citizens are also visible in everyday dancehall events. The uncompromising passion and enthusiasm among Japanese lovers of dancehall is evident from watching reggae fans at events such as Japansplash, which was modelled on the popular Jamaican festival Reggae Sunsplash. Tens of thousands of Japanese patrons turn out to hear the latest reggae and dancehall acts, along with performances by Japanese DJs.

FROM BOGLE TO USAIN BOLT

Perhaps the most exhilarating example of the journey across boundaries through dance is the trajectory from the dancemaster Bogle (see Chapter 5) to the sprinter Usain Bolt.

Bogle's contribution made an important statement about dancehall geography, history and identity. He stood on the shoulders of earlier dancers, such as Kid Harold, Pam Pam or Baskin, in the long trajectory of dancehall choreography and cultural heroes, but distinguished himself as the life of the dancehall party for several years through his participation in every major event. Dancing kept him out of a life of badness, and many have emulated his example. Most notably, his dance creations, alongside the rhythms he created, sustained increased levels of popularity and interest in dancehall during the two important high points, first between 1989 and 1994, and then between 1999 and 2004. His was and is the quintessential dancehall spirit, that which is going to be expressed by any means necessary as long as music and dance are its media. In the words of one who commented on Bogle at his funeral: "Fi mi, Bogle nuh gawn, because im stan' up pon di foreparents' back, im leave a legacy."

Bogle's legacy can be seen not only in the ways in which protégés have expanded the dance repertoire he left, but in the way in which his contributions have ignited those who have performed Jamaican dance moves on the largest world stages. Here I refer specifically to the Jamaican sprinter and world record phenomenon Usain Bolt, who allows us to consider deeper dimensions of a despatialized dancehall that has democratized itself and a performance ethos beyond Jamaican borders, with Bogle and his dancing disciples as major pillars. Bolt's performance at the Olympic Games in Beijing in 2008 made an important statement about Jamaica's identity, and its geopolitical and cultural distinctiveness. When Bolt performed the no linga and gully creepa moves, among others, during his victory laps, with several millions watching, the Jamaican dance floor became delocalized in its transplantation to Asian soil, where spectators momentarily became participants in the critical journey of largely lower-class dance pioneers such as Baskin, Persian the Cat, Pam Pam and Bogle.

Images of Bolt dancing as part of his athletic training routine as well as recreation are now used by the German shoe and sportswear company Puma AG. With fans eager to take photos and interact with Bolt, he was moved to ask for two hours in which dancing alone would be the focus to achieve heightened celebration after the hard work of training for and succeeding in the Olympics. Sealing his place as a Jamaican ambassador at large, Bolt succeeded in taking the Jamaican dance repertoire and performance aesthetic to the world.

The movement of Jamaican cultural identity across borders to sites as far away as East Asia provides ample evidence of this global transplantation of Jamaica's dance repertoire. Copeland Forbes, veteran promoter of reggae and dancehall, and former road manager of Peter Tosh, has disclosed that in August 2008, during a reggae/dancehall tour he promoted with Marcia Griffiths, Chuck Fenda, Sanchez, Voicemail, Bushman, Flourgon and the Stone Love sound system, special efforts were made at events in Nagoya in Japan, Ho Chi Minh City and Hanoi in Vietnam, and Samui Island in Thailand to please fans who had become familiar with Jamaica's dancing acumen through seeing Usain Bolt. Forbes stated in a television interview (2008) that, almost at the same time as Bolt was releasing the moves in Beijing, he had to demonstrate the no linga and gully creepa dances to dancehall fans across Asia.

Arguably, Bolt represented many ancestors, including cultural heroes such as the late dancemaster Bogle, who was never celebrated as a dancehall king until after his death, as well as Jamaica's National Hero Paul Bogle (c. 1820–1865), who fought for the poor black population but was defeated and hanged after leading the Morant Bay Rebellion. Metaphorically, then, Bolt's performance, which was received as the work of a hero by many Jamaicans, can be read as the fulfilment of national pride and agency, especially for the poor, who have been the creators of rebellions and performance cultures alike. Bolt represents the bodies that, through contestation, exploitation, discrimination and oppression, preserve themselves to tell tales of survival, tales of history and agency, which transcend time in their linking of old and new ways of toiling for freedom, while creating space and identity through performance on local yet transnational dance floors. Bolt's performance at the Olympics and at the homecoming celebrations following the Games was consistent with dancemaster Bogle's vision. Like Bogle, Bolt listened and responded with his feet to maintain dancehall dominance through dance. Bogle wore the attitude of dancehall and so did Bolt, who has extended Bogle's relevance through his performance of dances created by Bogle and his protégés such as Ice, creator of the gully creepa. Erasing the memory of marginalization, if only temporarily, such moments highlight the complexity that is dancehall, and popular culture more broadly, as well as the dynamic of transcending margins.

VIDEO LIGHT AND SPECTACLE

The role of the video light in the creation and maintenance of spectacle is an underresearched aspect of dancehall (see Crary 2005). By "spectacle" I mean any attempt to achieve a striking visual effect, through display or performance, beyond what is considered normative for a participant or an onlooker. Such attempts are often judged to be merely superficial and distracting, but they have important associations with the mass media, with consumer and celebrity culture, and, more broadly, with the psychogeography of the city.

The video light—a spotlight used to illuminate an object or event that is to be captured by a video camera—features prominently in the dancehall space, holding a degree of responsibility for the transmission of images beyond their place of origin. Within dancehall the phenomenon of the video light first came to prominence through the work of the early videographers, starting with Jack Sowah, who stood alone in the late 1980s as he recorded the happenings at dance events both large and small. Today the video light is present at many dance events, both at home in Jamaica and abroad. Footage recorded at events in Jamaica is mostly amateur, though it may often be sold to fans, while footage generated by prominent professional videographers such as Knight Rider or Scrappy is packaged for commercial distribution both in Kingston and other places in Jamaica, and in metropolitan centres such as London, New York or Tokyo. Generally, dancehall videotapes and, increasingly, DVDs circulate, at prices ranging between five and twenty US dollars, in those countries where reggae and dancehall are already established as popular forms, such as Germany, Brazil, South Africa, Kenya, Canada and Japan. More and more footage is also becoming available globally through general-interest websites, such as YouTube or MySpace, as well as specialist ones, such as DancehallTV.com.

Cameramen typically enter the dance space at or around the moment of transition from the "early dance" to more intense dancing, often marked by the presence of celebrity dancers, promoters, dons,

DJs and other dancehall notables. Once the cameraman has determined that there is something to be captured, the lights are turned on and the patrons vie for the spotlight, through their performances. The video light determines the space of activity, as accomplished or celebrity dancers often command its attention, while others compete to stay within its range. Many patrons attend events after experimenting with various devices, especially adornment, and during the event they seek to please the camera with emotionally charged vocalizations, such as "bigging up" their babyfathers or babymothers, or other performance modes such as dancing or "profiling," in order to command the attention of the videographer and his light. A typical dancehall event, whether community-based or commercial, has one to four cameras operating, depending on the scale of the performance. The making of videos has become such an integral part of the performance that finding an event in the Kingston Metropolitan Area without any camera present may be close to impossible.

Discussion forums and newspaper reports have documented some of the anxieties over the introduction of the video camera into the performance space, with claims being made that some women make greater efforts to attract the video light than they do to attract men, or dance less in order to continue looking fresh for the camera, or even get into fights over their positions in relation to the video light. One article in the *Daily Star* (see Evans 2007) reported,

> Some female dancers who attend street sessions like Passa Passa, Dutty Fridaze and other weekly dances have been known to go the extra mile to push their competition out of the spotlight, and have videographers and cameramen focus their lens on them.... [Some women have] climbed on roof tops, stripped down to their underwear, and others, without underwear, were clad in short skirts, wining on their head tops and assuming other sexually suggestive positions on the ground.

An important dimension to many of these claims and reports is the role of the mostly male videographer, his gaze, and the narratives he produces by editing the recorded images. The video light is both a useful technology and a figure, a personality, an instigator, so to speak, that creates the need and desire for recognition, while participating in preserving images of performers that can later be consumed by those who are far removed from them. There is thus a complex relationship between the videographer, the spectacular subject/object and the spectator who views the process or the final product. All are jointly authors, taking some control of the image, its representation and its ultimate marketing.

There is also a sense, however, in which the product is constructed by the community and belongs to that community. There is joint participation and ownership, as common identities and common interests build on each other. Through a range of media, from cursory references in songs to treatises on the video light by artists such as Frisco Kidd, TOK, Elephant Man, Lexxus, Macka Diamond or Mad Cobra, the dancehall "massive" (community) is encouraged to observe certain norms and rules governing readiness for, and consumption of, the video light. There are discourses linked to mature debates about economic security, "prime time" focus or centre stage appearance, and sexuality and performance, especially of females.

For example, in his single "Likkle and Cute" the DJ Frisco Kidd (1997) chastises a woman who has not taken enough care to maintain the health and strength of her vagina, and advances a discourse about the "good body gyal" who has no need to use alum to reduce the elasticity of her pudenda, as those who engage in too much sexual activity do. He further lauds a women whose pudenda have not been stretched to the capacity of an elastic band:

> Certain gyal ah walk inna video light crew
> And every man dun know she nah no glue
> She coulda have AIDS cause she no stop catch flu
> And tek man like Burger King drive-thru.

In "Make it Clap (Remix)" Busta Rhymes, Sean Paul and Spliff Star Star (2002) highlight the role of the video light as an apparatus for achieving "prime time" visibility, referring to "Dawn and Karen or Angie and Patsy inna di video light just like a big Sunday matinee." In other words, such is the power of the phenomenon of the video light that it can transform the scene of an event to proportions as grand as those of a Sunday matinee.

In the single "Taxi Fare" (2006) Mr. Vegas explains that walking from Asylum to Papine after clubbing is not right, since all "hot girls" should have their taxi fares to get home after partying. Hot girls should not have to walk or solicit rides to get to the dance event either, since they should have the means to use reliable and secure transportation. All the girls with their own taxi fares can therefore take centre stage:

> A who mi hear seh come a dancehall and a hype
> And don't even have a fifty fi buy a Sprite
> Gal, yuh have yuh money, then tek di video light
> And nuff a dem don't know how dem a reach home tonight.

The DJ Mad Cobra (2005) also adds to the database of lyrics about the video light with his song "Last Year Clothes," which contrasts the independent and fashionable dancehall woman whom the video light singles out—"Nah fi find di video man, di video man find yuh"—to women who are not ready to be illuminated by it:

> Cut inna face gal, nuh ready fi di video yet
> Two-colour face gal, nuh ready fi di video yet
> Nuh watch yuh mate, she nuh ready fi di video yet
> She nuh ready, she nuh ready fi di video yet.
>
> Beer bokkle shape, nuh ready fi di video yet
> Borrow clothes gal, dem nuh ready fi di video yet
> Repeat clothes gal, nuh ready fi di video yet
> Dash wey belly gal, dem nuh ready fi di video.

In "Grindacologist," a song by Beenie Man (2004) (featuring Kymberli), the DJ evokes much the same contrast:

> Gimme some a dem gal weh ever look bright,
> Face ever ready, coochie ever tight,
> Always ready, wah! fi di video light,
> Hotty hotty girl a fi mi type.

"Hotta" by TOK (featuring Maestro) is another single that highlights the video light as an important dimension of dancehall performance. The song speaks of a woman who has scars on her skin, a big belly and worn-out shoes: "Gal, yuh hotta, step out inna di video light yuh run Passa Passa, some gal a fi go stay behind di camera like Kassa, yuh man still in love like Sean Paul and Sasha."

As these examples from song lyrics suggest, the making of "community music videos" (as tapes or DVDs of amateur footage are known) often requires the participation of, mostly, women freely displaying intimate body parts and emotions. This focuses attention on the dancehall woman's agency in scripting her role in dancehall as a queen, or at least a would-be queen. Although males have gained access to the mostly female-dominated video light, especially with the emergence since 2003 of male dancers and crews, their place as dancers is vulnerable in a society where narratives of the construction of normative masculinity are still primarily centred around minimal display of the dancing male body, which is stigmatized as homoerotic.

The use of the term "community music videos" also calls attention to the way in which the video light has become part of a community-building strategy, occasioned by its role in the projection of community life within and outside dancehall. The video light did not exist thirty-five years ago, when Orlando Patterson (1974) recommended to the Jamaican government that every community should have its own sound system, but his reasoning can be applied to the video light too: that dancehall activities should be seen as part of the systematic construction of "bonds of solidarity" or economic potential, and encouraged by the authorities, especially in order to help young men to occupy themselves gainfully rather than engage in deviant behaviour. Today the video light is an integral element in dancehall culture, forming part of the mechanism for projecting communities and their citizenry beyond boundaries in concrete ways.

The entrance of the video camera and the video light has also assisted in the transformation of the ordinary into the fantastic through the adoption of camera-ready masks. The video light has played a significant role in shining selves into stardom and the celebration of personhood in an urban context where the phenomena of "sufferation" and the constant struggle to articulate identity are parts of the psychoscape. The alter-egos enacted through the wearing of masks are defined by dress (new outfit, nothing borrowed), hairstyles (wigs, braids) and behaviours (language, "profile") within the social celebration. Masks have to be contextualized, therefore, as tools for self-aggrandizement, in a tradition that has such antecedents as the Set Girls and Jonkonnu performances of the 19th century. The wearing of a different mask at each dance event is a criterion for attending the event and is seen as a means of guaranteeing the eventual broadcast of a well-worked-out visual product: the spectacle.

The video light shines people into recognition within and outside their communities, as videotapes and DVDs circulate within the local, national and international communities. It affords a certain "prime time" visibility, as well as status and access to resources outside the mainstream. Linked to the manifestation of the video light in dancehall, therefore, is the idea of the celebrity, in some instances created, but certainly maintained, by the video light. Constructions of certain types of celebrity under the video light are noteworthy, suggesting that modifications need to be made in the definition of the celebrity or star as a person given recognition for special achievements, especially in sport or entertainment, as typified by the film star (Turner 2004, 3–4). The mass appeal of such celebrities, and the consumption of facts and images connected to them, defines the sense of excessiveness that seems to attach to the development of such figures, to the point where it can be argued that "The cultural function of the celebrity today contains significant parallels with the functions normally ascribed to religion" (Turner 2004, 6). Analysis of celebrities has included ascriptions of godlike qualities to them, as well as anxiety about their effect on audiences (see also Chevannes 1999), and about the fickleness, faddishness and artificiality of the construction of celebrity itself, above all through the mass media and their role in the manufacturing and marketing of celebrities.

However, there are important differences in the way in which celebrity is produced and consumed in the Jamaican popular performance space, especially around dancehall culture. Many dancers, DJs, producers, promoters and other dancehall celebrities have their roots on the socioeconomic margins, and their rise to prominence has taken place beyond the reach of the mass media. Their fame is built on a significantly smaller scale than that which is generally the focus of analysis and criticism, requiring smaller inputs of technology, finance, production and marketing. The distribution of news and images is often centred in the small communities these dancehall celebrities originate from, even if these images then transcend those spaces. Especially at the level of the local community, these celebrities erupt into prominence, unlike the star who takes time to develop. For example, a dancer can reveal a new dance move and achieve community fame overnight. The achievement of such a dancer brings attention to the self, the dance and the community all at once, as it is made known through networks of fans, community media and international circulation. Here there are no strategic commercial plans backed by specialists in marketing and promotion, nor is there any corporate sponsorship. There are distinctions and modifications to be made, then, in analyzing the different roles of mass media and alternative media, or of professional image-makers and amateur image-makers, in the production of celebrities; the varying impact of the public performances of celebrities, as opposed to their private lives; their different relationships to audiences and fans; the incorporation and differential use of the video light and other technologies, ranging from the cheap and portable to the expensive and, for most people, unobtainable; and the ways in which different kinds of celebrities articulate constructions of national, gender, class and sexual identities, and function as local, regional or international "brands."

Jamaica's place on the music video production scene is now secure. Some two dozen music videos are shot in Jamaica each month, and cable channels such as Hype TV and RE TV often feature them, and thus promote many of the acts featured at dance events. Yet it is at these events that dancers, for example, must first gain exposure before they can hope for the opportunity to appear in a music video. Even now Jamaican culture is replete with examples of ordinary people creating and maintaining heroes, stars and celebrities in films, sport, music, rebellion and community activism or leadership. Visual representations of Jamaicans in the 21st century do not come from Hollywood, Broadway or the French Riviera, though they may well be influenced by the norms and standards generated in these spaces. Rather, they are more localized, being fashioned by the people for the people. Perhaps one of the most profound statements about celebrity in Jamaica is Barrington Levy's declaration: "I'm broad, I'm broad, I'm broader than Broadway" (Levy 2006). This simultaneous acknowledgement and rejection of Broadway is corroborated in Jamaicanisms powered on the engine of ancestral struggle and memory, such as "Wi likkle, but wi tallawah."

CONCLUSIONS

In this chapter I have explored the philosophical terrain of boundary-lessness, applied beyond the context of organizational behaviour to performance practice. I have argued that, even as dancehall culture is situated in a field of boundaries, its key participants have created several unbounded dancescapes and soundscapes, first, through everyday street events around music and dance that transcend the street; second, through travel across geopolitical borders allowing for the articulation of an urban dancehall "transnation"; and, third, in the ways in which participants inaugurate and expand categories that add prestige to, and invoke long histories in support of, these spaces.

As an aesthetic community, dancehall adherents imprint themselves on regional and international cityscapes, breaking boundaries that open the flow to other sites, and even fertilize other aesthetic communities. (It is this fertilization that forms the core of the discussion in Chapter 7.) A holistic view of dancehall practice centred on key performances and performers within their spheres of influence takes us through the dance space that yields important insights about how the disenfranchised citizens create and recreate spaces of celebration, renewal, transgression, and transcendence at various spatial, psychic and material levels.

A COMMON
TRANSNATIONAL SPACE

IN RECENT years cultural studies and related disciplines have increasingly aimed to take account of the global, the transnational or the international, especially in relation to the African Diaspora and other diasporas (see Clifford 2005). Often the transnational and the diasporic are treated as inextricably interlocked spheres of symbolic and material flows, involving routes/roots, tours, travel and borders. Khachig Tölölian (1991) argues that diasporas are the exemplary communities of the transnational moment. In this sense, a broad reading of the building of communities through solidarity, and of survival strategies that can erase borders of displacement and dispersal in the creation of home, place, networks of exchange and contact zones, can enter the discourse.

WORLD MUSICS AND THE BLACK ATLANTIC

One important context in both diaspora and transnational studies is the production of transnational cultures through music. Well before the term "world music" was coined in the 1980s (see Taylor 1997 and Bohlmann 2002) there was a crucible, a veritable sonic melting pot, of Black Atlantic cross-fertilization, occasioned by crossings, memory and syncretism, and producing much of the music now categorized under that term, which is understood to encompass "non-Western" musics outside the mainstream categories of commercial popular and classical music. In a literal sense "world music" is music that transcends national borders or is experienced by people all over the world, facilitated by increased travel and the use of digital technology, which has increased the movement, consumption and cross-fertilization of these musics. Examples such as the blues, ragtime, jazz, reggae, dancehall and kwaito have emerged in a context defined from the very outset as transnational, inhabiting one or more cultures through established routes of memory, travel, representation or performance. World musics thus preceded the use of the term "world music," a term that, in any case, is contested by the very existence and proliferation of Black Atlantic musical forms far beyond the popularity of the "mainstream" musics they are defined in opposition to.

As if the chain reaction from R&B to ska to rocksteady to reggae and dancehall was not enough for one small island in the Caribbean, their infectious rhythms have ensured fertilization beyond Jamaica for musics that remain unknown to most Jamaicans. The international significance of reggae and dancehall is unquestionable, but the extent to which they have crossed boundaries and created space at home and abroad is most evident in musical and performance genres that have

developed since the 1990s, including fuji, afrobeat, kwaito and makossa on the African continent, and bhangra in India and its diaspora.

Even before technological shifts in the mid-1980s enabled increased and multiple flows of music, the movement of Jamaican DJ style, its antecedents and its influence was effectively making a case for a reggae and dancehall transnation. Paul Gilroy (1993) highlighted transnational music cultures, from 19th-century singers to hip hop, reggae and rap, referencing ships, sound systems, phonographs, vinyl records and other technologies that have facilitated crossing, while Olu Oguibe (in an e-mail to this author, February, 25, 2005; see also Stanley Niaah and Niaah 2006) has pointed out that the Jamaican DJ

> U-Roy's [Ewart Beckford] prime historic place ... is not only the fact that he, more than any other, picked up, translocated and transformed [the African-American DJ Jocko] Henderson's techniques, shifting them out of the radio and recording studios into the streets, then back again, but also in the fact that he in turn provided the model for the expatriate Jamaican sound systems that would take over the Bronx in the early 1970s, and eventually form the foundation for hip hop and rap. "Your Ace from Space," [Henderson's moniker and name of a U-Roy album] as an expression and a cultural marker, establishes and signifies the transversal cultural history that unites African American and Jamaican popular culture across a half-century, from Henderson to Beckford to the Bronx and on to Shaggy, on one hand, and Ol' Dirty Bastard [ODB] on the other, ODB being a straight incarnation of late 1960s Beckford.

Reggae and its progeny, dancehall, long ago earned distinctive places on popular music charts and in racks in stores, while many other musics continue to be lumped into broad, all-embracing categories. A related point is that there are several subcategories of reggae, all of which were and are consumed in the dance. An advertisement by Irie FM (1996) identified some eighteen categories, including international reggae, conscious reggae, classic reggae, hip hop reggae, ska, reggae, bluebeat, mento, rocksteady, gospel reggae, jazz reggae, reggae philharmonic, reggae rock, rub-a-dub, dancehall, reggae ballads, lovers rock and dub poetry. Even this list excludes forms such as samba reggae and others identified more recently. The popularity of the genre is also evidenced by its estimated annual earnings of at least two billion US dollars, most of which remains in private holdings, largely overseas (see Chapter 1).

The transnational flow of reggae has received some attention (see Chude-Sokei 1997, Cooper 2004b and Marshall 2006), but I wish to

focus here on dancehall, kwaito and reggaetón, and the transnational terrain they reference in each other. Starting from the perspective that both kwaito and reggaetón have been influenced by dancehall culture, I seek to define these performance cultures, beyond their available musical perspectives, through their common genealogies, the common space linking the Old World with elements of the New World. Here, distance is inconsequential and space is about flows, with the local and global, temporal and spatial influences all feeding each other. This chapter analyzes the applicability of insights gleaned in the study of dancehall to other Black performance genres. I set up a conversation between dancehall, reggaetón and kwaito in order to reveal similarities, and differences, moving beyond current academic inquiry, which has focussed on their emergence, role and place in Jamaica on the one hand, and in, respectively, Puerto Rico and democratic South Africa on the other. I thus endeavour to expand the focus beyond musical and symbolic elements to include the space as an important category that reveals striking similarities across nations and their diasporas.

COMMON GENEALOGIES: KWAITO

First, if one considers post-apartheid South Africa as part of the democratized Atlantic world, kwaito's similarities with dancehall become clear. They are at once political, musical, social and cultural. Dancehall emerged in the 1950s and 1960s as an activity pioneered by the lower classes, in the generation seeking political independence from Britain, while kwaito emerged in the era of democratized South Africa, a new era of freedom.

Second, there are important commonalities and parallels in the spaces used by dancehall and kwaito. Both trace their origins to street dance events, which have always been held, to a greater or lesser degree, in contravention of state laws, although in South Africa under apartheid dance events were raided less often because police officers were generally afraid to enter the townships after dark. Like dancehall venues, the spaces now occupied by kwaito are varied and can be viewed on a continuum from community-based to commercial. They include refurbished warehouses, university stadiums, clubs, parks, private homes and train stations. At the highest commercial level there are free concerts hosted by record companies that attract sponsorship from multinational corporations such as PepsiCo. Clubs attract cover charges, and they range widely in the class of their clientele and their locations. Around the period of my research those in the Greater Johannesburg Metropolitan Area included Tandor and Rockefellars in

Yeoville, Horror Café (which has reggae/dancehall music on a Thursday night), Enigma and Sanyaki in Rosebank, and the Stage in Randburg, while Cape Town, Durban, Pretoria and other cities also have numerous clubs dotting their nightscapes. Events, which are more common in the summer, mark public holidays, birthdays, anniversaries, victories in soccer matches, marriages and interments.

Among all the spaces kwaito has been associated with, shebeens (informal drinking clubs in the townships) were important historically, as the music and culture around them spawned the "kwaito nation" much as the sound system culture of the 1950s and 1960s spawned dancehall culture. The shebeen always has a queen: it is her own house that is usually cleared of furniture so that, for a modest entrance fee, patrons may be treated to live music, beer and stew, sometimes all night long. Shebeens are to be understood as sites of control, spaces of surveillance and closure, especially under apartheid. However, dance and music performance construct an alternative political, spatial, and cultural narrative for shebeens, creating an identity inconsistent with dominant political interests, especially as different types of shebeen attract different audiences, from the "respectable" to the "low class." Shebeens still form an important part of today's social scene. Like the juke joints of the Mississippi Delta, they function as social institutions, building a sense of community and group identity, and helping to shape each city's cultural geography. However, many shebeens have been replaced by, or converted into, taverns, managed mostly by men rather than women, appealing to young adults in particular, with tables, chairs and decorated dance floors where kwaito, among other forms of music, can be heard and danced to.

Third, the accusations, mostly from international critics, about dancehall's "slackness," which reportedly flourished under the neoliberal approach of the governments formed by Edward Seaga and the Jamaica Labour Party from 1980 to 1989, resembles the branding that kwaito received for the supposed emptiness of its lyrics, which is thought to have thrived under neoliberal rule. Both are seen to have taken cues from the trends of new governments that supposedly encouraged the acquisition of personal wealth and the glamorizing of gangster lifestyles. Themes in kwaito, reggaetón and dancehall are also similar: social commentary about crime and violence, anti-politics, sexuality and sexual prowess, socially conscious songs about AIDS awareness, and violence against women in an era of reported increases in gang rapes, especially in South Africa. While there are criticisms to be made of the misogyny, sexuality and violence expressed in kwaito, reggaetón and dancehall, each of these musics also contains mature conversations about the place, nature, beauty and power of woman, whether as whore, wife or sweetheart, diseased, virtuous or conniving. These musics provide a way out of the township or ghetto or *barrio*, even as these spaces form the sources from which they receive their sustenance.

Kwaito, like dancehall, has distinct styles of dancing, performance, fashion and language, in the case of kwaito mostly drawn from township slang and indigenous languages (the band Bongo Maffin, for example, has used Shona, Sotho, Tswana, Xhosa and English in its lyrics). Unlike the protest music of Hugh Masekela, Miriam Makeba or Dolly Rathebe, kwaito, like dancehall music, is often thought to be "apolitical"—misleadingly, as already mentioned above. As Gavin Steingo (2005) has pointed out, kwaito's rejection of politics as a stance is itself political, and there is a new politics of riches beyond struggle, realized through opportunities made available through music. Kwaito, again like dancehall, often has misogynistic content, focused on girls, cars, partying and sexually explicit dance moves. The general opinion is that its arbiters seek to dissociate themselves from agony, struggle, conflict and exploitation, through "a culturated degree of estrangement" (Nuttall 2004, 451) from the generation that fought for the end of apartheid. This signals a movement into a new iteration of youth culture, ghetto youth culture, linked to city life and consciously distanced from the rural, seemingly unprogressive life of grandparents (see Stephens 2000, Satyo 2001 and Allen 2004b). Siswe Satyo (2001, 141) says that the performative language and ethos of Kwaito are "about throwing off the shackles of archaic rules imposed by some village schoolmaster or mistress," which is seen as "a benchmark of 'sophistication and creativity' within the peer group."

Kwaito stars are from a new generation. They include individuals such as Arthur, who is considered a founding father of kwaito, M'du, Oskido, Lebo, Mzekezeke, Mafikizolo, Mandoza, Mzambi, Chicco and Zola, and groups such as Boom Shaka, Bongo Maffin, Trompies, Aba Shante and Genesis. Kwaito is ubiquitous within South Africa, as dancehall music is in Jamaica. The music, seen as the "true music of the new South Africa" (Sicre 2004, 156), the "Rainbow Nation," pumps out of minibuses, taxis, clubs, radio bashes, shebeens and parties. It defines a generation of youth associated with popular radio and television programmes and advertisements, films, websites, magazines and fashion. It is a signifier for today's freedoms, and invokes age and locale at one and the same time (Allen 2004b, 86). Between 1999 and 2004, 30 percent of all hit songs in South Africa were kwaito tunes, and an analysis of the industry suggests that 31 percent of all adults are members of the "kwaito nation."

Kwaito draws its sustenance from the South African ghetto and generates dialogue with other ghettos around the world. With kwaito, urban youth can spend their nights in clubs rather than under curfew. Youth gangs are a real part of the everyday life of the ghetto and their members are also role models for the young who aspire to gain material wealth quickly (as discussed with my colleague David Coplan in July 2005). The wealth achieved through the music has fostered upward mobility and stimulated outmigration from ghettos, while technology has reordered the spaces of production and consumption of kwaito, making it possible, in South Africa as in Jamaica, to produce a recording, from start to finish, with just one or two persons in a single location. Kwaito moves beyond the sound economies, and the racialized "spatialities and temporalities of apartheid" (to borrow a characterization of township life from Achille Mbembe et al. 2004, 500). Like dancehall, it allows for the circulation of another version of local text and space through a sort of transnational or cosmopolitan performance. While kwaito's appeal is to the young, its purchase is clearly understood by the older generation, as evidenced by its incorporation into political campaigns intended to mobilize voters, reminiscent of the incorporation of Rastafari symbolism and Rastafari-inspired music, as well as dancehall music, into the election campaigns of the political parties in Jamaica, such as that of the People's National Party under the late Michael Manley in 1976 (see Charles 2005).

In a sense, kwaito has achieved in ten years what dancehall has achieved only very recently. Kwaito boasts its own musical entrepreneurs, who have built an all-inclusive approach to the production, distribution and marketing of the music. Solid artist–producers such as Oskido own recording studios, record labels and video production companies. Artists tour the world to perform, occupying soundscapes that are simultaneously local, national, regional and transnational. The kwaito band Bongo Maffin has performed in several other countries in Africa as well as in Europe and the United States, playing at events such as Reggae on the River at French's Camp, California, and Central Park Summer Stage in New York City.

Taking its cue from dancehall, kwaito has gained increased appeal through dance. Dance moves were popularized by the first kwaito band, Boom Shaka, which continues to create dance moves such as "chop di grass," performed to honour the men who cut grass when highways are being constructed. Junior Dread (2005) has even said that he was the first person in South Africa to perform ragga music. The presence of dancing girls is a motivation for men to go to kwaito parties and stage shows. Boom Shaka explain that their dancing is African and comes from the kwasa-kwasa, an urban dance that originated in the Democratic Republic of the Congo (formerly Zaïre) and became popular among South African youth, being performed mostly in the shebeens to kwaito music. Other popular dance moves are the butterfly, probably derived from the Jamaican dance of that name; the squga ("get down") dance, named after Mzekezeke's recent hit song of the year; the Madiba jive, named after one of Nelson Mandela's famous moves on his release from prison ("Madiba" being an honorific name for the former President); the chicken, a dance from the 1980s; the co-petsa; the sekele, derived from a traditional circle dance; the codesa, which takes its name from the Convention for a Democratic South Africa, the series of negotiations that ended apartheid); and the tobela, from Boom Shaka's song of that title, a Sotho word meaning "Thank you." Like Jamaican dance moves, these moves offer a window onto the everyday life of South Africans, while adding to the global conversation about meaning, representation and embodiment. DJs and producers have suggested that more than fifty dance moves have been created since the emergence of kwaito, building on traditions of South Africa's various peoples as well as dance influences from other countries in the region.

There are still deeper connections. It is well known that African music was influenced by vaudeville and ragtime performers touring parts of the continent, spawning a whole new culture of music production that culminated in the distinct genre of South African jazz and the colloquial renaming of Sophiatown as "Little Harlem." It has also been widely acknowledged that South African music in its turn influenced Jamaican music. Yet the reverse flow of influence has hardly been probed, even though Jimmy Cliff, Bob Marley and Peter Tosh significantly influenced the African musicscape, in Zimbabwe and South Africa in particular, through their performances and the export of their music.

The cross-cultural dimensions of kwaito in particular, specifically as seen through a reading of the Atlantic as a musical space of exchange, have been explored by David Coplan (2005a) and this chapter extends that reading (see also Allen 2004a and 2004b, Coplan 2005b, and Steingo 2005). A genealogy of kwaito reveals antecedents as far back as the 1950s, in Marabi nights, Kwela and Mbaqanga or jive, a musical experience around traditional songs heard in the shebeens; Mapantsula, a lower-class subculture of the 1980s, characterized by large groups of male dancers in synchronized movements very much resembling the male dancing crews in Jamaica after 2002; bubblegum, also from the 1980s, as well as township jazz, afro-pop, and Western musics such as R&B, jungle, hip hop, house, rap and ragga (the name by which dancehall is known especially in the European context). This is a musical potpourri, if there ever was one.

Simon Stephens argues that "kwaito's appropriation of the ragga vocal style and aspects of modern European dance music is a direct result of black South African exposure to these" and of a strategy employing "symbols of a black cultural ecumene and resistance" (Stephens 2000, 257). This tends to oversimplify the deeper relationship and conversations between Africa and its Diaspora, on the one hand, and the relationship between Jamaican reggae musicians and the South African liberation struggle, on the other. It is no coincidence that Junior Dread (a.k.a. Junior Sokhela), a former street boy from Hillbrow and leader of the first kwaito group, Boom Shaka, had a long relationship with Jamaican music through his uncle. According to Junior (2005),

> I've been a reggae fan since I was young because I had an uncle, and my uncle was an MK soldier [that is, a member of Umkhonto we Sizwe, the former military wing of the ANC]. So what he did, he used to play Bob Marley, but he loved Winston Rodney [Burning Spear]. They loved Burning Spear, Culture [Joseph Hill], and he had like Mutabaruka, I Roy and U Roy.... I used to hear all of them when I was young and I didn't know, but I got so interested, because he used to play them loud and they couldn't allow us to play any music which we want, so because it was his radio we had to listen to his music. So he'd put on a Prince Far I album and play it like non-stop every day. So we'd be singing to that and I got used to it, I started imitating it. By that time, as a youth I was still confused: I used to do break dancing, ragga, and do football, everything, [but] I just loved music.

Another kwaito singer, Stoan, and a member of Bongo Maffin, has explained (2005) the kind of conversation taking place across the Atlantic musicscape about aspiration, transformation, the politics of progress and freedom:

> If we had to look at any other example of Black people off the continent who have found their essence, it's Jamaicans, for us, for South Africans after the curtain was lifted, after we could see other things besides what was presented to us on television, which was blacksploitation movies and stuff like that, buffoons, you know, the picture of us. Any other successful picture of a black man was him behaving like a caricature of himself. So Jamaicans brought another element to a picture we had of us as an out-of-body experience. Yeah, so I think you'll find that a lot of people, you know, have

been touched by the culture, in South Africa, within ten years. Jah Seed has also really spread his influence.

Let me tell you a story. He started DJ-ing in Yeoville, at a place called Tandor, with Andy, the Admiral—this is his white selector— and he used to do this, he used to "wheel" the tunes, you know, and people used to complain. He'd be playing a tune and just as the people were going crazy he'd stop the tune and wheel it, you know: "Massive mi tune nice, yuh play it twice." And I go to him: "You know, Apple, South Africa is different, man, you just gotta play the song and people gotta enjoy it." And he's like: "No, a Stone Love, dem affi learn bwoy, if a tune nice, yuh affi play it twice, man. Now, wheel an' come again." By the end of that year—not even, within six months—people on the dance floor were the ones now screaming out: "Wheeeeeel, pull up man, wheel that tune an' come again."

COMMON GENEALOGIES: REGGAETÓN

Reggaetón is known as a pan-Latino culture that originated from and represents inner-city Latino youth. It enjoys immense popularity within US mainstream popular urban culture, with a strong presence on hip hop and R&B radio stations, and consistent rotation on MTV, VH1 Soul, Tempo and local cable channels, in Jamaica as well as in the United States. Reggaetón's relationship to a discourse of freedom is seen through the articulation of survival and independence by young Latinos and Latinas. Wayne Marshall, for example, declares (2006, 1): "From New York to Miami, Roxbury to Lowell to Springfield to Cambridge [in Massachusetts], Cuba to Colombia to Chile, young Latinos and Latinas are using reggaetón music and style to articulate a sense of community."

Reggaetón, symbiotically related to hip hop and reggae, was initially known as "Spanish reggae," a name that highlighted the spread and reach of its predecessor. Jamaican migrants to Panama took their music with them, and Panamanians started recording and performing "Spanish reggae" in the 1970s. Later, in the 1980s and 1990s, Panamanian artists updated their music with the latest dancehall reggae rhythms, in many cases maintaining the attitude and the stories being told. This music migrated with the movement of Latinos to metropolitan centres such as New York, where the migrants and their music encountered Puerto Rican rappers, and a new musical relationship was born. Dancehall already had strong appeal among Puerto Ricans because of the work of artists such as Shabba Ranks, Chakademus and Plyers/Pliers, and Buju Banton, so it was easy for Puerto Ricans to blend their rapping with deejaying in the Jamaican style. Elephant Man, TOK, Sasha and Cecile are just some of the Jamaican musicians who have collaborated with reggaetón artists. The underground scene of reggaetón ballooned in 1994–95, in much the same way as kwaito did, and reggaetón was directly influenced by the dancehall high point between 1989 and 1994. By 2004 reggaetón had gained widespread popularity in the United States, especially on the large club scene where much reggaetón is consumed.

Alternative marketing and distribution strategies eliminated the need for large companies to take control of reggaetón. Artists recording in home studios have been able to sell up to 200,000 copies of their albums or singles without the help of distribution companies. For ten years this was the mode of distribution, until connections for global reach became imperative, and record labels now pursue reggaetón artists, rather than the other way about. This mirrors the experience of kwaito musicians: in the early years of that genre, they could sell up to 500,000 copies of their recordings without help.

Patricia Meschino (2005) suggests that as much as 80 percent of reggaetón's beats come from reggae. Reggaetón takes the bass from reggae, blending it with the drums of hip hop. It is also influenced by techno and house music. Jamaican dancehall too is a wellspring for many of the rhythms, styles and techniques sampled by reggaetón. According to Wayne Marshall (2006, 3), "Reggaetón's unmistakable *boom-ch-boom-chick* relates directly to the late-80s/early-90s dancehall reggae that inspired it," although he acknowledges that, with early cross-fertilizations of Latin and Caribbean musics such as Cuban *son*, which influenced 20th-century calypso, the *boom-ch-boom-chick* also has Latin antecedents. The same musical patterns, with some variations of course, abound in many Caribbean musical styles, including reggae, mento, soca, calypso, salsa, son, mambo, merengue and bachata. However, one distinct feature of a very high proportion of reggaetón tracks is the "dem bow" rhythm taken from Shabba Ranks's single of that title (1991). No doubt reggaetón's rhythmic structure has served to remind Jamaican sound engineers of older rhythms, some of which triumphantly resurfaced on the dancehall scene between 2005 and 2007. While there are cases where old rhythms are used for new recordings in dancehall, the cross-fertilization inherent in the construction and emergence of reggaetón has also affected Jamaica. Perhaps the best example of this is the sampling of the "taxi" rhythm in Buju Banton's highly successful hit song "Driver A" on the album *Too Bad* (2006).

Reggaetón circulates in clubs, in cars, on radio and via the internet.

Clubs in Puerto Rico, Cuba, New York City and elsewhere, including those considered ghetto clubs, such as De Noise in old San Juan, allow youths to consume the music via the performance space, using the dance floors to put their daily troubles in a temporary vacuum (see Bentley 2005). Hardcore barrios also have street events where reggaetón DJs and reggae bands can be found side by side. The rule of the local don imprints itself on these events in the form of rules that residents and visitors to certain communities must abide by. For example, cellphones or cameras are not allowed in some areas because these devices can easily transmit information to the authorities.

As with dancehall and kwaito, reggaetón has been accused of having excessively sexual content, in the form of descriptions of sexual acts, sexual desire, bodily fluids and female body parts, often expressed in very explicit language. There are, of course, other types of lyric, including socially uplifting songs to encourage barrio youth, and social commentary against domestic violence, reliance on guns or cheating in relationships. Dance styles such as the doggy style or *perreo* are sometimes subjected to censorship in Puerto Rico and Cuba, for the reasons suggested in this description by Sarah Bentley (2005, 44) of a typical reggaetón dance event:

> Some couples face each other, arms locked around the waist, banging their crotches together hard, while for others the guy stands behind the girl, pushing it up against her as she gyrates her *culos* [batty]. Ladies without partners shake their butt cheeks and dip their knees. Solo guys dip, pull suggestive faces and dance as if riding an imaginary horse.

When reggaetón dance styles and lyrics have come under attack— whether from legislators trying to impose puritan mores, or police officers, who have sometimes destroyed musical equipment, or from radio, television and retail outlets that have banned performers or recordings—musicians and other cultural workers have responded with resounding defences of the genre (see Fairley 2006). As they point out, the emphasis on body parts such as the hip and the sensuality depicted in reggaetón dance moves are both linked to a long tradition of dance in Africa and its Diaspora. Other examples include samba; the calenda of Louisiana and Uruguay, which is noted for its belly-to-belly contact; the Cuban rumba, a dance intended to depict the courting experience between men and women; the pana-livio and the sereno, belly-to-belly dances with African origins that became popular in Peru in the 18th century; the currulao performed in Colombia (see Wright 2004); the tango, which was born in Argentina and has spread around the world; and the Cuban and Mexican danzón, which, like so many other dances in this tradition, have been regarded as transgressive and shocking because of their explicit sexual display. These examples (and there are many others) reveal a sort of instinctive impulse expressed through dance, linking it to the intimate play between men and women that is at the core of human existence. Just as the Jamaican dancehall space has to be understood within a wider history and practice, so too these dance moves have to be located as historically embodied African/Caribbean Diasporic practice. The kinaesthetics, philosophy and practice of Jamaican, Caribbean and other African Diasporic movement patterns predominantly have their origins in the dances of West Africa in particular.

COMMON SPACE: FROM GHETTO STREETS TO WORLD STAGE

When reggaetón was blowing up the airwaves in the early years of the 21st century it was having a conversation with other musical forms such as kwaito, bhangra, afrobeat and fuji. It is as though, in some real as well as imaginary senses, these performance cultures travel through a ghetto geography, spanning the Black Atlantic, in which knowing subjects surrender to the "ghetto allegiance" around dancehall, as described by Edwin Houghton (2004, 90):

It's not just the sound, the code to which the youthful soldiers of the New World's roughest ghetto swear allegiance. Increasingly, it's also the glue that holds disparate strands of urban music together in the world's international centres, from New York City to Rio to Tokyo. It is the sound that displaced Punjabis like Apache Indian and Bally Sagoo use with bhangra, and reimport to the Indian subcontinent as the next big thing. It is the only worthy symbol of cutting-edge modernity to artificially tanned and dreadlocked Japanese dancehall queens. It is the inexhaustible source of street cred that reinvigorates both hip hop and UK garage in ongoing waves. To *favela* youth in Brazil and across Latin America, it is the rhythmic marker of their separation from a Eurocentric colonial past. In short, it is the anti-world beat, the perfect global music ... and it might just be the soundtrack of the 21st bloodclot century.

The production and consumption of this transnational ghetto music, this "anti-world beat" and its performance practices shaped in the margins, share common histories, geographies and identities. Local politics and communities occupy national and transnational geographies, at the same time as they engage in dialogue with each other through performance.

Kingston, Johannesburg and San Juan hold important sites of memory for dancehall, kwaito and reggaetón respectively. Their ghettos, townships or barrios are all associated with high levels of murder, police harassment, hardship and squalid conditions. Visual representation of such poor neighbourhoods features dirt roads, mud-brick homes, barefoot children, intense overcrowding, derelict buildings and corrugated metal fences that hide rotting wooden sheds. From the 1930s to 1970s there were few services in such locations as Soweto and Sophiatown in South Africa, or Trench Town in Kingston. Paved roads, street lighting and clean water were non-existent, and families survived on little or no cash from formal employment, hustling or "juggling" to make a living. Today, as in the past, gangs, often involved in illicit activities, institutionalized warfare and partisan political banditry, come to occupy the spaces from which dancehall, kwaito and reggaetón emerged, and in which they thrive.

Based on his fieldwork in Washington, DC, in the late 1960s, Ulf Hannerz (2004, p. 11) contextualized the concept of the ghetto as an "anti-euphemism" for inner city or slum, indicating poor, rundown conditions, but also the "nature of community and its relationship to the outside world," ethnicity, family ties and other factors that keep people living in the same space. The difference between the early ghettos and contemporary ones is that their status as communities is not necessarily determined by strong dependence on relationships with dominant outsiders. Fundamentally, economic stability is low relative to other communities, and even though some residents have low-paid work as gardeners, garbage collectors or domestic helpers (not seen as "real work"), there is still relatively high unemployment. There are also relatively low levels of movement inwards or outwards on a daily basis by residents or visitors. However, there are transnational networks that they operate within, distributing news of the struggles and victories of daily life through music, and maintaining tangible links among ghetto citizens via Brixton, the Bronx, Lagos and Soweto. There is a proliferation of bonds of solidarity around music and dance performance.

There are other significant and largely unexplored ways in which kwaito, dancehall and reggaetón share a common space. First, there is the abiding parallel between the spatiality of the slave ship or the plantation and the spatiality of the ghetto, township or barrio. Like the slave ship and the plantation, the inner city has offered little provision for celebration. Much of the social life of these areas was therefore erected around uninhabited spaces, streets and other policed spaces that were appropriated for performance in spite of curfews, enforcement of laws about noise and other pressures. Dance events, generally peripatetic in nature, evolved from the need to surmount everyday tensions, celebrate life and survive against all odds. Deprivation, poverty and neglect generated the cultures of survival out of which these musical forms emerged. By the 1950s beer, music and dancing had come together, especially at weekends, around the sound systems in Kingston, the shebeens in Soweto and other townships, and the clubs and bars of the barrios.

Dance halls, bars and clubs, and the street together construct a politics of enjoyment, even as everyday life militates against it. The existence of such enjoyment assaults and mocks oppression, and those who construct and maintain it. Enjoyment can reduce the potential to incite violence against the self and the community, because it channels energies in a pleasurable way. Where ghetto, township and barrio folk are allowed to self-destruct in the quagmire of oppression, they survive it in mockery of oppressive forces. Thus the very spaces created for consumption and production of cultural forms and access to pleasure constitute sites of political power for that practice and the people who create them. The street in particular is an important site. At weekends streets are taken over by jams, bashes or dances, at which aspiring performers try to woo audiences and attract the attention of producers. The street is thus the first stage for many aspirants, whether they are DJs, musical selectors or sound system operators.

Spreading out from these sites of origin, beside and beyond the transnational networks of capital, dancehall, reggaetón and kwaito occupy significant places within youth consciousness, even as they have increasingly ambivalent relationships with the nations that spawned them. At the same time as they are appropriated and projected in the media, and in official campaigns to attract tourists, they receive sanctions from the state and its apparatuses in the form of legislation and police raids. There is little or no institutional support for the establishment, management and maintenance of these creative industries. As I noted earlier (see Chapter 2), one dancehall DJ, Mr. G (2002), has summed up the situation by saying, "Over the years we've got our support not from the government or the court." Liminality (as discussed in Chapter 4) is seen in the ways in which dancehall, kwaito and reggaetón occupy in-between spaces, locations that are neither here nor there, and yet are central to national and transnational identities, even while maintaining their home bases and their links at the margins. This in-betweenness, this liminality, is an important characteristic of the cultures of marginalized youth. The liminal location is one means by which such performance cultures maintain themselves, since the power of popular support serves to negate the ways in which the state disciplines and controls their growth. Essentially, therefore, there is a sense in which the liminal is inextricably linked to the transformatory potential and reality of performance.

Invoking and expanding on work by James Scott, Lara Allen (2004a) argues that music inherently has "hidden transcripts," sets of private meanings that are made public by transmission to various audiences, transgressing and rebutting hegemonic discourses—in contrast to conceptions of leisure, including the consumption of music, in which pleasure is emphasized as the sole or main use. The creators and perpetuators of performance cultures such as dancehall make important statements about agency in their daily existence, and mock the oppressive forces that prepare for and predict their demise.

Putting this into language closer to home, the notion of "nation language" proffered by Kamau Brathwaite (1995) helps in understanding the possibilities shaped in the kind of affirmative action facilitated by indigenous vernaculars, such as Jamaican creole, that still fight to shed their marginal beginnings and the classed/racialized cloud around acceptance into the mainstream. Such languages speak through their citizens, of them and for them, to the world, and, in the case of Jamaican creole, to a world of growing converts who, especially in Japan, learn it before or instead of Standard English, propelled by the distance education provided by reggae and dancehall music. In the case of music, it is a Diasporic language that is transmitted through performance. This performance, be it through language use or embodied practice, can be seen, like spiritual practice, as a means of making links to one's source of existence through ritual, to inner selves, unmasked selves, as well as each other, across different terrains, nations and cultures.

More so than either kwaito or reggaetón, the very name dancehall, derived from the venue in which dance events occurred, immediately invokes space (see Table 7.1). I use the category "spatial divides" to distinguish the ways in which the personal—that which is of the body, private, mostly invisible—can be separated analytically from, and yet is always closely intertwined with, the public spaces that increase visibility. Within these spaces systems of violence, politics, and memory operate to contribute an overall understanding of the major analytical markers that can classify dancehall within (although not limited to) its Kingston habitus, its ghetto geography and by extension, its transnation.

PERFORMING GEOGRAPHY, PERFORMING IDENTITY

In 2008 Jamaicans, like many others in the Black Atlantic world, paused to observe the bicentennial of the abolition of the trans-Atlantic trade

TABLE 7.1
Summary of Dancehall's Spaces

Spatial divides	Spatial systems	Spatial descriptors (analytical tools)
personal/communal	ritual	liminal
body/ghetto area (urban, street, pub, yard)	memory	real/imagined
private/public	economy	contested/contesting
exclusive/inclusive	politics	marginal/legitimate
closed/open, inner/outer	performance	nomadic
anonymous/visible	identity	limitless/boundaryless/ transnational
female/male	aesthetics	transformatory
autonomous/policed	violence	siege

in enslaved Africans. However, even now many pay little attention to the importance of history. There still remains a mental block that prevents them from engaging with other histories, sometimes and especially those that come closest to them, even though completing the task of emancipation that Erna Brodber (1996) writes of requires an ability to see oneself in history.

I have sliced off a piece of that history as it relates to performance spaces with the aim of helping to bridge gaps in the unexplored transnational record of "submarine connections" (see Brathwaite 1974) across the Caribbean and the Black Atlantic more broadly. While my invocation of submarine connections here has some resonance with Brathwaite's understanding of it, I extend his reading beyond the Caribbean by remembering and citing the poignant words of Amiri Baraka (1995):

It's my brother, my sister.
At the bottom of the Atlantic Ocean there's a
railroad made of human bones.
Black ivory
Black ivory.

Baraka leads us to push outside the confines of the Caribbean to build an understanding of the submarine connections to the wider "Black Atlantic" world of the African continent and its Diaspora. This conception helps to construct a bridge on which we can meet and talk with intellectuals such as Wole Soyinka, as well as the host of Africans, continental and Diasporic, who live to perform and perform to live despite the odds. Baraka's poem invokes an underground city and an underground railroad as the track of history, where the past, the present and the future come together as one. Here there are no time and space as separate entities. Rather, they are rhythms of life that do not exist without each other.

In many ways this book is about responding to David Scott's assertion (1999, 192) that "there is as yet no adequate cultural history of dancehall." He was making a statement about the volume, state and status of research on dancehall, but also about the kinds of cultural histories constructed about and through performance. Reflection on the project of delineating performance geography, which is part of the making of cultural history for dancehall, makes it evident that cultural histories are written by combining multiple approaches and navigating multiple terrains. Not only is the engagement with history different in particular spaces, but histories are determined by relationships of power that implicate different degrees of legitimacy, acceptance, circulation or censorship. Therefore, in looking deeper at what it means to write cultural history we find implications for research on performance geographies and, more generally, the nexus between the recording of time, and its negotiation within space and through culture.

Michel Foucault's clarity about the way in which historical imagination has been privileged over geographical imagination inspired my engagement with the intersection between performance, geography, and the history of survival, and of identities being constructed and reconstructed in that nexus. While acknowledging that the terrain of analysis was different in Foucault's case, I suggest that there is a basic point of convergence around history sharing centre stage with the space that gives it context and meaning. In this light I have engaged with history and performance practices that bind us within concrete historical but also locational indices. Performing everyday life brings both space and time into focus, moving beyond each as separate domains. Time without space is meaningless, and space belongs to time as time owes its life to space. Performance geography brings both time and space into focus in a way that privileges both across a variety of connected performance sites.

This book began with literal and metaphorical readings of the movement limbo as a poignant answer to certain questions. How have displaced peoples survived in the New World? How have they fashioned identities beyond those that were imposed upon slaves? The answers lie in the feet that stomped, danced and called up spirits under the banyan tree on the plantation; in the drumming that accompanied the singing of the Jamaican folk song "Moon Shine Tonight" ("Moon shine tonight / Come mek we dance and sing"), and that continues to reverberate in the contemporary movement in dance halls; in the perspiration that melts from the excitement and the tension in the armpits of those who have had to dance in order to do more than merely survive, and to live. They have danced on the slave ships and, in Congo Square, and continue to dance in the streets of the townships, ghettos and barrios, in open lots, clubs and other venues that are all dance halls in varying degrees.

While I have engaged with Kingston's dancehall culture as my first point of departure, I have located its logic, form, celebratory ethos, institutional networks and discourses in a wider field of performance and intellectual practice. Dancehall is at once a field of performance and a set of multiple spaces and iterations. A mapping of Kingston's dancehall spaces, their history, evolution, character, use and classification, reveals that the city's dancehall memory is bound up in these spaces where histories, selves, new modes of community, ritual, survival and nation have evolved. Dancehall space, physical and political, is central to urban, national and transnational identities. It is contradictory, nomadic, communal, hierarchical, competitive, as it is also and at the same time spectacular, celebratory and sacred. The citizens at the heart of dancehall culture live a profound and resistant cartography of survival, where history and their everyday lives contradict their ability to name their existence in a world that negates them.

The performance sociology of "the subcultural dance" (see White 1984) has been expanded, building on the long tradition of recorded dance activity in the New World. Crucially, dancehall, kwaito and reggaetón are racialized performance sites of contestation, travel and transience, transcendence and boundarylessness, pleasure and ritual, innovation, hybridity, and social integration that have fed each other and continue so to do. The citizens of their respective massives, nations or communities simultaneously enact, reclaim, reconnect and renew self and Diasporic cultural identity. Dancehall, kwaito and reggaetón constitute sites of psychic relocation (see Allen 2004b), embodying questions and paths toward making space, a new self and nation.

In closing, I want to echo the plea made by Wole Soyinka (2001) for a "millennial indaba" as the point at which I conclude my argument on the local yet transnational performance geography explored in this book. Soyinka, once an exiled citizen of Africa and now a citizen of its Diaspora, has actively contemplated the relationship between the children of the Diaspora and those on the continent. Speaking of the "oceans of ignorance" that "still separate the general black population from the mother continent," Soyinka asserts that a "percussive impact is required, a mammoth-scale, extended event that celebrates and contextualizes both the African past and contemporary reality." Such a millennial indaba would involve conferences, exhibitions, films, performing arts and celebrations to promote exchange. However, the transnational performance terrain navigated here reveals an alternative way of viewing the concept of a millennial indaba. The sounds of Africa and the Caribbean travelled to the United States with enslaved and free Africans. They in turn influenced the emergence of the blues, which then influenced the musics of Jamaica, South Africa and West Africa in particular. More recently, Africa has been influenced by the Diasporic musics of the United States and Jamaica, while the Caribbean territories continue to influence each other, and their own diasporas, with the latest digital beats and performance aesthetic. There is an enormous network of travel and cross-fertilization through which exchange and learning have helped to dry out the "oceans of ignorance" that Soyinka identified and deplored. Just as other indabas have occurred all over the African continent, the millennial indaba has already been achieved, to some extent, using what ordinary people have always had: the common impulse to create and perform in spite of the odds. In instances where performers have had to create spaces to meet their need to celebrate in the face of oppression and repression, the articulation of a philosophy of limitless space and boundaryless-ness allows for the reclamation, multiplication and transcendence of spaces. This is what performers in the contexts where repression propels struggle have achieved, creating formidable ways in which to use space as a strategy of power, dwelling within but outside, peripherally but centrally, simultaneously transcending micro- and macrospatialities through performance.

REFERENCES

Ahye, Molly. (2002). "In Search of the Limbo: An Investigation into its Folklore as a Wake Dance." in *Caribbean Dance From Abakuá to Zouk: How Movement Shapes Identity*, ed. Susanna Sloat. Gainesville: University Press of Florida, 247–61.

Ajayi, Omofolabo. (1996). "In Contest: The Dynamics of African Religious Dances," in *African Dance: An Artistic, Historical and Philosophical Inquiry*, ed. Kariamu Welsh-Asante. Trenton, NJ: Africa World Press, 183–202.

Ajayi, Omofolabo. (1998). *Yoruba Dance: The Semiotics of Movement and Body Attitude in a Nigerian Culture*. Trenton, NJ: Africa World Press.

Akon. (2004). "Ghetto." Song on the album *Trouble*. Universal Music Enterprises.

Allen, Lara (2004a). "Music and Politics in South Africa." *Social Dynamics* 30:2, 1–19.

Allen, Lara. (2004b). "Kwaito versus Crossed-Over: Music and Identity during South Africa's Rainbow Years, 1994–99." *Social Dynamics* 30:2, 82–111.

Alleyne, Mervyn. (1988). *Roots of Jamaican Culture*. London: Pluto Press.

Appadurai, Arjun. (1990). "Disjuncture and Difference in the Global Cultural Economy." *Public Culture*, 2:2, 1–24.

Assassin. (2006). "Gully Sit'n". Single. Zero G Music Label.

Austin-Broos, Diane. (1997). *Jamaica Genesis: Religion and the Politics of Moral Orders*. Chicago: University of Chicago Press.

Baby Cham. (2006). "Ghetto Story." Song on the album *Ghetto Story*. Atlantic Records.

Bailey, C. (1999). "Intra-Urban Variations in Fear of Crime: Kingston Metropolitan Area." BA thesis, University of the West Indies.

Bailey, Richie "Feelings." (2007, April 4). Author's interview.

Bailey, Wilma R. (1974). "Kingston 1692–1843: A Colonial City." PhD thesis, University of the West Indies.

Bakare-Yusuf, Bibi. (2006). "Fabricating Identities: Survival and the Imagination in Jamaican Dancehall Culture", *Fashion Theory*. 10: 3, pp. 1–24

Baraka, Amiri [formerly Leroi Jones]. (1968 [originally 1963]). *Blues People: Negro Experience in White America and the Music that Developed From It*. New York: William Morrow.

Baraka, Amiri. (1995). "Improvisations on 'Wise, Why's, Y'z' (excerpts from Africa Section)," in *Fooling with Words with Bill Moyers: The Poets Read*. New York: WNET. Online at http://www.pbs.org/wnet/foolingwithwords/Pbaraka_poem11.html [consulted August 5, 2009].

Barrow, Steve, and Peter Dalton. (2001 [originally 1997]). *The Rough Guide to Reggae: The Definitive Guide to Jamaican Music from Ska through Roots to Ragga*. 2nd ed. London: Rough Guides/Penguin Books.

Baxter, Ivy. (1970). *The Arts of an Island: The Development of the Culture and the Folk and Creative Arts in Jamaica, 1494–1962*. Metuchen, NJ: Scarecrow Press.

Beckles, Hilary. (2002). "'War Dances': Slave Leisure and Anti-Slavery in the British-Colonized Caribbean," in *Working Slavery, Pricing Freedom: Perspectives from the Caribbean and the African Diaspora*, ed. Verene Shepherd. Kingston, Jamaica: Ian Randle Publishers, 223–46.

Beckwith, Jane (producer and director) (2000). *Dancehall Queens*. London: Diverse Productions for Channel 4 Television.

Beenie Man. (1994). "World Dance." Song on the album *Strictly the Best, Volume 13*. VP Records.

Beenie Man (1999) "Gospel Time," song on the album *The Doctor*, VP Records: USA

Beenie Man (2004) 'Grindacologist' single on the album *Back to Basics*, USA : Virgin Records America

Beenie Man. (2004) "Row Like a Boat." Song on the album *Back to Basics*. Virgin.

Bennett, Andy. (2000). *Popular Music and Youth Culture*. London: Palgrave Macmillan.

Bentley, Sarah. (2005). "Reggaetón in Puerto Rico: Three Worlds Collide." *Riddim* 1, 42–47.

Bohlmann, Philip (2002). *World Music: A Very Short Introduction*. Oxford and New York: Oxford University Press.

Bounti Killa. (2003, October). Interview. Kingston, Jamaica: CVM TV.

Boyne, Ian. (2002a, December 15). "How Dancehall Promotes Violence." *Sunday Gleaner* (Kingston, Jamaica), G1.

Boyne, Ian. (2002b, December 29). "How Dancehall Holds Us Back." *Sunday Gleaner* (Kingston, Jamaica). Online at www.jamaica-gleaner.com/gleaner/20021229/focus/focus1.html [consulted August 5, 2009].

Branche, Clement. (1998). "Boys in Conflict: Community, Gender, Inequality and Sex," in *Gender and the Family in the Caribbean*, ed. Wilma R. Bailey. Mona, Jamaica: Institute of Social and Economic Research, University of the West Indies, 185–201.

Brathwaite, (Edward) Kamau. (1971). *The Development of Creole Society in the British West Indies, 1770–1820*. Oxford: Clarendon Press.

Brathwaite, (Edward) Kamau. (1973). *The Arrivants: A New World Trilogy*. Oxford: Oxford University Press.

Brathwaite, (Edward) Kamau. (1974). *Contradictory Omens*. Mona, Jamaica: Savacou Publications.

Brathwaite, (Edward) Kamau. (1994a). *Trench Town Rock*. Providence, RI: Lost Roads Publishers.

Brathwaite, (Edward) Kamau. (1994b). *Dreamstories*. London: Long-man.

Brathwaite, (Edward) Kamau. (1995 [originally 1984]). *History of the Voice: The Development of Nation Language in Anglophone Caribbean Poetry*. London: New Beacon Books.

Brewster, Bill, and Frank Broughton. (1999). *Last Night a DJ Saved My Life: The History of the Disc Jockey*. London: Headline.

Brodber, Erna. (1975). "A Study of Yards in Kingston." Mona, Jamaica: Institute of Social and Economic Research, University of the West Indies.

Brodber, Erna. (1996). "Re-engineering Black Space." Plenary Presentation at the Conference on Caribbean Culture, University of the West Indies, Mona Campus.

Brodber, Erna. (2003). *Standing Tall: Affirmation of the Jamaican Male: Twenty Four Self-Portraits*, Mona, Jamaica: Sir Arthur Lewis Institute of Social and Economic Studies, University of the West Indies.

Browning, Barbara. (1997). *Infectious Rhythm: Metaphors of Contagion and the Spread of African Culture*. New York and London: Routledge.

Buju Banton (featuring Beres Hammond). (1999). "Pull It Up." Single. Anti Inc.

Buju Banton. (1990). *Mr Mention*. Album. Penthouse Productions.

Buju Banton. (1992). "Bogle Dance." Single. Mango.

Buju Banton. (1993). "No Respect" and "Operation Ardent." Songs on the album *Voice of Jamaica*. Polygram Records.

Buju Banton. (2001 [first released 1990]). "How the World a Run." Song on the album *Ultimate Collection*. Universal Music Enter-prises.

Buju Banton. (2006). "Driver A." Song on the album *Too Bad*. Gargamel Music.

Buju Banton. (2007, March 28). Interview on *The Buzz*. Kingston, Jamaica: Irie FM.

Busta Rhymes (featuring Sean Paul & Spliff Star) (2002). *Make it Clap* [single], USA: J Records

Butler, Judith. (2000). "Agencies of Style for a Liminal Subject," in *Without Guarantees: In Honour of Stuart Hall*, ed. Paul Gilroy, Lawrence Grossberg and Angela McRobbie. London and New York: Verso, 30–37.

Campbell, Kenneth "Bop." (2003, September). Author's interview.

Capleton (2000). "Jah Jah City." Song on the album *More Fire*. VP Records.

Captain Barkey (1996). "Go Go Wine." Song on the album *Strictly the Best, Volume 17*. VP Records.

Carty, Hilary. (1988). *Folk Dances of Jamaica: An Insight*. London: Dance Books.

Certeau, Michel de. (1984). *The Practice of Everyday Life*. Berkeley and Los Angeles: University of California Press.

Charles, Christopher. (2003). "Skin Bleaching, Self-Hate, and Black Identity in Jamaica." *Journal of Black Studies*, 33:6, 711–28.

Charles, Christopher. (2005). "The Psychology of Music in Jamaican Political Campaigns, 2002." Paper presented at the 30th Annual Conference of the Caribbean Association, Santo Domingo, Dominican Republic, May.

Chevannes, Barry. (1999). "Between the Living and the Dead: The Apotheosis of Rastafari Heroes," in *Religion, Diaspora, and Cultural Identity: A Reader in the Anglophone Caribbean*, ed. John W. Pulis. Amsterdam: Gordon & Breach Publishers, 337–56.

Chevannes, Barry. (2001, March 22). "Ambiguity and the Search for Knowledge: An Open-Ended Adventure of Imagination." Inaugural Lecture at the University of the West Indies, Mona Campus, Jamaica.

Chin, Timothy. (2004, March 12). Author's interview.

Chude-Sokei, Louis. (1997). "Postnationalist Geographies: Rasta, Ragga, and Reinventing Africa," in *Reggae, Rasta, Revolution: Jamaican Music from Ska to Dub*, ed. Chris Potash. New York: Schirmer Books, and London: Prentice Hall International, 215–27.

Clifford, James. (2005). "Diasporas," in *Internationalizing Cultural Studies: An Anthology*, ed. Ackbar Abbas and John Nguyet Erni. Malden, MA, and Oxford: Blackwell, 524–58.

Cohen-Cruz, Jan, ed. (1998). *Radical Street Performance: An International Anthology*. London: Routledge.

Comaroff, John. (1985). *Body of Power, Spirit of Resistance: The Culture and History of a South African People*. Chicago: University of Chicago Press

Connell, John, and Chris Gibson. (2003). *Sound Tracks: Popular Music, Identity and Place*. London and New York: Routledge

Connerton, Paul. (1989). *How Societies Remember*. Cambridge: Cambridge University Press.

Conquergood, Dwight. (1991, June). "Rethinking Ethnography: Towards a Critical Cultural Politics." *Communication Monographs* 59, 179–94.

Cooper, Carolyn. (1993). "Slackness Hiding From Culture: Erotic Play in the Dancehall," in Carolyn Cooper, *Noises in the Blood: Orality, Gender and the "Vulgar" Body of Jamaican Popular Culture*. London: Macmillan, 136–73.

Cooper, Carolyn. (2000, Spring). "Punany Powah." in *Black Media Journal* 2, 50–52.

Cooper, Carolyn. (2002). "Erotic Disguises: (Un)dressing the Body in Jamaican Dancehall Culture." Walter Rodney Memorial Lecture at the Centre for Caribbean Studies, University of Warwick. Online at http://www2.warwick.ac.uk/fac/arts/ccs/rodney/ [consulted August 5, 2009].

Cooper, Carolyn. (2004a). "Lady Saw Cuts Loose: Female Fertility Rituals in the Dancehall." *Jamaica Journal* 27:2–3, 13–19.

Cooper, Carolyn. (2004b). *Sound Clash: Jamaican Dancehall Culture at Large*, New York: Palgrave Macmillan

Coplan, David (2005a). "Born to Win: Music of the 'Black Atlantic' Revisited." Paper presented at the National Art Festival, Grahamstown, South Africa, July 6.

Coplan, David. (2005b, July). "God Rock Africa: Thoughts on Politics in Popular Black Performance in South Africa." *African Studies* 64:1, 9–27.

Corr, Norman, Jr., and Rachel Corr (1999). ""Imagery of Blackness in Indigenous Myth, Discourse, and Ritual," *Representations of Blackness and the Performance of Identities*, ed. Jean Rahier. Westport, CT, and London: Bergin & Garvey, 213–34.

Crary, Jonathan. (2005). "Spectacle," in *New Keywords: A Revised Vocabulary of Culture and Society*, ed. Tony Bennett, Lawrence Grossberg and

Meaghan Morris. Malden, MA, Oxford, and Carlton, VIC: Blackwell, 335–36.

Cressey, Paul Goalby. (2008 [originally 1932]). *The Taxi-Dance Hall: A Sociological Study in Commercialized Recreation and City Life.* Chicago: University of Chicago Press.

Dagan, E. A. (1997). "Origin and Meaning of Dance's Essential Body Position and Movements," in *The Spirit's Dance in Africa: Evolution, Transformation and Continuity in Sub-Sahara,* ed. E. A. Dagan. Montreal: Galerie Amrad, 102–16.

"Dancers' Duel" (January 23, 2005). *Sunday Gleaner* (Kingston, Jamaica). Online at http://www.jamaica-gleaner.com/gleaner/20050123/ent/ent1.html [consulted August 5, 2009].

Davis, Marcia. (2002, April 17). Author's interview.

Dempster, Beth. (2002). "Boundarylessness: Introducing a Systems Heuristic for Conceptualizing Complexity." Paper presented at the Toward a Taxonomy of Boundaries Conference, Land Institute, Matfield Green, KS, May/June.

Derouet, Nicolas. (2006). "Biography [of Ras Mortimo Planno]." Online at http://www.mortimoplanno.com/biography.html [consulted August 5, 2009].

Douglass, Lisa. (1992). *The Power of Sentiment: Love, Hierarchy, and the Jamaican Family.* Boulder, CO: Westview Press.

Durkheim, Émile. (1915 [originally 1912]). *The Elementary Forms of Religious Life: A Study in Religious Sociology,* tr. Joseph Ward Swain from *Les formes élémentaires de la vie religieuse.* London: George Allen & Unwin.

"Dutty Wine Didn't Kill Girl: Forensic Test Clears Popular Dance" (September 10, 2008). *Jamaica Star.* Online at http://www.jamaica-star.com/the-star/20080910/news/news2.html [consulted August 5, 2009].

Dyema Attitude. (2006, November 1). Interview on *Direct.* Kingston, Jamaica: CVM TV.

Edgerton, Robert B. (1995). *The Fall of the Asante Empire: The Hundred-Year War for Africa's Gold Coast.* New York: Free Press.

Edmondson, Belinda. (2003, March). "Public Spectacles: Caribbean Women and the Politics of Public Performance." *Small Axe: A Caribbean Journal of Criticism* 7:1, 1–16.

Elephant Man. (2001). "Log On." Song on the album *Strictly the Best, Volume 27.* VP Records.

Elephant Man. (2002). "Wining Queen." Single. Studio 2000.

Elephant Man. (2003). "Blasé," "Fan Dem Off," "Pon di River, Pon di Bank" and "Signal di Plane." Songs on the album *Good 2 Go.* Atlantic Records.

Elephant Man. (2008). "Gully Creepa." Song. Seanizzle.

Eskamp, K., and F. de Geus. (1993). "The Pelvis as Shock Absorber: Modern and African Dance." *Journal of Popular Culture* 27:1, 55–65.

Evans, Teino. (2007, March 24). "Women Get X-Rated for Video Light." *Daily*

Star (Kingston, Jamaica). Online at http://www.jamaica-star.com/the-star/20070324/ent/ent1.html [consulted August 5, 2009].

Fabre, Geneviève. (1999). "The Slave Ship Dance," in *Black Imagination and the Middle Passage*, ed. Maria Diedrich, Henry Louis Gates, Jr., and Carl Pedersen. Oxford and New York: Oxford University Press, 33–46.

Fairley, Jan. (2006). "Dancing Back to Front: Regeton, Sexuality, Gender and Transnationalism in Cuba." *Popular Music* 25:3, 471–88.

Fanon, Frantz. (1963 [originally 1961]). *The Wretched of the Earth*, tr. Constance Farrington from *Les damnés de la terre*. New York: Grove Press.

Figueroa, Mark, and Amanda Sives. (2002). "Homogeneous Voting, Electoral Manipulation and the 'Garrison' Process in Post-Independence Jamaica." *Commonwealth and Comparative Politics* 40:1, 81–108.

Forbes, Copeland. (2008, September 20). Interview on *On Stage*. Kingston, Jamaica: CVM TV.

Forman, Murray. (2002). *The Hood Comes First: Race, Space, and Place in Rap and Hip Hop*. Middleton, CT: Wesleyan University Press.

Foster, Chuck. (1999). *Roots Rock Reggae: An Oral History of Reggae Music from Ska to Dancehall*. New York: Billboard Books.

Foucault, Michel. (1986). "Of Other Spaces," tr. Jay Miskowiec. *Diacritics* 1:11, 22–27.

Frisco Kidd (1997) 'Little and Cute' single on the Compilation Album *Dancehall Queen – Original Motion Picture Soundtrack, Kingston*: Island Jamaic

Fullberg-Stolberg, Claus, ed. (1990). *Jamaica 1938: The Living Conditions of the Urban and Rural Poor: Two Social Surveys*. Mona, Jamaica: Social History Project, Department of History, University of the West Indies.

Gayle, Herbert. (1997). "Hustling and Juggling in Inner-City Communities in Kingston." MSc thesis, University of the West Indies.

Gayle, Herbert. (2002, April). Correspondence with author.

Gelder, Ken, and Sarah Thornton, ed. (2005 [originally 1997]). *The Subcultures Reader*. 2nd ed. London: Routledge.

Gilroy, Paul. (1987). *There Ain't No Black in the Union Jack*. London: Hutchinson

Gilroy, Paul. (1993). *The Black Atlantic: Modernity and Double Consciousness*. Cambridge, MA: Harvard University Press.

Goodison, Bunny. (2002, April 29). Author's interview.

Grazian, David (2003). *Blue Chicago: The Search for Authenticity in Urban Blues Clubs*. Chicago and London: University of Chicago Press.

Gunst, Laurie. (1995). *Born Fi Dead: A Journey Through the Jamaican Posse Underworld*. New York: Henry Holt.

Guthrie, Gwen. (1986). "Ain't Nothin' Goin' On But the Rent." Single. Polydor Records.

Hall, Stuart, and Tony Jefferson. (1976). *Resistance Through Rituals: Youth Subcultures in Post-War Britain*. London: Hutchinson.

Halley, Alexis A. (1998). "Applications of Boundary Theory to Organizational and Inter-Organizational Culture." *Public Administration and Management: An Interactive Journal* 3:2. Online at http://web.archive.org/web/19960101-re_/http://www.pamij.com/halley.html [consulted August 5, 2009].

Hamilton, Beverly. (1994). "Marcus Garvey and Cultural Development in Jamaica: A Preliminary Survey," in *Garvey: His Work and Impact*, ed. Rupert Lewis and Patrick Bryan. Trenton, NJ: Africa World Press, 87–111.

Hannerz, Ulf. (2004 [originally 1969]). *Soulside: Inquiries into Ghetto Culture and Community.* 2nd ed. Chicago: University of Chicago Press.

Harriott, Anthony. (2000). *Police and Crime Control in Jamaica: Problems of Reforming Ex-Colonial Constabularies.* Mona, Jamaica: University of the West Indies Press.

Harris, Wilson. (1999 [originally 1970]). "History, Fable and Myth in the Caribbean and Guianas," in Wilson Harris, *Selected Essays of Wilson Harris: The Unfinished Genesis of the Imagination*, ed. Andrew Bundy. London and New York: Routledge, 152–66.

Harrison-Pepper, Sally. (1990). *Drawing a Circle in the Square: Street Performing in New York's Washington Square.* Jackson and London: University Press of Mississippi.

"Harry T." (2002, April 24). Author's interview.

Hartman, Saidiya V. (1997). *Scenes of Subjection: Terror, Slavery and Self-Making in Nineteenth-Century America.* New York and London: Oxford University Press.

Hazzard-Gordon, K. (1996). "Dancing under the Lash: Sociocultural Disruption, Continuity, and Synthesis," in *African Dance: An Artistic, Historical and Philosophical Inquiry*, ed. Kariamu Welsh-Asante. Trenton, NJ: Africa World Press, 101–30.

Headley, Bernard. (2002). *A Spade Is Still a Spade: Essays on Crime and the Politics of Jamaica.* Kingston, Jamaica: LMH Publishing.

Hebdige, Dick. (1979). *Subcultures: The Meaning of Style.* London: Methuen.

Hebdige, Dick. (1997 [originally 1974]). "Reggae, Rastas and Rudies: Style and the Subversion of Form," in *Reggae, Rasta, Revolution: Jamaican Music from Ska to Dub*, ed. Chris Potash. New York: Schirmer Books, and London: Prentice Hall International, 121–128.

Hebdige, Dick. (2005 [originally 1979]). "Subcultures and the Meaning of Style," in *The Subcultures Reader*, ed. Ken Gelder and Sarah Thornton. London: Routledge, 130–43.

Hemmings, Marcia. (2002, March 29). Author's interview.

Hohn, Brian. (2007, July/August). "Bembe Fever Takes Over Thursdays." *Buzz Caribbean Lifestyle Magazine* 3:3, 22.

Holt, John. (2002 [originally 1980]). "Ghetto Queen." Song on the album *The Biggest Dancehall Anthems, 1979–82.* Greensleeves Records.

Hope, Donna P. (2004). "The British Link-up Crew: Consumption Masquerading as Masculinity in Dancehall." *Interventions* 6:1, 101–17.

Hope, Donna P. (2006). *Inna Di Dancehall: Popular Culture and the Politics of Identity in Jamaica*. Mona, Jamaica: University of the West Indies Press.

Houghton, Edwin. *(2004, August)*. "The Year Dancehall Ate the City." *Fader Magazine*, 86–94.

Hurston, Zora Neale. (1999 [originally 1933]). "Characteristics of Negro Expression," in *Signifyin(g), Sanctifyin', and Slam Dunking: A Reader in African American Expressive Culture*, ed. G. D. Caponi. Amherst: University of Massachusetts Press, 293–308.

Irie FM. (1996). Advertisement. *Reggae Times* 1:8, 13.

Jackson, Steven. (2009, May 10). "2008: 43 Entertainment Events Held Each Day." *Jamaica Observer* (Kingston). Online at https://www.jamaicaobserver.com/magazines/Entertainment/html/20090509T200000-05 00_151114_OBS_ENTERTAINMENT_EVENTS_HELD_EACH_DAY_.asp [consulted August 5, 2009].

Jamaica Intellectual Property Office. (no date given). "Music Could Expand Economy." Online at http://www.jipo.gov.jm/pages/aboutus/musicandeconomy.htm [consulted August 5, 2009].

Johnny P. (1991). "Bike Back." Song, now available on the album *Punanny*. Greensleeves Records (2000).

Jones, Grace. (1985). "Slave to the Rhythm." Single. Island Records.

Junior Dread (2005, July). Author's interview.

Katz, David. (2003). *Solid Foundation: An Oral History of Reggae*. London: Bloomsbury.

Keith, Michael, and Steve Pile, ed. (1993). *Place and the Politics of Identity*. London: Routledge.

Kelly, R. (featuring Wyclef Jean). (2003) "Ghetto Religion." Song on the album *The R. in R&B Collection Volume 1*. Jive/Tavdash.

Kertzer, David I. (1988). *Ritual, Politics and Power*. New Haven, CT, and London: Yale University Press.

Kincaid, Jamaica (1988). *A Small Place*. New York: Farrar, Straus, & Giroux.

King, Stephen (2004). "Blues Tourism in the Mississippi Delta: The Functions of Blues Festivals." *Popular Music and Society* 27:4, 455–75.

Kurasawa, Minako (director). (2007) *Born in JAHpan*. Video. New York: Arthur L. Carter Journalism Institute, New York University.

Lady Saw. (1996). "What is Slackness." Song on the album *Give Me the Reason*. Diamond Rush Promotions.

Laidley, Thaddeus "Teddy," with Charles Campbell and Jade Lee. (2009, June 19). "Events, Artistes and Live Productions." Excerpt from *Inside the Muzik Biz*, broadcast June 17, 2009, on HOT 102 FM, in *Jamaica Observer* (Kingston). Online at http://www.jamaicaobserver.com/magazines/Entertainment/html/20090619T030000-0500_153778_OBS_EVENTS__ARTISTES_AND_LIVE_PRODUCTIONS.asp [consulted August 5, 2009].

Lal, Kanwar. (1967). *The Cult of Desire: An Interpretation of Erotic Sculpture of India*. New Hyde Park, NY: University Books.

Lamming, George. (1992). *Conversations: Essays, Addresses and Interviews, 1953–1990*, ed. Richard Drayton and Andaiye. London: Karia Press.

Levy, Barrington. (2006). "Here I Come (Broader than Broadway)," on the album *The Best of Barrington Levy: Broader than Broadway*. Time 1 Jamaica.

Levy, Horace. (1996). *They Cry Respect: Urban Violence and Poverty in Jamaica*. Mona, Jamaica: Centre for Population, Community and Social Change, Department of Sociology and Social Work, University of the West Indies.

Liebes, Tamar, and James Curran, ed. (1998). *Media, Ritual and Identity*. London and New York: Routledge.

Lipsitz, George. (1994). *Dangerous Crossroads: Popular Music, Postmodernism, and the Poetics of Place*. London and New York: Verso.

Lomax, Alan (1943). "I Got the Blues." *Common Ground* 8:4, 38–52.

Mad Cobra (2005) 'Last Year Clothes', single on the compilation album *The Biggest Ragga Dancehall Anthems*, UK : Greensleeves

Madonna. (1984). "Like a Virgin." Single. Sire Records.

Marcuse, Peter. (2003). "Cities in Quarters," in *A Companion to the City*, ed. Gary Bridge and Sophie Watson. Malden, MA, and Oxford: Blackwell, 120–281

Marley, Bob, and The Wailers. (1976). "Dem Belly Full (But We Hungry)" and "Talking Blues." Songs on the album *Natty Dread*. Island Records.

Marley, Bob, and The Wailers. (1976). "Johnny Was." Lady Saw. (1996). Song on the album *Rastaman Vibration*. Island Records.

Marley, Damian. (2001). "Halfway Tree." Song on the album *Halfway Tree*. Motown Records.

Marshall, Wayne. (2006, January 19). "The Rise of Reggaeton." *Boston Phoenix*. Online at http://thephoenix.com/Boston/Music/1595-rise-of-reggaeton [consulted August 5, 2009].

Matterhorn, Tony. (2006, June 24). Interview on *On Stage*. Kingston, Jamaica: CVM TV.

Matterhorn, Tony. (2007, April 4). Author's interview.

Mavado. (2007). "Don't Cry" and "Gully Side," on the album *Gangsta for Life: The Symphony of David Brooks*. Album. VP Records.

Mbembe, Achille, et al. (2004). "Soweto Now." *Public Culture* 16:3, 499–506.

Mbembe, Achille. (2001). *On the Postcolony*. Berkeley and Los Angeles: University of California Press.

McCall, Michael M. (2000). "Performance Ethnography: A Brief History and Some Advice," in *Strategies of Qualitative Research*, ed. Norman K. Denzin and Yvonna S. Lincoln. Thousand Oaks, CA, and London: Sage Publications, 112–33.

Meschino, Patricia. (2005, July/August). "Reggaetón's Rise from the Underground." *SkyWritings: The Inflight Magazine of Air Jamaica*, 52–53.

Mills, Charles. (1997, June). "Smadditizin'." *Caribbean Quarterly* 43:2, 54–68.

Minott, S., and Branche, Clement. (1994). "Caribbean Sociological Social Psychology." Paper presented at the Annual Meeting of the Midwest Sociological Society, St. Louis, MO, March 10–13.

Mintz, Sidney W., and Richard Price. (1976). *The Birth of African American Culture: An Anthropological Perspective*, Boston, MA: Beacon Press.

Moore, Brian L., and Michele A. Johnson, ed. (2000). *Squalid Kingston, 1890–1920: How the Poor Lived, Moved and Had Their Being*. Mona, Jamaica: Social History Project, University of the West Indies.

Moten, Fred. (2003). *In the Break: The Aesthetics of the Black Radical Tradition*. Minneapolis: University of Minnesota Press.

Mr. G (a.k.a. Goofy). (2002, March 15). Interview on *Entertainment Report*. Kingston: Television Jamaica.

Murray, Albert (2000 [originally 1976]). *Stomping the Blues*. 25th anniversary ed. New York: DaCapo Press.

Nash, Catherine. (2000). "Performativity in Practice: Some Recent Work in Cultural Geography." *Progress in Human Geography* 24: 4, 653–64.

Nettleford, Rex. (1978). *Caribbean Cultural Identity: The Case of Jamaica. An Essay in Cultural Dynamics*, Kingston: Institute of Jamaica.

Nettleford, Rex. (1993, July 18). "Fancy Dress and the Roots of Culture: From Jonkonnu to Dancehall." *Sunday Gleaner* (Kingston, Jamaica), 1D and 16D.

Nettleford, Rex. (2000 [originally 1995]). "Introduction," in George Lamming, *Coming, Coming Home: Conversations II: Western Education and the Caribbean Intellectual*. Philipsburg, Netherlands Antilles: House of Nehesi Publishers, ix–xii.

Nettleford, Rex. (2001, February 15). "Different Tune Same Dance." *Daily Star* (Kingston, Jamaica), 11.

Nuttall, Sarah. (2004). "Stylizing the Self: The Y Generation in Rosebank, Johannesburg." *Public Culture* 16:3, 430–52.

Obrebski, Josef, and Tamara Obrebski. (1948, June 29). "Village Institutions." File 25, no. 9, Box 13, Folder 11, in Special Collections and Archives, University of Massachusetts at Amherst, as recorded by Daniel T. Neely.

Patterson, Orlando. (1964). *Children of Sisyphus*. London: Hutchinson, and Boston, MA: Houghton Mifflin.

Patterson, Orlando. (1967). *The Sociology of Slavery: An Analysis of the Origins, Development and Structure of Negro Slave Society in Jamaica*. London: MacGibbon & Kee.

Patterson, Orlando. (1974). "The Condition of the Low-Income Population in the Kingston Metropolitan Area." Kingston, Jamaica: Office of the Prime Minister.

Pelias, Ronald (2008). "Performative Inquiry: Embodiment and its Challenges," in *Handbook of the Arts in Qualitative Research: Perspectives,*

Methodologies, Examples, and Issues, ed. J. Gary Knowles and Ardra Cole. Thousand Oaks, CA, and London: Sage Publications, 185–93.

Pelton, Robert D. (1980). *The Trickster in West Africa: A Study of Mythic Irony and Sacred Delight*. Berkeley and Los Angeles: University of California Press.

Planning Institute of Jamaica. (2003–08). *Economic and Social Survey Jamaica, 2002–07*. Kingston: Planning Institute of Jamaica.

Planno, Mortimo. (2002, March 23). Author's interview.

Powell, Winston "Wee Pow." (2002, April 5 and 22, and 2003, September). Author's interviews.

Reckord, Verena. (1997). "Reggae, Rastafarianism and Cultural Identity," in *Reggae, Rasta, Revolution: Jamaican Music from Ska to Dub*, ed. Chris Potash. New York: Schirmer Books, and London: Prentice Hall International, 3–13.

Red Rat. (1997). "Nuh Live Nuh Weh." Song on the album *Oh No ... It's Red Rat*. Greensleeves Records.

Regis, Helen (2001). "Blackness and the Politics of Memory in the New Orleans Second Line." *American Ethnologist* 28:4, 752–77.

Reyes, C. (1993). "Investigation into Dancehall." Unpublished research paper, School of Dance, Edna Manley College for the Visual and Performing Arts, Kingston, Jamaica.

Riley, Tarrus, and Jimmy Riley. (2007). "Pull Up Selector." Single. Lyrics online at http://www.jamaica-star.com/thestar/20080710/ent/ent4.html [consulted August 5, 2009].

Robotham, Don. (2005). *Culture, Society and Economy: Bringing Production Back In*. Thousand Oaks, CA, and London: Sage Publications.

Rudder, David. (1998). "High Mas." Song on the album *Beloved*. Lypsoland.

Ryman, Cheryl. (1980). "The Jamaican Heritage in Dance." *Jamaica Journal* 44, 2–13.

Ryman, Cheryl. (1993). "Bouyaka Boo-ya'h-kah: A Salute to Dancehall." Unpublished paper.

Ryman, Cheryl. (2003). "Jamaican Body Moves: Source and Continuity of Jamaican Movement," in *Tapestry of Jamaica: The Best of SkyWritings, Air Jamaica's Inflight Magazine*, ed. Linda Gambrill. Kingston, Jamaica, and Oxford: Macmillan, 170–71.

Salewics, Chris, and Adrian Boot. (2001). *Reggae Explosion*. Kingston, Jamaica: Ian Randle.

Satyo, Siswe. (2001). "Kwaito-Speak: A Language Variety Created by the Youth for the Youth," in *Freedom and Discipline: Essays in Applied Linguistics from Southern Africa*, ed. Elaine Ridge, Sunfree Makoni and Stanley G. M. Ridge. New Delhi: Bahri Publications, 139–48.

Scher, Philip W. (2003). *Carnival and the Formation of a Caribbean Transnation*. Gainesville: University Press of Florida.

Scott, David. (1999). *Refashioning Futures: Criticism After Postcoloniality.* Princeton, NJ: Princeton University Press.

Scott, Michelle (2002). "The Realm of a Blues Empress: Blues Culture and Bessie Smith in Black Chattanooga, Tennessee, 1880–1923." PhD dissertation, Cornell University.

Señor Daley (2003, September 30). Author's interview.

Shabba Ranks. (1991). "Dem Bow" and "Wicked inna Bed." Songs on the album *Just Reality.* VP Records.

Shabba Ranks. (1995). "Girls Wine." Song on the album *Caan Dun.* VP Records.

Shore, Shandon. (2007). "Dancehall Bad Boys in the Spotlight." *Buzz Caribbean Lifestyle Magazine* 3:3, 46–47 and 52.

Sicre, Frederic, ed. (2004). *South Africa at Ten: Perspectives by Political, Business and Civil Leaders.* Cape Town and Pretoria: Human & Rousseau, for the World Economic Forum.

Simpson, George E. (1956, December). "Jamaican Revivalist Cults." *Social and Economic Studies* 5:4, 321–442.

Skelton, Tracey. (1995). "'I Sing Dirty Reality, I am Out There for the Ladies': Lady Saw, Women and Jamaican Ragga Music, Resisting Patriarchy." *Phoebe: Journal of Feminist Theory, Scholarship and Aesthetics* 7, 86–104.

Skelton, Tracey. (1996). "Women's Spaces/Space for Women?: Feminine Identity and Ragga Music." Paper presented at the 21st Annual Conference of the Caribbean Studies Association, San Juan, Puerto Rico, May 27–31.

Skelton, Tracey. (1998). "Ghetto Girls/Urban Music: Jamaican Ragga Music and Female Performance," in Rosa Ainley, *New Frontiers of Space, Bodies, and Gender.* London: Routledge, 142–54.

Slack, Jennifer Daryl. (1996). "The Theory and Method of Articulation in Cultural Studies," in *Stuart Hall: Critical Dialogues in Cultural Studies*, ed. David Morley and Kuan-Hsing Chen. London and New York: Routledge, 113–27.

Soja, Edward. (1993). "History: Geography: Modernity," in *The Cultural Studies Reader*, ed. Simon During. London and New York: Routledge, 114–25.

Soja, Edward. (1996). *Thirdspace.* Malden, MA, and Oxford: Blackwell.

Somé, Malidoma. (1999). *The Healing Wisdom of Africa: Finding Life Purpose Through Nature, Ritual and Community.* New York: Penguin Putnam.

Soyinka, Wole. (1976). *Myth, Literature and the African World.* Cambridge: Cambridge University Press.

Soyinka, Wole. (2001, July 4). "A Millennial Indaba?" *Washington Informer.* Online at http://www.edofolks.com/html/pub34 [consulted August 5, 2009].

Stacey. (2003, September). Author's interview.

Stanbury, Lloyd. (2006). "Mapping the Creative Industries: The Experience of Jamaica." Paper presented at the CARICOM–WIPO Experts Meeting on Creative Industries and Intellectual Property, CARICOM Secretariat,

Georgetown, Guyana, February 8–9. Online at http://www.caricom. org/jsp/community_organs/cohsod_culture/caricom-wipo_news. jsp?menu=cob [consulted August 5, 2009].

Stanley Niaah, Sonjah, and Jalani Niaah. (2006). "'Ace' of the Dancehall Space: A Preliminary Look at U Roy's Version and Subversion in Sound." *Social and Economic Studies* 55: 1 and 2, 167–89.

Stedman, John Gabriel. (1992 [originally 1796]). *Stedman's Surinam: Life in an Eighteenth-Century Slave Society*, ed. Richard Price and Sally Price [abridged and modernized text of *Narrative of a Five Years Expedition Against the Revolted Negroes of Surinam*]. Baltimore, MD, and London: Johns Hopkins University Press.

Steingo, Gavin. (2005). "South African Music after Apartheid: Kwaito, the "Party Politic" and the Appropriation of Gold as a Sign of Success." *Popular Music and Society* 28:3, 333–57.

Stephens, Simon (2000). "Kwaito," in *Senses of Culture: South African Culture Studies*, ed. Sarah Nuttall and Cheryl-Ann Michael. Oxford and New York: Oxford University Press.

Sterling, Marvin Dale. (2000). "In the Shadow of the Universal Other: Performative Identifications with Jamaican Culture in Japan." PhD thesis, University of California, Los Angeles.

Stewart, Kingsley. (2002). "'So Wha, Mi Nuh Fi Live To?': Interpreting Violence in Jamaica through the Dancehall Culture."*Ideaz* 1:1, 17–28.

Stoan. (2005, July). Author's interview.

Stolzoff, Norman. (2000). *Wake the Town and Tell the People: Dancehall Culture in Jamaica*. Durham, NC: Duke University Press

Stone, Ruth M. (1998). "African Music Performed," in *Africa*, ed. Phyllis M. Martin and Patrick O'Meara. 3rd ed. Bloomington: Indiana University Press, 257–72.

Sugar Dee. (1992). "Armstrong." Song on the album *Turn It Over 2: Bogle Meets Armstrong*. Island Records.

Super Cat. (1986). "Trash an' Ready." Song on the album *Si Boops Deh*. Kingston.

Super Cat. (1992). "Ghetto Red Hot" and "Nuff Man a Die." Songs on the album *Don Dada*. Sony.

Sutherland, Peter (1999). "In Memory of the Slaves: An African View of the Diaspora in the Americas," in *Representations of Blackness and the Performance of Identities*, ed. Jean Rahier. Westport, CT, and London: Bergin & Garvey, 195–212.

Taylor, Diana. (2003). *The Archive and the Repertoire: Performing Cultural Memory in the Americas*, Durham, NC: Duke University Press.

Taylor, G. (1983). "A Preliminary Look at Slim and Sam: Jamaican Street Singers" *Jamaica Journal* 1, 39–45.

Taylor, Timothy. (1997). *Global Pop: World Music, World Markets*. London and New York: Routledge.

"The Uncrowned King of the Dancehall: Montana Interviews Bogle" (October 31, 2002). Online at http://www.chicagoreggae.com/bogle.htm [consulted August 5, 2009].

Thompson, Dave. (2002). *Reggae and Caribbean Music: The Essential Listening Companion*. San Francisco: Backbeat Books.

Thrift, Nigel. (1997). "The Still Point: Resistance, Expressive Embodiment and Dance," in *Geographies of Resistance*, ed. Steve Pile and Michael Keith. London: Routledge, 124–52.

Toddler, Harry. (2002a). "Dance the Angel." Single. Ward 21.

Toddler, Harry. (2002b, May 25). Interview on *The Party*. Kingston, Jamaica: CVM TV.

Tölölian, Khachig. (1991). "The Nation State and Its Others: In Lieu of a Preface." *Diaspora* 1:1, 3–7.

Trouillot, Michael-Rolph. (1992). "The Caribbean Region: An Open Frontier in Anthropological Theory." *Annual Review of Anthropology* 21, 19–42.

Turner, Graeme. (2004). *Understanding Celebrity*. Thousand Oaks, CA, and London: Sage.

Turner, Rasbert. (2006, October 30). "Dance of Death?—Beacon Hill Residents Blame 'Dutty Wine' for Teen's Death." *Daily Gleaner* (Kingston, Jamaica).

Turner, Victor. (1967). "Betwixt and Between: The Liminal Period in *Rites de Passage*," in Victor Turner, *The Forest of Symbols: Aspects of Ndembu Ritual*. Ithaca, NY: Cornell University Press.

Turner, Victor. (1969). *The Ritual Process: Structure and Anti-Structure*. Chicago: Aldine.

U Roy (2002). Author's interview.

Various Artists. (1995). *Reggae Gold*. Album. VP Records.

Waddell, Hope Masterton. (1970). *Twenty-Nine Years in the West Indies and Central Africa: A Review of Missionary Work and Adventure, 1829–1858*. London: Frank Cass.

Warner-Lewis, Maureen. (2003). *Central Africa in the Caribbean: Transcending Time, Transforming Cultures*. Mona, Jamaica: University of the West Indies Press.

Welsh-Asante, Kariamu. (1985). "Commonalities in African Dance: An Aesthetic Foundation," in *African Culture: The Rhythms of Unity*, ed. Molefi Kete Asante and Kariamu Welsh-Asante. Westport, CT: Greenwood Press.

White, Garth. (1984). "The Development of Jamaican Popular Music, Part 2: Urbanization of the Folk, the Merger of Traditional and the Popular in Jamaican Music." *ACIJ* [African–Caribbean Institute of Jamaica] *Research Review* 1.

Williams, Jason (director and writer). (2006). *It's All about Dancing: A Jamaican Dance-U-Mentary*. DVD. Penalty Recordings and Fine Gold Productions [now Fine Gold Music].

Willis, W. Bruce. (1998). *The Adinkra Dictionary: A Visual Primer on the Language of Adinkra*. Washington, DC: Pyramid Complex.

"Winston." (2003, April 7). Interview on *Our Voices*. Kingston, Jamaica: CVM TV.

Witmer, Robert. (1989, February to April). "A History of Kingston's Popular Music Culture: Neocolonialism to Nationalism." *Jamaica Journal* 22:1, 11–18.

Wright, Beth-Sarah. (2004). "Speaking the Unspeakable: Politics of the Vagina in Dancehall Docuvideos." *Discourses in Dance* 2: 2, 45–59.

Wright, Keril. (2007, July 31). "Anger over Winner Spoils Dancehall Queen Competition." *Jamaica Observer* (Kingston). Online at http://www.jamaicaobserver.com/lifestyle/html/20070730t200000-0500_125740_obs_anger_over_winner_spoils_dancehall_queen_competition.asp [consulted August 5, 2009].

Wynter, Sylvia. (1977, November). "We Know Where We Are From: The Politics of Black Culture from Myal to Marley." Unpublished paper archived in the C. L. R. James Collection, Africana Studies Department, Brown University, Providence, RI.

INDEX

"f" refers to figure; "t" to table.

Composed by Sandra Friesen in Meta and Meta Serif. Meta was designed by Eric Spiekermann in 1991. Meta Serif was designed by Christian Schwartz, Erik Spiekermann and Kris Sowersby in 2007.

CPSIA information can be obtained
at www.ICGtesting.com
Printed in the USA
LVHW031558100321
681107LV00001B/232